The
European Union
in the World
Community

The
European Union
in the World
Community

edited by
Carolyn Rhodes

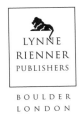

LYNNE
RIENNER
PUBLISHERS

BOULDER
LONDON

Published in the United States of America in 1998 by
Lynne Rienner Publishers, Inc.
1800 30th Street, Boulder, Colorado 80301

and in the United Kingdom by
Lynne Rienner Publishers, Inc.
3 Henrietta Street, Covent Garden, London WC2E 8LU

Library of Congress Cataloging-in-Publication Data
The European Union in the world community / edited by Carolyn Rhodes.
    Includes bibliographical references and index.
    ISBN 1-55587-780-X (alk. paper)
    1. European Union. I. Rhodes, Carolyn, 1953– .
JN30.E9474   1998
341.242'2—dc21
                                          97-48272
                                              CIP

British Cataloguing in Publication Data
A Cataloguing in Publication record for this book
is available from the British Library.

Printed and bound in the United States of America

The paper used in this publication meets the requirements
of the American National Standard for Permanence of
Paper for Printed Library Materials Z39.48-1984.

5 4 3 2 1

Contents

Preface

This book is the culmination of a project that began with a European Community Studies Association (ECSA) workshop held in Jackson Hole, Wyoming, in May 1996 on "The Role of the European Union as an Actor in International Affairs." The workshop was funded by grants from the European Union Delegation of the Commission in Washington, D.C., and from the Milton R. Merrill Endowment at Utah State University. While the weather proved to be disappointing, the workshop discussion certainly did not, and a number of the chapters contained in this volume were developed from the papers presented. I am deeply appreciative of ECSA's support for this very worthwhile workshop, as well as for the funding we received from the Delegation and the Merrill Endowment.

Participants included the following paper presenters and discussants: David Allen, William Burros, Fraser Cameron, James A. Caporaso, Jonathan Davidson, Roy Ginsberg, Antje Herrberg, Madeleine Hosli, Leon Hurwitz, Joseph Jupille, Carl Lankowski, Pierre-Henri Laurent, Sophie Meunier, Alberta Sbragia, Stefan Schirm, Michael Smith, and myself. In addition, students from Utah State University's Department of Political Science attended as observers, adding a lively dimension to the informal discussions that followed the regular workshop sessions.

The workshop proved to be a fruitful forum for discussing the challenging issue of how to define and characterize the European Union (EU) as an international actor. In papers ranging from global environmental policy to European security policy, attempts were made to pin down what we mean by "actorhood" in international affairs and to measure recent EU activities against the criteria raised. The discussions that ensued provided valuable feedback to paper presenters, and also helped to refine the parameters of this book project. In the end, seven papers from the workshop were selected to be developed into chapters for the book, and three other chapters were solicited from individuals who did not give papers at the workshop, but whose research efforts fit well with the book's overall plan (Olufemi Babarinde, Alberta Sbragia, and Alan Mayhew).

The book has been designed to capture the "essence" of the European Union as an international actor in the world community, first by offering an overview of its activities and challenges and then by turning to a series of issue area case studies that examine specific external-relationship arrangements and patterns of behavior. In addition, internal institutional and historical influences and constraints are taken into account, allowing individual authors to reflect upon both the international dimension of European Union integration and the internal factors that contribute to, or limit, purposeful external action. The result is a set of substantively rich and analytically informative case studies that together contribute to our understanding of this emerging actor in international affairs.

Given the historical development of European integration and the changes in terminology adopted in the Treaty on European Union (TEU), a note regarding various usages of the terms "European Union," "European Community," and "European Economic Community" is warranted. Generally, I have made the editorial decision to utilize the term "European Union" in references made to it after the ratification of the Treaty on European Union. Even when an author is referring to activities generated within pillar one of the TEU, where the term "European Community" is technically correct, I have decided to utilize European Union because the case discussions often involve consideration of the larger EU role as an international actor. Even the case studies involving trade and the environment make reference to the EU. However, specific references to major EC initiatives prior to the creation of the European Union utilize the term "European Community." Furthermore, when a chapter deals historically with the Treaty of Rome and trade agreements under the EEC portion of the treaty, references are made to the European Economic Community, rather than to the EC.

A number of individuals have helped in the development and production of this manuscript, and I would like to thank them at this time. First and foremost, I would like to thank my former student and current colleague Jeannie Johnson for her tireless, attentive, and good-humored assistance with the preparation of the final manuscript. Her knowledge of the subject matter, as well as her responsible and caring attitude, were crucial to the completion of a quality volume. I also thank Rachel Hurst, Sally Okelberry, Charles DeLaney, and Sonia Bose of Utah State University for a variety of typing, computer support, and bibliographic assistance; and Sally Glover and Steve Barr at Lynne Rienner Publishers for their development and editorial assistance. In addition, I would like to acknowledge the support of my department head, Randy Simmons, who does his utmost to ensure that his faculty have the resources necessary to complete research and writing projects. By example and through tangible support, he has been instrumental in encouraging my professional development. Lynne Rienner also merits a note of thanks beyond the obvious. She is a dedicated student of European Union studies and has been a key factor in the encouragement of EU studies and publication in the United States. In addition to my admiration for her in this capacity I am personally grateful for her encouragement of this particular scholarly project. Finally, I want to express heartfelt appreciation to my husband, Tod, and daughter, Brett, who were often ignored because of my preoccupation with this project, and whose support and love I treasure above all things.

1

Introduction: The Identity of the European Union in International Affairs

Carolyn Rhodes

Anyone observing the integration and enlargement undertaken by the European Union during the past two decades cannot help but wonder about the impact of these changes on the EU's capability in the global arena. We know that changes have occurred in the distribution of sovereign influence between the EU and its member states, and we know that intentions to broaden EU-level activity abroad are evidenced in the Treaty on European Union (TEU) and voiced in many quarters. We remain uncertain, however, about the character of these changes and the extent to which member state sovereignty has been diminished in favor of EU-level foreign policy initiative and execution. Furthermore, as scholars and observers in the field, we need to assess whether expectations about EU influence in the international context correspond with reality.

While the European Union's visibility in the international arena grew substantially after the passage of the Single European Act, the signing of the TEU, and the end of the Cold War, the actual content and influence of EU activity in the international arena has received less scrutiny. This project was launched to help redress this deficiency—to urge scholars to delve into a range of issue areas, examine the role of the European Union in those contexts, and generate analytical descriptions about EU external capability and influence that can be compared and contrasted in juxtaposition.

While most observers would agree that the European Union is becoming an important international actor, and while some noteworthy chronicles of EU external affairs have been produced,[1] few have attempted to identify and systematically assess the nature of EU influence across issue areas.[2] Yet, for students of international relations and European Union studies, clarification of the role of the EU in international affairs is of considerable interest, since it addresses a dimension of the EU "persona" that is increasingly important: how the EU is shaped by, and in turn shapes, the international system. If we are to understand the sources of influence in the global arena as we approach the twenty-first century, it is vital that we consider and assess the role of this evolving and increasingly important actor.

The European Union consists of a set of arrangements that is unlike any other in the history of international relations. It was spawned from a range of integrative agreements undertaken by its member states to solve age-old rivalries and conflicts for the purpose of facilitating regional co-operation, market interdependence, and economic development.[3] The de-gree to which its member states have voluntarily transferred their respec-tive sovereignty to a supranational arrangement is unprecedented in international relations. Only in the process of nation building and the cre-ation of new sovereign nation-states can one find historical parallels.[4]

Yet, its development has not been linear, particularly in the realm of EU foreign policy. Some areas of integration have developed much more than others, and steps to deepen integration have often followed periods of noncooperation and skepticism. Thus, even the label "Union" must be con-sidered advisedly, because agreement on the degree to which integration is desirable or the degree to which member states should submit to a com-mon voice has not been reached. This has been apparent in intra-EU pol-icy development but is even more obvious in external policies. The shar-ing of sovereignty between the member states and the European Union affects how policy is projected abroad and how others in the world inter-act with the EU and its constituent parts.

Member states have committed themselves to a set of common poli-cies aimed at creating a single market and at achieving unity of purpose on a wide range of associated political-economic goals. These member states have willingly transferred some of their individual sovereignty to the col-lective institutions of the Union. Yet, they continue to retain sovereignty where it has not been expressly transferred to the supranational arrange-ments of the Union. Intergovernmental decisionmaking clearly prevails in many realms, yet neofunctionalist views about the development of inte-gration also seem relevant as EU-level institutions continue to advance in-tegrationist policies.[5] This dichotomous character of the EU has prompted some to describe it as a "multilevel system of governance," wherein dif-ferent degrees of integration and varying levels of member state intrusive-ness coexist across various issue areas.[6] Consequently, one cannot classify the European Union merely as an international organization, yet neither can one classify it as a sovereign actor in its own right. Attempts to ex-plain and predict its behavior as an international actor must take into ac-count this hybrid character, as well as the evolving nature of the Union enterprise.

As this book reveals, the degree to which member states are willing to forgo individual policies in favor of influencing a common European-level policy, and the degree to which other international actors are forced to take into account the European Union's structure and influence, both depend heavily on the particular issue at hand, the historical patterns of interaction involved, and the ability of individual member states legally or credibly to "go it alone." The European Union's capacity to act as a separate and influential entity, therefore, has much to do with its legitimacy at home and abroad, and this in turn varies from issue area to issue area.

Drawing upon the contributions to this book, this introductory chapter discusses the outward personification of the European Union as it is expressed in four different realms: (1) its potential for influence arising both from changes in the international system as well as from internal EU developments; (2) its capacity to act as determined by historical and institutional constraints; (3) its legitimacy and responsibility in both internal and external terms; and (4) how others view the EU as an international actor. In examining these four factors, this chapter links the international personification of the European Union with both the international and the domestic factors that produce it, revealing how the external persona is created and projected across a variety of issue areas. This linkage allows us to examine the tension that exists between the EU's potential for influence and the institutional capacity to translate that potential into policies and external activities. The chapter highlights the fact that even though the European Union's institutional structure is in a state of evolution, some general observations can be made about the EU's decisionmaking capability, its perception by other actors in the world arena, and its resulting behavior in international affairs.

Sources of EU Influence in International Affairs

Potential for Influence:
International System Change and EU Opportunities

Opportunities for EU influence abroad have been created by shifts in the structure of the international system as well as by deepening institutional commitments within the Union. Nearly coincidental with the creation of the single market and the signing of the Union Treaty, the Cold War ended. With its end came the disappearance of many of the structures it had created, including a divided Germany and the indefinitely prolonged presence of an extensive U.S. military force in Western Europe. These changes opened the way for EU initiatives regarding security issues and cooperation with Central and Eastern Europe and the former Soviet Union, but they also posed a number of challenges for the future of the European Union in international affairs. The new circumstances created high expectations both inside and outside the European Union about the new role it could play—expectations that member states have proven reluctant to meet.

In addition to the impressive success of the single-market program, ongoing interdependent economic forces had been at work to influence Sweden, Norway, Finland, Austria, and Switzerland to apply for membership. The eventual enlargement (which omitted Switzerland and Norway, whose populations rejected their respective referenda) was largely a response to the changing international system, which encouraged stronger economic ties with the EU and freed national governments to pursue those ties without interference from Cold War structures.

The development of more complex interdependent economic relations has not only prompted neighboring states to seek membership, but has also caused many trade and investment partners—most notably the United States—to recognize the tremendous importance of the single market as well as the increasing potential influence of the European Union in bilateral commercial and financial affairs. Dynamic international investment and trade patterns during the past several decades have altered the relative economic power positions of these two global actors, creating more truly interdependent economic relationships, which are shaping policy goals and influencing the character of actual bilateral negotiations in commercial affairs. Increasingly, the EU is perceived as, and acts as, an equal with the United States in this realm.

Historical and Institutional Limitations on the EU's Capacity to Act

Despite the influence of the international environment, and despite the success of European integration and enlargement, the ability of the European Union to respond to new challenges abroad has been affected by its own institutional shortcomings as well as by the persistence of the historical positions taken and the relationships maintained by member states.

The role of historical relationships and existing institutional arrangements in influencing EU foreign policy is evident in member states' positions regarding new member state accession. For example, the member states that border and have strong ties to Central and Eastern European nations have been much stronger advocates of enlarging the Union eastward, while those with a Mediterranean orientation favor enlargement in that region and worry about the consequences of eastern accessions. From the perspective of the former group, enlargement eastward, despite its disadvantages, will stabilize the economic and political relationships that these countries have cultivated because of historical connections and geographical proximity. The Mediterranean states, on the other hand, worry that eastward enlargement will directly threaten their existing welfare within the Union by forcing major institutional and budgetary reform at their expense.

In addition, institutional factors within the European Union, which reflect member state reluctance to cede further prerogative to Brussels, constrain the development and execution of a coherent and purposeful foreign policy. Common Foreign and Security Policy (CFSP) in particular has highlighted the differences in member state traditions and historical relationships, as well as the absence of supranational structures for formulating and dispatching defense policy. As member states with widely divergent backgrounds—neutral states, North Atlantic Treaty Organization (NATO) members, and Western European Union (WEU) members—try to come together in the creation of a unified but comfortable foreign and security policy, past approaches to security affairs emerge as strong and persisting impediments to deeper integration in this area. While a certain degree of progress was made in the Amsterdam treaty in laying a new institutional foundation for CFSP, it was also clear from the treaty that member states remain reluctant to give up their sovereign prerogative in foreign affairs.[7]

EU Legitimacy and Responsibility

Capability in foreign relations is clearly influenced by issues of legitimacy and responsibility both within the European Union and outside. It is obvious that the balance of power between individual member states and the Union is in a constant state of flux, with definite shifts in weight toward Brussels for a range of policy areas, but with ongoing resistance by some member states and sporadic reassertions of sovereignty by others. This makes any across-the-board generalization about the character of shared responsibility between the member states and the Union difficult. What can be said is that here again historical relationships and patterns of decisionmaking provide useful insights into how EU policy will be made.

The legitimacy of EU-level foreign policy is grounded in a number of areas. At the most basic level it begins where there is a legal foundation in the treaties for the collective representation of EU interests abroad. This may be endowed upon the Commission, the Council, the Parliament, or some other designate such as the European Central Bank or the Secretary General of the Council, and comprises the source of "authority" for external roles.[8] Whether common external policies can be developed and/or pursued by the Commission is fundamentally a legal question with ever present political overtones. For example, interpretations by the Court of Justice have endorsed common policies in areas not strictly the purview of the single-market enterprise, but which have trade implications, such as environmental regulation.[9] Council mandates to the Commission to negotiate on behalf of the Union also tend to reinforce the Union's supranational activities abroad.

However, even when these so-called mandates are awarded to the Commission for carrying out a single EU external policy, it is always possible for individual member states, responding to domestic interests, to resist the collective enterprise, thus altering the actual policy outcome. This resistance has been evident in EU negotiations within the GATT framework, despite a longstanding commitment to grant the Commission the authority to negotiate on behalf of the Community.[10] Depending upon how frequently such roadblocks occur in a given issue area, the European Union's legitimacy abroad is affected. If it becomes apparent to observers that the member states are refusing to grant responsibility to the Union for particular negotiations or policy arrangements, they may attempt to deal directly with the key member states, or may even opt to pursue relationships entirely separate from the EU, further undermining the European Union's legitimacy in the area in question. If member states refuse to allow the EU to take responsibility (or continually block Commission initiatives) for key external relationships and policies, then the EU's capacity to act is severely constrained, and its international role diminished.

On the other hand, when initiatives are taken by EU representatives, such as the Commission or the Parliament, and their legitimacy is not seriously challenged, then new frontiers in external relations can be created. This seems to have been the case with EU policy toward Russia in recent years, demonstrating that while institutional constraints may limit the purview of EU-level foreign policy, some opportunities to "push those limits" have been seized by entrepreneurial actors.[11]

External Perceptions About the EU: Judging the EU as an International Actor

The EU's capacity to act is in part a function of how other international actors evaluate the legitimacy of EU-level agents. External perceptions about the EU's presence and capability in international affairs are important indicators of how well intentions have been translated into observable actions.[12] Paying attention to how the European Union is viewed abroad helps us to evaluate whether gaps between expectations and realities have affected the "reach" of EU influence.[13] While perceptions of other actors in the international system may not always consitute an accurate measure of EU activity, they do provide insights into how the EU is judged as an international actor. Moreover, as Herrberg explains in Chapter 5, the process by which an actor such as the EU shapes its foreign policy in response to others (and vice versa) actually contributes to the creation of its own identity. Much can be learned about the European Union from the development of its relationship with others. Demands placed on the EU by its neighbors and the EU's responses (from the Commission or the European Parliament or the Council) to those demands provide rich sources of information about the emerging character of the European Union in the world community.

Characterizing the EU's Identity
in the World Community Across Issue Areas

Successive enlargements of the membership of the EC/EU demonstrate that neighboring states have generally determined that the costs of accepting some degree of supranational governance have been worth paying in exchange for the advantages of the common market. In the most recent enlargement, countries that were already members of the European Economic Area, and therefore already assured market access, clearly felt their interests would be better served if they also had a role in EU decision-making.[14] As a critical mass of European countries achieved membership status, it became increasingly unacceptable to be left out.

This "bandwagon"[15] effect alone has made the European Union one of the most significant entities in the world political economy. With its 370 million people and $7.2 billion GDP, it comprises the single largest economy in the world, as well as the world's largest trading partner. (The EU's external trade accounts for nearly 20 percent of the world's commercial transactions.)[16] As additional nations join the Union, its presence as a single economic power will become even more impressive. Being a member of the EU "club" affords nations a set of opportunities and potential influence in the realm of commercial and financial affairs that makes the loss of a degree of individual national influence palatable. Moreover, the interdependent nature of the global economy, coupled with the presence of the EU's increasingly integrated market, makes staying "outside" more and more costly in terms of trade, finance, and policy input. The perception abounds that joining the European Union will create considerable advantage, leading nearly all of the nations of Europe to line up in hopes of someday becoming members, even if that membership comes with its own set of costs and responsibilities.

Of course, joining the European Union is a very complicated process, involving the acceptance of the *acquis communautaire* and all that this means in terms of conforming with the principles and procedures laid down in the treaties and subsequent legislation. Since the process demands a high degree of harmonization of policy practices before membership can be implemented, it provides the European Union with an incredible amount of influence on the prospective member state. This was especially apparent in the Mediterranean enlargements when Greece, Portugal, and Spain were delayed from joining the European Union until they had adopted democratic and market-oriented governments. Similarly, in the course of EU negotiations with the Central and Eastern European Countries (CEEC), governments have been scrambling to reform their command-style economies and to adjust to the democratic expectations of the European Union. Thus, becoming a member of the European Union means much more than merely accessing its internal market or joining in future decisions. In acceding to the European Union, member states agree to conduct their affairs on a sweeping range of issues according to specified principles and procedures.

This is significant because it demonstrates that the European Union, while a part of the international system, actually affects the structure of that system by its very existence and potential for enlargement. The map of Europe, as well as its economic configuration, has changed dramatically since 1957, not only because of the increasingly interdependent nature of the global economy, but also because of the purposeful institutional arrangements and successive enlargements of the European Community. To borrow David Allen and Michael Smith's term, the very "presence" of the European Union has had a profound impact on the structure of the international economic system.[17]

As other countries have observed the tremendous cooperative success of the European Union's commercial enterprise, they have sought to imitate it to varying degrees. The European Union has become a "model" and a "mentor" for a number of cooperative regional efforts such as the Association of South East Asian Nations (ASEAN), founded in 1991, as well as Latin America's Southern Cone Common Market (MERCOSUR) and the North American Free Trade Agreement (NAFTA), each signed in 1992. These efforts reflect an interest in emulating the regional free trade aspects of the EU experience, if not in duplicating its unique institutional structures.[18] In the realm of trade, therefore, it is possible to observe the influence of the European Union on patterns of commercial exchange and cooperation *elsewhere,* in addition to its more obvious influence as a trading entity itself.

Other changes in the international system have presented opportunities for EU influence, particularly in Europe. David Allen and Michael Smith provide in Chapter 3 an insightful assessment of the changes that have taken place in the European security order since 1990. They argue that any measure of the EU presence in European security must first take into account the international environment within which this presence is felt. They observe that the relatively stable Cold War system was replaced by "a shifting mosaic of authority and actors" that created "a highly uncertain milieu for policy making." In addition, they observe, the very concept of "security" itself is being challenged—along with changing "notions of threat and alliance" and growing expectations (particularly in Central and Eastern Europe) that pan-European security can be achieved via EU institutions.[19] These expectations, however, have confronted the European Union at a time when it is unclear whether it has the "institutional capacity" and "collective will" to take action in the realm of security policy.[20] Allen and Smith argue that the European Union is handicapped by the pillar structure of the Maastricht Treaty, where no centralized institution was created to collect information, coordinate activity, and mobilize resources. While success in EU foreign policy has been seen in the diplomatic sphere, there remain strong impediments to a significant military role. Moreover, the contradictions among NATO planning, EU overtures toward Russia, enlargement, and basic alliance issues call into question the ability of the European Union to "manage" the changing European security order.

This perspective is supported by several other authors in this volume, who note that demands placed on the European Union by changes in the international system have overtaken the ability of the EU decisionmaking machinery to respond. They observe that initiating and maintaining a clear-cut foreign policy agenda in the security sphere has been particularly elusive. Fraser Cameron's relatively positive assessment of the performance of the European Union as an international actor is tempered, for example, by reservations about its abilities in the security arena; he notes that "ambitious statements and numerous declarations from Brussels do not compensate for a political system and society in the EU that does not generate a strong common will, assertiveness and self-confidence in international relations."[21]

Stefan Schirm, in Chapter 4, reinforces this perspective but takes the issue further and challenges whether the European Union should even pursue a militarily oriented security policy at all. He observes that, despite the opportunities created by the remarkable systemic changes of the latter 1980s and early 1990s, the EU's role in international security has been disappointing. The effort to create a genuine Common Foreign and Security Policy within the framework of the European Union has been met with considerable reluctance by member states. Moreover, he argues, CFSP "often duplicates functions better accomplished by NATO, the United States, United Nations, or even the Organization for Security and Cooperation in Europe (OSCE)."[22] He offers an interesting assessment of the "necessity, viability and adequacy" of the EU's CFSP, and concludes that the European Union is currently best suited to play a "civil socio-economic" role in external affairs and not a military role, which remains better performed by other actors in the international arena.

While their focus is very different from Schirm's, Antje Herrberg's examination of the European Union's evolving relationship toward Russia and Alan Mayhew's analysis of the European Union's policy toward Central and Eastern Europe tend to reinforce the view that the EU has been quite capable in pursuing what Cameron calls "soft security"—diplomatic relations and assistance efforts by the EU aimed at stabilizing its neighbors to the east.[23] Although the end of the Cold War, the collapse of the Council for Mutual Economic Assistance (CMEA) in Central and Eastern Europe, and the disintegration of the Soviet Union clearly took Western European leaders by surprise, the EU has managed to forge a fairly influential set of policies toward the former Soviet bloc, even if member states remain reluctant to embrace eastern enlargement.

Although Russia is not one of the countries in the queue for EU accession, the revolution of its political and economic orientation has absorbed much of the European Union's attention. In fact, according to Mayhew, Germany's concern with maintaining positive relations with Russia at times impeded progress on the Europe agreements, because the German government did not want to alienate or radicalize the fledgling Russian government. European Union–Russian relations have been one of the most important features of the post–Cold War era. As Russia has considered its new role in the world, EU officials have hoped to influence it in a friendly, market-oriented direction. The European Union's ability to do so, as Antje Herrberg explains in Chapter 5, has much to do with past patterns of relations between the two as well as the international context that has shaped them.

Her case study focuses on the interaction between the European Economic Community (and later the European Union) and the Soviet Union (and later Russia), the relationship that developed between them over time, and its significance for EU foreign policy. She notes that the international context has, since the Second World War, created barriers between Russia and the European Union—especially because of pressures emanating from the EU's relationship with the United States—but that paradoxically this same international context has also at times created opportunities for rapprochement, as the European Union offered Russia a means of access to the West without having to deal directly with the United States.

The European Union moved from a role of interlocutor to a more proactive role of policy advocate with the dissolution of the Soviet Union and the effort within its successor states to adopt more democratic and market-oriented institutional structures. The dynamic nature of developments within Russia, coupled with the high value the EU placed on a cooperative and progressive relationship, with that country, often compelled the European Union to assume a leadership role in influencing other international actors to embrace the reforms taking place, as well as to refine its own institutional structures for dealing with Russia. On both counts the European Union demonstrated not only an identifiable "presence" but also the capability to adapt to a highly dynamic and evolving situation. According to Herrberg, the end of the Cold War and the concomitant changes within Russia opened the way for a significant new *ostpolitik* on the part of the European Union; this in turn contributed meaningfully to the maturity of the EU's capacity for foreign policy and to distinction within the international arena. Here too, however, the EU's capacity to initiate foreign policy was linked to institutional capabilities back home in Brussels.[24] Interestingly, Herrberg notes that the European Parliament, often cited as the least-effectual EU institution, proved to play a key role alongside the Commission in pressing forward EU-Russian rapprochement.

As Alan Mayhew explains in Chapter 6, Western officials welcomed the changes that were taking place and voiced support for stronger ties with the East, but they were somewhat unprepared for the task ahead. Mayhew discusses, for example, how the dramatic changes in the structure of the international system, with their accompanying challenges and opportunities, occurred during the period when EC states were trying to cope with demanding economic and political issues such as unemployment and ratification of the Treaty on European Union.

The challenges posed by the CEEC have aimed at the very heart of the European Union's historical mission—to offer eventual membership to any European nation that qualified. Because both European Union members and the CEEC have favored anchoring the CEEC to the West in order to help transform them into market-oriented, democratic nations, closer ties with the European Union appear to be a logical response to the abrupt structural changes caused by the dissolution of the Soviet empire. However, as Mayhew explains, a clear agenda beyond that vague concept has not existed within the European Union, while in the CEEC the eventual goal of EU membership has been paramount. This imbalance in purpose is a reflection not only of the divergent national interests involved but also of the dramatic and distressing impact of systemic change on the CEEC, in comparison with EU countries who have not faced the same kinds of immediate demands and threats. Consequently, for the countries of Central and Eastern Europe, the Union has been woefully slow and self-serving, and therefore not responsive to their needs and expectations. For a number of EU member states, on the other hand, the overtures toward the East have been almost alarming. Many of them remain unprepared to accept all that enlargement entails, including structural adjustment and Common Agricultural Policy reform, as well as the most fundamental of Community principles—full market access for prospective member states.

Even so, the European Union has developed very strong ties with the CEEC, negotiating association (or "Europe") agreements with Estonia, Latvia, Lithuania, Bulgaria, The Czech Republic, Hungary, Poland, Slovakia, Slovenia, and Romania. In addition, its economic and technical assistance programs toward Central and Eastern Europe and Russia have been the most generous and proactive international efforts mustered to assist in the reform and stabilization of the former Communist bloc countries.

One of the most interesting aspects of these arrangements is the fact that in many respects they mirror the trade agreements reached over the years with less-developed countries (LDCs). Olufemi Babarinde's examination of EU-South relations in Chapter 7 reveals not only the character of these relations over time, but also that they clearly were a model for the association agreements with the CEEC in the 1990s. Reflecting past Commission experience with such arrangements, as well as EC/EU norms regarding development assistance in general, the Europe agreements obviously benefited from the EU's longstanding effort in development policy toward the LDCs.

There is much to be learned from Babarinde's analysis of EU relations with the LDCs in a broader sense as well—both in terms of future trade relations with the CEEC and in terms of general lessons about the institutional capacity of the EU to initiate and maintain foreign policies that have the potential for affecting member state privileges. First, he notes that the ability of the Commission to move the EU into concessionary trade agreements has in fact been impressive over the years despite member state concerns; however, arrangements have definitely been affected by the historical relationship between key member states and particular LDCs. Moreover, as Mayhew notes with regard to the CEEC, Babarinde confirms that enlargement has brought both opportunities and frustration to LDCs seeking trade association status with the EU, depending upon the countries involved. Some member states want to maintain special relations with former colonies; others have no such affinity. Odd variations in the EU's relations with developing countries can be explained in part by such differences.

The changing international system is profoundly affecting the many aspects of the role of the European Union within it. The EU's economic weight, as well as the character of its economic involvement in the world, has begun seriously to alter the way that it behaves and the way that others behave in response. Alberta Sbragia in Chapter 8 makes a strong case that the shift in the balance of economic power between the United States and the European Union that has occurred since the early 1980s has been due primarily to increased symmetry in bilateral investment patterns, as well as to a growing recognition in the United States of the influence of Brussels in the policymaking process. European foreign direct investment (FDI) in the United States is now very similar in value to U.S. FDI in Europe. This symmetry in investment interdependence has created a very different set of negotiating circumstances for U.S. and EU trade and finance officials who now must take into account the consequences of their actions for their domestic producers and investors in a truly multinational environment. "Us" and "them" can have little meaning during trade negotiations when foreign direct investment makes employment and profits transnational phenomena. This new state of affairs influences agenda formation in the transatlantic relationship, propelling the private sector into an increasingly visible role in determining which issues should be on the negotiating table.[25] The current Transatlantic Business Dialogue is a prime example.

Moreover, Sbragia observes, the European Commission is increasingly recognized within U.S. government circles, as well as among private business, as the most appropriate contact point in Europe to register economic policy concerns or initiate bilateral discussions. This "upgrading" of European Union institutions over national capitals further demonstrates recognition in the

United States of the growing influence of the European Union as an economic actor. Because of its commercial power, transnational investment strength, and institutional character, the European Union is becoming the focal point for the transatlantic relationship.[26]

As Madeleine Hosli explains in Chapter 9, this evolution of the European Union into one of the most important actors in the international system will be further reinforced by intra-EU efforts to achieve economic and monetary union. Her analysis of the potential that the new euro has as a globally important currency is compelling, alerting all economic observers to the fact that the European Union (and other euro investors) will have considerable influence in global monetary affairs in the future. The weight of this emerging currency will signal not only the combined wealth of the EU nations involved but also the need for other nations and investors to take into account the collective monetary policy that supports it. However, Hosli also notes that the EU's ability to manipulate the value of the euro for macroeconomic purposes will have limits.

She argues that European Economic and Monetary Union (EMU) has the potential for having a significant global impact as a new unit of account, means of payment, and store of value. Depending on which member states meet the Union's economic and monetary convergence criteria, the resulting euro could seriously compete with other important currencies in the world, particularly the U.S. dollar and the British pound sterling (the yen's largest role is in the Asian Pacific region). However, the EMU's priority of price level stability, strengthened by the institutional decision-making rules set forth at Maastricht, may impede its flexibility with respect to concluding international exchange rate agreements. Thus, the euro may exist as a new powerful "presence" in the realm of global monetary investment and relations, but its influence in engineering future exchange rate arrangements (or in utilizing monetary policy to stimulate intra-EU economic growth) may be limited by the institutional constraints of the EMU regime. Still, it is important to note that the existence of a strong centralized authority for monetary policy will clearly mark a new milestone in the supranational development of the EU.

In the commercial sphere, where one would expect that symmetrical power resources and deepening interdependence between the United States and the EU ensure a fairly equal match in terms of negotiating capability, the European Union faces unique challenges. For example, despite the reforms of the Single European Act, its decisionmaking structure continues to leave member states with the ability to block major international agreements and therefore creates some interesting bargaining situations. The one area in EU foreign policy that most analysts have agreed has been characterized by unity of purpose and strength of collective will has been trade policy. However, the fact that the Commission has enjoyed a mandate from Community member states to conduct trade negotiations on behalf of their collective membership has not ensured "cohesiveness" in every situation. This absence of unity does not mean that the EU cannot effectively enter into and secure important international agreements. Nonetheless, according to Sophie Meunier, who explores this dynamic in Chapter 10, it does mean that outcomes of trade negotiations often depend on whether recalcitrant member states agree to go along with the majority, or whether they force the EU to hold out against foreign demands despite the position of the rest of the member states.

The EU is clearly a pluralist entity whose decisions and behaviors are shaped by the differing voting rules and levels of the assertiveness of its respective member states. As such it often lacks sufficient cohesiveness to engage effectively in international negotiations. Initial agreements reached by the Commission, negotiating on behalf of the entire Union, may be overturned or blocked by recalcitrant member states. On the other hand, this same lack of cohesiveness can at times serve certain interests within the EU well. If a member state refuses to cooperate with the majority and thus blocks an international agreement, its stance can force the Community to bargain harder and thus may have the useful effect of eventually securing for the EU a better arrangement than it might have settled for in the first place. Given this character of the EU, negotiating partners must consider the impact of intergovernmentalism and voting rules as factors bearing on their ability to secure an agreement. At those times when Commission autonomy is relatively high because the Council has extended it a mandate to proceed with negotiations, breakthroughs in international discussions may result; however, Council oversight can still undo what has been achieved, making it necessary for the trading partner to pay close attention to member state preferences. Basically, this means that even though negotiators on both sides might enter into good-faith efforts, the bottom line is that the EU member states still wield ultimate power.

Meunier's examination of U.S.-EU trade negotiations also reinforces the idea that lowest-common-denominator (reflecting member state positions) outcomes are the most likely ones when negotiating with the EU in this realm. Despite an informal "flirtation" with majority rule regarding trade negotiations, the norm remains one of consensus because of the threat by member states to invoke their veto power. Genuine majority rule could move the negotiating position of the EU from the lowest common denominator to the median realm where a majority determines policy; however, recent events do not indicate a move in this direction. Under consensus decisionmaking, raising the level of acceptance of agreements among member states may be achieved by more generous concessions on the part of the trading partner or by internal (within the EU) side payments that "coopt" the recalcitrant state(s).

Meunier's case study is useful because it traces the EU's negotiating effort through a series of institutional (formal and informal) changes. This allows us to determine the effect of voting rules, relative Commission autonomy, and the negotiating positions of the trading partner on the outcomes that were produced. In turn, these determinations help us to generate observations about the capacity of the EU to negotiate effectively and about its general character as an international actor. As we have seen above, member state reluctance to adhere to the principle of majority rule is considered by most analysts to be the single largest impediment to an effective foreign policy in the security realm, yet EU foreign trade policy has been viewed as relatively successful. Perhaps the most important lesson from this case study, therefore, is that by focusing critically on the area most likely to produce a collective EU-level foreign policy, it offers a useful set of insights about the conditions under which agreement is most or least likely. In addition to identifying structural limits to coherent and proactive foreign policy, it also demonstrates how those limits actually affect the dynamics of international negotiations and their eventual outcomes. Thus, these insights may be equally applicable to other areas of European Union foreign policy, including security, enlargement, development, or the environment.

During the last three decades, more and more attention has been given to the increasingly interdependent nature of the global environment. As with international economic interdependence, water and air pollution and resource depletion have forced nation-states to recognize the transboundary character of environmental issues. Within the European Union there has been an increased effort to adopt Union-wide environmental protection policies, and this has also prompted the EU Commission to undertake a more visible role externally as well.

Probably the most theoretically ambitious contribution to this volume is the last chapter, by Joseph Jupille and James Caporaso, which utilizes an environmental case study to draw generalizations about the European Union's capacity to act in external affairs. Moving beyond a simple analysis of the EU's behavior in international environmental politics, the authors offer four criteria that they consider useful in assessing the European Union's role in world politics and then apply those criteria to the case under examination. Each of the following criteria—recognition, authority, autonomy, and cohesion—is considered important in assessing the EU's capacity to act in the world arena. "Recognition" refers to how "others" view the EU (and thus bears much similarity to Herrberg's concept of others' perception). Is the EU accepted as an international actor, and do others "interact" with it as such? "Authority" refers to the "legal competence to act." "Autonomy" refers to whether the EU is institutionally distinct and independent from other actors (most specifically member states). "Cohesion" refers to the "degree to which an entity is able to formulate and articulate internally consistent policy preferences," and it includes both "procedural" and "value" cohesion.[27]

Measured against these criteria in the case of the Rio de Janeiro Earth Summit, the European Union received mixed reviews. It did receive the recognition of others involved in the international negotiations, and its legal authority to act externally in the environmental area has been established. However, as with Meunier's examination of EU trade negotiations, Jupille and Caporaso found that the ability of member states to resist EU-level efforts to establish and carry out international environmental policies undermined the ability of the Union to act effectively. Where legal authority was not firmly established or where voting rules allowed dissenters the right of veto (as in the case of development aid at the Rio conference), EU capacity to act as a collective entity was thwarted. Under these conditions—which, the authors noted, were more often produced from political circumstances (a lack of cohesion of values) than from simple institutional limits—EU autonomy from the member states was difficult to achieve. Autonomy, they observe, is the most demanding of their criteria, and the most elusive for the European Union. Thus, even though they acknowledge that the Commission is becoming recognized as a distinct actor in international environmental affairs, their assessment of the EU ultimately hinges on its capacity to project policy without interference from the member states, and this remains limited.

Summary

Despite limitations on its capacity as a cohesive actor, the following chapters clearly demonstrate that the EU's role in the world community is significant and multidimensional, yet that factors bearing on this role—such as its own institutional development, member state influence, and external perceptions—continue to evolve. A product of progressive internal integration, historical relationships, and international system opportunities, its role is increasingly shaped by dichotomous forces. On the one hand, there is stronger and stronger pressure on the EU to be more assertive and active in international affairs, but on the other hand member state discomfort with an expanded EU role remains a serious check on the pursuit of a proactive external policy. Existing decisionmaking procedures tend to reinforce the latter at the expense of the former. To better understand the balance between these forces and the development of the EU's unique external character, the chapters in this volume offer rich substantive and analytical insights into the role of the EU as an international actor.

Notes

1. An excellent new book on the subject is Peining 1997.
2. Noteworthy efforts to develop our understanding of the EU as an international actor in more specific realms include Allen and Smith 1990; Hill, 1994; Sandholtz and Zysman 1992; and Smith 1996.

3. Dinan 1994 provides an excellent overview of the development of the European Union.

4. See Caporaso 1996 for a related discussion.

5. A number of very useful analyses of the character of EU decisionmaking, policy development, and institutional structure grapple with this issue. Two edited books that explore a range of factors affecting the character of the EU are Keohane and Hoffmann 1991 and Sbragia 1992a. The most influential recent intergovernmentalist perspective is represented by Moravscik 1991, 1993. Influential institutionalist perspectives are represented by Garrett 1992, 1995.

6. Marks 1993 introduced the concept of multilevel governance as a way to account for differing sources of decisions in the EU. Pollack 1997 further develops our understanding of how agendas are set and authority delegated by examining the relationship between "principals" (e.g., member states) and the supranational institutions of the EU.

7. See Fraser Cameron's assessment of the Amsterdam treaty in this area in Chapter 2.

8. See Jupille and Caporaso's exploration of the concept of authority in Chapter 11.

9. Ibid.

10. This is explored in a rich case study by Meunier in Chapter 10.

11. See Herrberg's observations in Chapter 5.

12. Antje Herrberg's discussion in this volume of the value of how others view the EU informs my approach. See Chapter 5.

13. See Smith 1996 for a useful discussion of the politics of inclusion and exclusion with regard to the EU in Europe.

14. Alan Mayhew makes this observation in Chapter 6 of this volume.

15. I am borrowing this term from the alliance and security literature, which utilizes it to distinguish the phenomenon of nations joining "the most likely powerful" nation in an alliance rather than joining together in alliance against its power. My meaning here is not associated with balance of power politics. Rather it refers simply to nations expecting advantages from associating themselves with the EU as opposed to other alternatives.

16. See Fraser Cameron's overview of the EU's economic importance in Chapter 2 of this volume.

17. Allen and Smith 1990.

18. Rhodes 1997.

19. Allen and Smith, Chapter 3 of this volume.

20. Ibid.

21. Cameron, Chapter 2.

22. Schirm, Chapter 4.

23. Cameron, Chapter 2.

24. Herrberg, Chapter 5.

25. See Vogel 1995.

26. Sbragia, Chapter 8.

27. Jupille and Caporaso, Chapter 11.

2

The European Union as a Global Actor: Far from Pushing Its Political Weight Around[1]

Fraser Cameron

The president of the European Commission, Jacques Santer, was correct in drawing attention to the glaring discrepancy between the economic and political influence of the European Union (EU) when he observed that "the European Union is simply not punching its weight on the international stage in the foreign and security policy areas."[2] A year later, in the same forum, Richard Holbrooke, the U.S. chief negotiator in the Bosnian peace process, castigated the EU for its inability to take decisive action in its own backyard. He criticized the EU for failing to use military force in ex-Yugoslavia and for "sleeping" during a security crisis between Greece and Turkey. But almost as he spoke, two U.S. ambassadors, Stewart Eizenstadt (Brussels, EU) and Richard Gardner (Madrid, Spain), were writing complimentary articles on the EU's expanding role on the world stage, emphasizing its important contribution in terms of "soft security."[3]

What kind of actor then is the EU? There is no doubt that along with the United States and Japan, the EU is a key player in world trade negotiations. It made a major contribution to the success of the Uruguay Round and is the principal driving force behind proposals to establish an effective World Trade Organization (WTO). It is the prime organizer of the economic rescue of Eastern Europe and the former Soviet Union. It is drawing its northern, eastern, and southern neighbors into a complex web of agreements as a magnet attracts bits of metal. It is the main source of development assistance to the Third World. It is a main player in an increasingly complex international arena encompassing political, economic, social, environmental, and technological issues. As a significant global economic power, it is a much-sought-after interlocutor on political affairs by an increasing number of countries and regional groupings.

These political discussions, important in their own right, should not obscure the general failure of the EU to exercise decisive political influence on world events, particularly those involving the use of force. The EU continues to suffer from what one observer has termed an "expectations-capability

gap."[4] In other words, the Union's aggregation of size, economic performance, and military arsenals do not automatically qualify it as a major
world power. Ambitious statements and numerous declarations from Brussels do not compensate for a political system and society in the EU that
does not generate a strong common will, assertiveness, and self-confidence
in international relations. Recognizing both the strengths and weaknesses
of EU foreign policy, this chapter examines how the EU became a global
power, discusses the roots of such power, reviews current external policies
and priorities, assesses the operation of the Treaty on European Union, and
concludes by discussing the 1997Amsterdam Treaty and offering some
proposals to improve the EU's effectiveness in external affairs.

The Slow Path to Global Power

The EU has always had a foreign and security policy dimension. The 1951
Treaty of Paris establishing the European Coal and Steel Community
(ECSC) defined its creation in the preamble as a contribution to the safeguarding of world peace.[5] In the early years of the EU this mission was
achieved principally through the elimination of age-old rivalries within
Western Europe rather than through specific actions on the world stage
outside.

To the extent that the early European Community (EC) had external
policies, they were in the first instance a necessary consequence of the
EC's internal progress toward integrating foreign policy patterns of individual member states, particularly toward their former colonies. As a result, the EC's external policies were lopsided both in substantive terms,
concentrating as they did on trade and development, and in geographical
terms, with their heavy bias toward the African, Caribbean, and Pacific
(ACP) countries rather than the developing world in general. The EU's increasingly important international role was in part a byproduct of its own
considerable internal achievements and in part a necessity imposed upon it
by changes in the global system over which it had little direct control.[6]

The clearest example of how internal success implied external responsibility was provided by the 1992 single-market program, which immediately precipitated far-reaching reactions in the international community. At
first there were fears, mainly in the United States and Japan, of the EU becoming a "Fortress Europe," but as business began to understand the liberalizing effects of the single market, these fears diminished and were replaced by a scramble to secure optimal placement within the EU to take
advantage of them. External developments, however, were still more important in pushing the EU forward as an international actor. The rapid and
radical internationalization of the global economy, the problems surrounding

the collapse of Communism, the Gulf War, and the Yugoslav crisis exposed the limitations of any one European state to influence events.

An Economic Giant

Whatever the EU's deficiencies in political coherence, cultural identity, and military organization may be, it does not lack economic power. Following the January 1995 enlargement to include Austria, Sweden, and Finland, it has a larger population than the United States (370 million) and a GDP a third higher than the United States, and twice that of Japan. Although it has only 7 percent of the world's population, the enlarged EU is the principal provider of foreign direct investment (FDI), both as a host economy and as a source economy; it also provides 53 percent of all official development assistance, holds 37 percent of global financial reserves, produces 27 percent of the world's automobiles, and is responsible for 19 percent of world trade (excluding intra-EU trade).[7] If and when the EU forms a currency union, the EU could well topple the dollar from its perch as the world's top currency. Moreover, that unique self-aggrandizing feature of the Union known as enlargement will continue to increase this economic primacy.

The EU is also extending the scope of its free trade area gradually to the entire continent and even reaching into North Africa. The first step was the creation of the European Economic Area (EEA) to include several European Free Trade Association (EFTA) countries; the second stage was the extension of the free trade area to Central and Eastern Europe; the third stage (as from 1998) envisions exploring the possibility of free trade areas with Russia and Ukraine; and a fourth stage (beginning early next century) would extend this free trade area to the countries of the North African littoral. Taken together this would create a free trade area of just under one billion in population, which would be significantly higher than that of the North American Free Trade Agreement (NAFTA) or Asian Pacific Economic Cooperation (APEC).

The process of internal integration brought home to member states the reality of interdependence between countries well before the concept of globalization became widely accepted. Interdependence between the EU and the United States was always very high, and a similar pattern has developed in recent years between the EU and Asia. The EU has sought to take a single position at the numerous international conferences dealing with environmental, social, and economic issues. The Union's role and status in international institutions varies considerably. In most UN bodies, the Commission enjoys observer status; in the Organization for Economic Cooperation and Development (OECD) it has a sui generis status; and in the Food and Agriculture Organization (FAO) it is a full member.

One of the oddities of the Union is its role in the General Agreement on Tariffs and Trade (GATT). Formally speaking, it is not a contracting party to the GATT; only its individual member states are. Yet, the Union is recognized as having all the rights and obligations of a full GATT signatory, and by the early 1960s the European Commission had established itself as the EU's single negotiating voice. There was never any dispute about this, as the member states were quick to see the negotiating advantage of pooling their combined weight.

The EU has also had an impact on GATT by deepening the nature, as well as widening the geographical scope, of its own integration. As the Union has grown steadily more ambitious in forging a single market—in creating a free flow of capital, services, and labor as well as goods—so GATT has set its sights higher. The Uruguay round of negotiations was vastly more ambitious than earlier rounds, seeking for the first time international regulation of agriculture and services. The newly established World Trade Organization (WTO) has an ambitious agenda, largely formulated by the EU, reaching into new areas of international trade such as public procurement, trade and investment, and social and environmental issues. As a result of the interplay between EU integration and GATT liberalization, trade "creation" has outweighed trade "diversion." This growth has resulted in a steady increase in manufactured imports from third countries (4.7 percent of the EU's output in 1980 and 6.3 percent in 1994).[8]

The EU's positive influence is even more evident if one examines the Union's record in development assistance. The Union has steadily increased the proportion of its budget devoted to aid and international action.[9] Between 1989 and 1995 the aid budget rose from 2.7 percent to 4.2 percent. The Union and its member states devote 0.51 percent of GNP to development aid compared to 0.15 percent for the United States and 0.32 percent for Japan. In 1994 this amounted to more than ECU 21 billion, which is more than 40 percent of all global assistance. The Lomé convention, with sixty-nine developing countries, is the largest single aid program in the world. The fourth Lomé convention (1990–2000) provides for ECU 12 billion in the form of grants, soft loans, and interest rate rebates in the first half of the decade. A similar sum was agreed upon in December 1995 for the second half of the decade, despite a trend in some member states toward renationalization of development assistance. Increasingly, aid is being targeted toward structural adjustment programs and the provision of stabilization funds for specific sectors. In South Africa, the EU played an important role in supporting the transition process and is preparing a comprehensive agreement with the new democratic government in Pretoria. The ending of the Cold War has led the Union to adopt more political criteria in determining aid programs. Democracy, respect for human rights, and good governance are now basic conditions for Union assistance.[10]

Another growth area has been the demand for emergency aid as a result of natural and man-made disasters. The EU has taken the lead in providing aid to the Kurds in northern Iraq and to Somalia, Ethiopia, southern Africa, Bangladesh, Rwanda, Bosnia, and many other countries requiring assistance. It has now established a humanitarian aid office (ECHO) within the Commission in Brussels. Its budget has grown rapidly from ECU 368 million in 1992 to ECU 605 million in 1993 and ECU 760 million in 1994.[11]

External Priorities

Inevitably, the EU had to give first priority to its eastern neighbors who had finally broken free after decades under Communist rule. But the EU could not neglect its southern flank, nor ignore changes in U.S. policy, nor the emergence of Asia as an important political as well as economic factor in world affairs. Moreover, the EU found itself playing an increasingly important role in international forums dealing with transnational issues such as the environment, population control, jobs, and information technology. A first attempt to define external priorities was made by the European Council at Lisbon in June 1992.[12] Successive European Councils have added to these priorities, emphasizing the EU's immediate neighborhood.

Central and Eastern Europe Countries (CEEC)

Since 1989, the European Union has been in the forefront of international efforts to support the reform process and thus to increase stability in the eastern half of the continent. The Union's involvement includes ever closer political links, wide-ranging association or "Europe" agreements, rapidly growing trade, economic assistance (especially through PHARE and TACIS),[13] and now a pre-accession strategy designed to prepare the CEEC for EU membership.[14] The Union also provides considerable financial assistance through the European Investment Bank (EIB) and, collectively, is the largest shareholder in the European Bank for Reconstruction and Development (EBRD).

Key to the EU's approach toward the CEEC are the Europe agreements, which are in force with ten countries (Estonia, Latvia, Lithuania, Bulgaria, Czech Republic, Hungary, Poland, Slovakia, Slovenia, and Romania). These Europe agreements, which build on the trade and cooperation agreements signed with most of the CEEC in 1989–1990, are extremely wide-ranging in that they provide the framework for cooperation in the political, economic, industrial, trade, scientific, technical, environmental, and cultural spheres.

The Europe agreements are important milestones in the process of reintegrating the CEEC, after decades of Communist suppression, into the mainstream of European political and economic life. Successful implementation of the agreements is prerequisite to future EU membership, an objective shared by all the CEECs. The agreements, which are similar for each country, contain provisions for regular meetings at the executive, ministerial, and official levels to discuss all subjects of common interest. The agreements envision an asymmetrical, industrial, free trade area between the EU and the CEEC whereby the EU is opening its markets (apart from agriculture) completely and the CEEC will have a number of years to adjust before barriers are removed. In progress under the auspices of the Europe Agreement, negotiations involved asymmetrical progress toward a free trade area over a ten-year period.

In terms of economic cooperation, a large number of specific areas of mutual interest are identified in the agreements, including industrial cooperation, protection of investments, norms and standards, scientific and technological cooperation, education and training, regional and social cooperation, small and medium-sized enterprises, statistics, environment, transport, telecommunication, and drugs. There are also provisions for financial and cultural cooperation. Association councils meet at regular intervals to review progress and to decide on additional measures. A consultative parliamentary group also brings members of the national parliaments together with representatives from the European Parliament.[15]

Since 1989 the EU has played the leading role in the provision of international economic assistance to the CEEC. Total OECD assistance from 1990 through 1994 totaled ECU 75 billion, of which the EU and its member states were by far the largest contributors with 37 percent, compared to 13 percent for the United States, 9 percent EFTA, and 4 percent Japan. The EU's PHARE program budget has also risen substantially, with further increases foreseen in the period up to 1999. The program has concentrated on the following priority areas: training, private investment, market access, environment, and modernization of agriculture. Despite occasional difficulties with local implementation, the coordinating process has developed satisfactorily both on the political and operational level. The CEEC have all embarked on major economic reforms, and the assistance is constantly adapted to meet individual and changing requirements.

The European Union is by far the main trading partner of the CEEC, importing ECU 23 billion out of CEEC total exports to the OECD in 1994 of ECU 29 billion. It is also their main supplier, exporting to them ECU 30 billion out of total imports of ECU 39 billion from the OECD. The EU has also been a major factor in promoting the dynamic growth of their trade. Against the backdrop of an economic take-off, and a complete restructuring of external trade following the collapse of the Council for Mutual Economic Assistance (CMEA), exports to the European Union from the CEEC grew by 74 percent from 1989 to 1994, during which time exports to the United States, Japan, and Canada either increased very slowly or even declined. The same dynamism is reflected in the explosion of the CEEC's imports from the EU, which rose by 120 percent between 1989 and 1994. These changes in trade flows are all the more astonishing if one considers that 78 percent of total CEEC trade was within the CMEA area in 1989 and that 65 percent of its trade is now with the EU.[16]

Another important step was taken at Copenhagen in June 1993, when the European Council accepted the goal of Union membership for Europe agreement countries and agreed on the necessity of creating a "structured institutionalized relationship" with the CEEC. Regarding membership in the EU, the European Council specified the following conditions: (1) stability of institutions guaranteeing democracy, the rule of law, human rights, and respect for and protection of minorities; (2) the existence of a functioning market economy; (3) capacity to cope with competitive pressure and market forces within the Union; and (4) ability to take on the obligations of membership (*acquis communautaire*), including adherence to the aims of political, economic, and monetary union. The European Council also concluded that "the Union's capacity to absorb new members, while maintaining the momentum of European integration, is also an important consideration in the general interest of both the Union and the candidate countries."[17]

After Copenhagen, contacts at all levels between the Union and the CEEC intensified, leading to agreement at the Essen European Council in December 1994 on a "pre-accession strategy." The two major elements of this pre-accession strategy are:

1. A "structured relationship," which means that there are now regular meetings at ministerial level to consider a wide range of policy areas such as Foreign and Security Policy, Justice and Home Affairs, Environment, Transport, Energy, Internal Market, etc. This practical experience of working together in areas of common interest is helping to create a climate of mutual confidence and to reinforce ties between the Union and the associated states.

2. The establishment of a White Paper listing the measures that the CEEC will have to undertake in order to meet the requirements of the single market. The single market involves acceptance of free trade and strict rules regarding competition policy. In May 1995 the Commission published a White Paper that sets out the requirements for participation in the single market. Each associated country will now be able to draw up a list of priorities and a timetable, which can be jointly monitored with the Union and for which help can be obtained through a technical assistance office based in Brussels. The White Paper process will help make clear over time the extent to which countries are ready for membership.[18]

At the Madrid European Council in December 1995, it was agreed that the Commission should start preparing the opinions on the applicant states with a view to their completion for Council perusal "as soon as possible after the conclusion of the Inter-governmental conference."[19] It was hoped that preliminary negotiations on accession might begin at the same time as those with Malta and Cyprus, that is, six months after the conclusion of the IGC. The European Council also requested the Commission to continue its work analyzing the likely impact of CEEC enlargement on EU policies including agriculture and the structural funds.[20]

The effects of enlargement were outlined in an interim report made by the Commission for Madrid, which emphasized that the political benefits of enlargement, although not quantifiable in the same way as the economic effects, were most important. Enlargement would allow the EU to extend to the rest of Europe the zone of stability and security that it itself has enjoyed. Economically, the accession of Central and East European countries will be a major challenge for them. Together they add less than 5 percent of EU GDP and have an average per capita income less than 30 percent of that of the EU. Enlargement will also be a challenge for the Union's policies. Although no precise budgetary estimates can be given, since the common agricultural policy is in constant development, and the cohesion funds are due to be reviewed in 1999, enlargement will require significant budgetary efforts on the part of the Union. But in the long term, the enlargement of the internal market to include more than 100 million in additional population should bring a new boost and dynamism to the European economy.

The EU is also making a substantial contribution to the resolution of outstanding political problems in the region through the Stability Pact, a joint action of the CFSP. The pact was an attempt to enhance stability through the promotion of good neighborly relations, concentrating on questions relating to frontiers and minorities, as well as regional cooperation and the strengthening of democratic institutions. The EU did not intend that the pact should develop into a new institution. Following conclusion of the Final Conference in March 1995, the pact was entrusted to the OSCE, which has responsibility for the follow-up. Existing principles and commitments established by the UN, OSCE, and Council of Europe on the inviolability of frontiers and the treatment of minorities serve as the basic principles of the Stability Pact. Essentially, the Union sought to bring "added value," for example by financing proposals within the framework of the PHARE program in areas such as language training for native Russian speakers in Estonia and Latvia so that they can learn Estonian and Latvian requirements for citizenship; cross-border cooperation; training of customs officials; and encouraging cultural links between citizens of neighboring countries.[21]

In addition to measures under the Stability Pact, the EU is also undertaking a number of initiatives to promote interregional cooperation and good neighborly relations. These include increasing PHARE financing of multicountry programs, cross-border projects, and democratic institution building. Among the most important of these projects are the Baltic Sea Cooperation Council, the Barents Sea Initiative, the Central Free Trade Area, and the Black Sea Cooperation project. These initiatives clearly have a security element, in that they deal with concrete risks such as storage of nuclear material and lessen tension by promoting greater transparency and cooperation.

Russia/CIS

Developments in Russia, Ukraine, and the Commonwealth of Independent States (CIS) also have major implications for the security and prosperity of the Union, and it remains the EU's intention to establish a strategic political partnership with Russia and Ukraine. The EU's interest in the success of the reform process in Russia and Ukraine and in the establishment of stable and prosperous systems throughout the CIS is evident. Not only is this an essential element for security and stability in general, but it also opens new prospects for addressing a wide range of global and regional security issues. In addition, the EU has an interest in Russia and Ukraine as viable economic partners. At present the economic links between the EU and these countries are rather limited, but the potential for a mutually beneficial economic relationship is substantial.

The EU has responded to the situation in Russia/CIS by negotiating Partnership and Cooperation Agreements (PCAs) that provide for cooperation on political, economic, and technical issues. The PCA is the most ambitious agreement ever signed between the Russian Federation and one of its major world partners.[22] It aims gradually to draw the economies of Russia and the EU closer together by lifting trade barriers, providing a more favorable business environment, and promoting the direct investment that the Russian economy so desperately needs. It also paves the way for a potential free trade area after 1998, while establishing regular political contacts at all levels and promoting respect for democracy and human rights.

EU policy toward the Ukraine, until recently, has been hampered because of lack of reform. There are, however, encouraging signs of a greater commitment to reform under President Kuchma, and the PCA signed in April 1994 should provide the framework for a comprehensive development of relations between the EU and Ukraine. The EU has agreed to greater support for Ukraine in macroeconomic assistance, agriculture, and energy sectors, provided Ukraine itself proceeds with a much needed reform program, including moves to close down the Chernobyl nuclear power station.

The EU has become the most important trading partner of Russia, Ukraine, and the CIS, which together imported nearly ECU 18 billion worth of goods out of ECU exports to the OECD totalling ECU 23 billion in 1992, and which accounted for more than ECU 13 billion of the EC's total imports from the OECD, worth ECU 19 billion. As is the case with the CEEC, the EU's trade with the CIS countries is flourishing. Their exports to the EU rose by 22 percent between 1989 and 1993, and the EU's exports to the CIS over the same period rose by 19 percent. In contrast to its trade surplus with Central and Eastern Europe, the EU had a trade deficit with the CIS (ECU 3.5 billion in 1994).

In terms of technical assistance to Russia and the CIS since 1991, the EU and its member states have provided ECU 54 billion (59 percent) in OECD aid out of a total of ECU 92 billion. The TACIS program has spent over ECU 500 million in Russia alone over the past three years, concentrating on projects to restructure state enterprises and to promote private sector development, agricultural reform, infrastructure development (energy, telecommunications, transport), nuclear safety and the environment, public administration reform, social services, education, and democratic institutions. TACIS is constantly changing to reflect local needs. For example, there is now more emphasis on regional projects and a greater concentration on priority sectors of the economy.

The Balkans

Without doubt the tragedy of the events in former Yugoslavia has dealt a severe blow to the EU's pretensions on the international stage. Yet, the EU is the only actor to have been involved in all stages of the effort to secure a peaceful settlement of the conflict and is by far the main provider of humanitarian assistance to the former republics of Yugoslavia. As far as diplomatic pressure and economic sanctions are concerned, the Union went to the limits of its powers, but these were clearly not sufficient to bring an end to the conflict. A number of member states refused to entertain the prospect of military action without full U.S. involvement, a move that the Clinton administration was reluctant to accept. During 1993–1994, therefore, there were significant transatlantic differences on how to proceed in Bosnia.

The Union's lack of political will to use military power finally resulted in the United States taking the lead in 1995, with NATO air strikes leading to the peace agreement negotiated at Dayton and signed in Paris on 14 December. It remains to be seen whether the settlement will hold, but what is certain is that the successor states will continue to look to the EU for economic and other assistance to recover after the war. Unlike other donors, including the United States, the EU was prompt in committing its share of funds for reconstruction. The end of hostilities has also opened the prospect of new trade and cooperation agreements between the EU and the successor states to former Yugoslavia, as well as Albania.[23]

The Mediterranean and Middle East

While concentrating attention eastward, the EU has not neglected its neighbors to the south. The EU has association or trade and cooperation agreements with most Mediterranean countries (Libya is the exception) dating back several years. In 1990 the EU adopted the Renovated Mediterranean Policy, which provided for a substantial increase in aid for horizontal cooperation in areas such as the environment (to supplement existing bilateral agreements with the EU) and improvements to the trade agreements for both industrial and agricultural products.

At the European Council in December 1994, the EU accepted a Commission proposal to work toward a Euro-Mediterranean Partnership by developing a long-term program in the political and economic spheres, including the prospect of a free trade area. A further increase in financial assistance to nearly ECU 5 billion was agreed for the period 1995–1999. The main thrust of EU policy was to support indigenous economic development, to create employment, and to reduce migratory pressures, coupled with measures to support human rights and the consolidation of democracy in the region. The promotion of regional integration was another main objective.

The Barcelona Euro-Med Conference in November 1995 was an important landmark in the EU's relations with its Mediterranean partners. For the first time, member states, the Commission, and the twelve Mediterranean partners sat down at at the foreign minister level and endorsed an ambitious plan for the future of their relationship. The mixture was potentially explosive (Cyprus, Greece, Turkey, Israel, Syria, and Lebanon), and the text of the political section of the Barcelona Declaration was not agreed upon until the very last moment, but the Spanish presidency handled the discussions skillfully, and the result was a resounding success. The outcome of the conference was agreement on a declaration and a work program, with the emphasis on three main areas:

1. Political and security relations: the partners recognize a number of fundamental principles and a joint high-level working group to discuss practical measures for securing their implementation.

2. Economic and financial relations: the principles of free trade and the market economy, together with substantially increased financial assistance from the EU (ECU 4.685 billion for 1995–1999) form the basis of future relations. The work program, additionally, outlines areas for increased cooperation, including industry, transport, energy, telecommunications, tourism, and environment.

3. Social, cultural, and human affairs: the text outlines ways in which civil society will become more involved in the partnership and in which exchanges of people can be encouraged. Under this heading, sensitive issues

such as terrorism, drug trafficking, and illegal immigration will be tackled jointly.[24]

The Barcelona process complements at the multilateral level the development of the EU's bilateral relations with partners. Negotiations for Euro-Mediterranean association agreements were concluded in 1995 with Israel, Tunisia, and Morocco. Progress has been made with Egypt, Jordan, and Lebanon. Of the other partners, Algeria is keen to start negotiations, and even Syria seems likely to do so before long; the EU is also prepared to enter into an agreement with the Palestinian Authority, subject to the special legal situation. Within the broad rubric of the Mediterranean, there remain, however, important differences among the various states of the region. Three countries—Turkey, Malta, and Cyprus—have applied to join the EU, whereas others, such as Libya, remain pariah states.

Regarding the Middle East, the Union has a vital interest in securing stability in the region and uninterrupted access to oil supplies. The Gulf War, during which the EU provided substantial humanitarian and economic assistance to the frontline states, has led to increased EU involvement in the region both on the political and economic fronts. The EU is the main trading partner for all countries of the region and is also a main player in the Middle East peace process. It is the principal provider of financial and other assistance to Palestine and organized a successful monitoring mission for the first elections in Palestine.

Transatlantic Relations

With the end of the Cold War, relations between the EU and the United States have changed significantly. The previous lopsided security relationship has given way to a more equal partnership.[25] In November 1990 a Transatlantic Declaration was signed codifying relations between the Union and the United States (a similar declaration was signed with Canada). The declaration was based on U.S. recognition of the Union's growing weight in world affairs as well as a common heritage and shared values. Cooperation now takes place over a wide spectrum of policy areas ranging from foreign and security, economics and trade, science and culture, to terrorism and drugs. The most visible result of the declaration, which commits both parties "to inform and consult each other on matters of common political and economic interest," was to initiate a series of semiannual summit meetings that are now a major feature of the international agenda.[26]

The Clinton administration has been a strong supporter of closer European integration, particularly on the security front. In major speeches in Brussels in January 1994 and Paris in June 1994, President Clinton gave his support to efforts to establish a European Security and Defense Identity

(ESDI). The United States would clearly like the EU to develop into a genuine partner, in order to deal with a growing array of international problems.

An important step toward a strengthened EU-U.S. partnership was taken at the Madrid summit in December 1995, when Presidents Clinton and Santer plus Prime Minister Gonzalez signed an action plan designed to increase transatlantic cooperation in a wide range of areas. The aim of the new approach is to translate common political and economic goals into concrete joint measures. The new agenda will be revised and updated at each semiannual EU-U.S. Summit. Four shared goals were identified: (1) promoting peace and stability; (2) encouraging democracy and development around the world; (3) responding to global challenges; and (4) contributing to the expansion of world trade and closer economic relations.

The summit agreed that there should be a move "from consultation to joint action."[27] First, for example, a commitment was made for EU and U.S. missions to work more closely in third countries on a variety of concrete issues, in particular in the fields of development cooperation, humanitarian assistance, and economic restructuring. Second, it was recognized that it was now opportune to foster EU-U.S. ties in all existing policy areas, thus taking full advantage of the widened scope provided by the Maastricht Treaty. The third guideline takes into account that the EU and the United States, when joining forces, can better promote stability, increase prosperity, and advance development on a global scale. Finally it was decided to go beyond traditional government contacts to increase contacts on a personal level, from exchanges through university cooperation and "sister cities" to more scholarships and internship programs.[28]

Asia

In 1993 Asia became the EU's largest trade partner, ahead of the United States. In terms of assistance to the region, the EU is the second largest aid donor, behind Japan, but far ahead of the United States; most aid is concentrated on the poorest countries of the region. For the period 1995–1999 the EU has agreed on a budget of ECU 2.16 billion for financial assistance to Asia. In light of the impressive economic development in the region, the EU has recognized the importance of developing a dialogue on political as well as economic and trade issues. Political consultations are already held, for example, with ASEAN, Japan, China, India, and Pakistan. Moreover, the EU wishes to develop an expanding EU-Asian partnership. A new Asia strategy paper adopted by the EU at the end of 1994 called for: (1) an increased EU profile in Asia; (2) support for regional cooperation in Asia; (3) strengthened links with Asian countries in international forums; (4) expansion of EU-Asian trade and investment; and (5) contribution to alleviating poverty in the poorer Asian countries.

Most of these themes were on the agenda of the first EU-Asia summit, which took place in Bangkok on 1–2 March 1996, bringing together twenty-five heads of state from Asia and Europe. Closer economic ties with Asia are of paramount importance to the EU's own welfare. Years of inattention to the region have resulted in the loss of market share to the United States and other trading partners, and investments as well have lagged behind those of Japan and the United States. Europe has a strong interest also in pursuing political dialogue with its Asian partners and in making a modest contribution to Asia's efforts to achieve regional stability. Other areas where the EU would like to see closer cooperation are human resources, energy, and environment. The EU's main objectives at the summit were:

- To raise the mutual awareness of the potential for cooperation, particularly in the area of trade and investment;
- To support an open world trade system and sustainable development, and initiate a process of multilateral trade liberalization as well as unilateral measures to facilitate trade and investments among participating countries;
- To promote political dialogue between the two regions with a view to peace and stability;
- To promote more cooperation between Asia and Europe in a number of fields.

Latin America

The EU is also the principal aid donor to Latin America (60 percent of all aid in 1993), emphasizing support for rural development and regional cooperation. Recently, emphasis on support for human rights and on development of democracy has increased. The EU has also negotiated agreements with both MERCOSUR and the Andean Pact while deepening its relations with Mexico and other Central American countries (Dialogue San José). In October 1995 the Commission presented new proposals to the Council to strengthen ties between the EU and Latin America. The emphasis would be on political dialogue, measures to promote regional integration and free trade, and cooperation on a wide range of other issues including the environment, drugs, and poverty.[29]

The Administration and Budget for External Relations

As the TEU went into effect, both the Council and Commission were forced to undergo an internal reorganization to cope with the new demands on the external front. For the Council this meant doubling the staff in the CFSP unit to around twenty-four, half from the Council and half from member states. For the Commission it involved changing the division of responsibilities agreed upon in 1993, when Sir Leon Brittan took responsibility for external economic relations and Hans van den Broek responsibility for external political relations. This rather unsatisfactory division was ended in 1995 by the creation of geographic responsibilities involving four Commissioners. The main external relations directorate general (DG I) was split into DG I (responsible for external trade and the G-7 countries), DG I-A (responsible for all of Europe, Russia, and the CIS, CFSP, and the new unified external service), DG I-B (responsible for the Middle East, Mediterranean, and Southeast Asia), plus DG VIII with its traditional responsibility for the developing world. This geographical split was partly necessitated by the increased number of commissioners following the EFTA enlargement.[30] The decision to create the Commission's unified external service and its management structure in 1993 was followed at the beginning of 1995 by the creation of the commissioners' and directors' general external relations groups, known as Relex. Despite early predictions, the Relex group has worked well. Early warning of new initiatives to allow for policy coordination at a preparatory stage has become a regular feature, and informal and pragmatic cooperation among external-relations staff has become increasingly common in everyday work. It is perhaps also worth noting that the unified external service of the Commission now employs 2,452 staff spread over 126 missions. In DG I-A a further 729 staff are employed. These numbers mean that the Commission possesses the fifth largest diplomatic service in Europe.

With regard to the budget, just under 6 percent of the Union's ECU 86.5 billion budget for 1996 was earmarked for foreign spending, on projects ranging from supporting the transition in South Africa (ECU 125 million), monitoring the elections in Palestine (ECU 80 million), and administering the Bosnian town of Mostar (ECU 32 million) to promoting EU exports to Japan (ECU 13 million). But the bulk of spending—some ECU 2 billion—was earmarked for Central and Eastern Europe, Russia, and the CIS, with a further ECU 900 million for North Africa and the Mediterranean. Food aid totalled some ECU 850 million, with another ECU 730 million for development aid, followed by ECU 550 million for specific development projects in Cuba, Vietnam, Latin America, and Africa. Much of these sums were to be disbursed by the European Community Humanitarian Aid Office (ECHO). In what is perhaps a sign of how immature the CFSP remains, its administrative budget line was a mere ECU 30 million.

The Maastricht Treaty

The Maastricht Treaty on Economic Union (TEU) gave a further boost to European integration. The twin driving forces were Economic and Monetary

Union (EMU) and the prospect of a Common European Defense. The agreement to proceed with a three-stage plan to achieve EMU by the end of the century was as much a political as an economic decision. The eventual adoption of the euro as the common currency for the Union could have major political implications both within member states and in the wider world. Externally, the euro could well rival the dollar and yen as a reserve currency and increase the influence of the Europeans in international monetary institutions (see Hosli's analysis in Chapter 9). It should logically lead to a G-3 world economic structure (EU, United States, and Japan).

On the political side, EU leaders agreed at Maastricht to a number of new common policies, albeit some outside the Union framework. CFSP and Interior/Justice matters were established under separate pillars organized on an intergovernmental basis. The European Parliament won a number of extra powers, including the right to codecision in areas such as the single market, consumer protection, free circulation of workers, education and vocational training, research and development, environment, communications, public health, and culture. Many of these subjects were new policy areas for the Union. It also won the right to confirm the president of the Commission and other Commissioners in January 1995. Since the TEU was signed, however, debate has persisted on the future of Europe, leading to a range of proposals for institutional reform.

Amsterdam and CFSP Reform

Despite the extensive preparations leading up to the 1996–1997 IGC, and the lengthy negotiations themselves, few politicians or commentators considered the outcome a major success. "Disappointing" and "modest" were the adjectives most frequently used to describe the results. Jacques Delors was perhaps the most trenchant critic, stating that the conclusions were "catastrophic" for Europe. What was originally conceived largely as an internal policy-developing exercise, notably toward CFSP, became overshadowed by the twin pressures of the single currency and enlargement. It was no surprise, therefore, that meeting deadlines and keeping to timetables gradually assumed more importance than the actual substance of reform. In the end agreement was reached, but largely through a mixture of exhaustion, frustration, and prevarication. In the aftermath of the summit, it was not surprising to hear calls for a different approach to preparing constitutional change in the Union.

There is little doubt that the agenda for the Amsterdam summit was heavily overloaded. The energetic Dutch presidency had toured capitals to seek possible compromise solutions to difficult outstanding issues such as institutional reform, but had failed to narrow down the options to manageable proportions for the heads of government. The agenda had also taken on many issues that should have been dealt with at a lower level, including animal welfare, the position of the German Sparkassen, etc. An added problem, sparked by the election of a new Socialist government in France, was the row that surfaced immediately before the summit regarding the interpretation of the Maastricht criteria for entry into the third stage of Economic and Monetary Union (EMU). This dispute took up the entire first day of the summit, which meant that little time remained to resolve the most contentious issues of institutional reform. CFSP reforms were, however, largely agreed upon in advance of the European Council meeting. The principal changes were as follows:

Consistency of external activities. The pillar structure of the Maastricht Treaty was not changed, but the Amsterdam treaty demonstrates an increased awareness of the need for consistency in external relations. Article C has been amended and it now foresees the duty of both the Council and the Commission to cooperate to ensure consistency. The new Article J(4) Par. 4 states that the Council may request the Commission to submit proposals on CFSP to ensure the implementation of a joint action. The declaration on the new planning unit explicitly says that appropriate cooperation with the Commission shall be established in order to ensure full coherence.

CFSP objectives. Article J(1) has added a new CFSP objective: the safeguarding of the "integrity of the Union in conformity with the principles of the UN Charter." The same article introduces a new obligation for member states: they "shall work together to enhance and develop their mutual political solidarity."

CFSP instruments. The treaty clarified the distinction between joint actions and common positions and introduced a new instrument (common strategies) without defining it clearly. Article J(2) sets the list of CFSP instruments: principles and general guidelines; common strategies; joint actions; common positions and systematic cooperation. Article J(3) specifies that principles/general guidelines and common strategies are defined by the European Council. Common strategies are to be adopted in areas where member states have important interests in common. Article J(3) reinforces the role of the European Council in CFSP but poses the risk of making decisionmaking in CFSP relatively cumbersome. Article J(4) defines joint actions, saying that they shall address specific situations where operational action is needed. Article J(5) defines common positions: they "shall define the approach of the Union to a particular matter of a geographical or thematic nature."

Institutional set-up. Apart from enhancing the role of the European Council, the treaty also reinforced the Secretary General of the Council. He or she will act as the high representative for CFSP, will assist the Council in CFSP matters, in particular conducting political dialogue with third parties, and will head the new policy-planning and early warning unit. The presidency, the Secretary General, and the Commission will constitute a new troika. The Commission's role has not been substantially modified: it remains "fully associated" with all areas of the CFSP work. The Parliament's involvement in CFSP also remains unchanged, continuing its right to be consulted and informed.

Preparation of decisions. The initiative in CFSP is still shared between member states and the Commission. In practice, proposals presented by the presidency, perhaps resulting from the work of the new planning unit, will have the greatest chance of success. A declaration to the final act provided for the creation of a policy-planning and early warning unit, to be established in the General Secretariat of the Council under the responsibility of its Secretary General. The unit will consist of personnel drawn from the General Secretariat, member states, the Commission, and WEU. Its tasks shall include, among others, "producing at the request of either the Council or the presidency or on its own initiative, argued policy options papers to be presented under the responsibility of the presidency."

Decisionmaking. The Treaty of Amsterdam increases the use of majority voting in CFSP but still considers unanimity as the general principle. Article J(13) envisages three voting procedures for the Council: unanimity, qualified majority voting (QMV), and majority voting of its members. The principle of unanimity is nuanced by the possibility of constructive abstention. The member state abstaining will not be obliged to apply the decision but shall accept that the decision commits the Union and shall refrain from any action likely to conflict with EU action. However, if the member states abstaining constructively represent more than one-third of the votes (weighted according to the QMV rules), the decision will not be adopted. The Council will be able to act by QMV (sixty-two votes in favor cast by at least ten members) when adopting decisions on the basis of a common strategy (adopted by unanimity by the European Council) or decisions implementing a joint action/common position. However, a member state can oppose the adoption of a decision by QMV for "important and stated reasons of national policy." In this case, the Council may, by QMV, refer the matter to the European Council, which will decide by unanimity. QMV will not apply to military decisions. The Council will act by majority of its members for procedural questions.

Implementation and representation. Article J(8) of the treaty confers the implementation and representation tasks on the presidency, who shall be assisted by the Secretary General, acting as high representative for the

CFSP. He will be assisted by a deputy Secretary General, responsible for the running of the General Secretariat. The Commission shall be fully associated to the tasks of implementation and representation and with CFSP work in general. The Council may also appoint special representatives for particular issues. Article J(16) states that the Secretary General will assist the Council in the implementation of its decisions and will conduct political dialogue with third parties "when appropriate and acting on behalf of the Council at the request of the Presidency."

International organizations. The Treaty provisions on the member states' behavior in international organizations have not been substantially changed.

CFSP financing. The new Article J(18) states the principle that CFSP operational expenditure shall be charged to the budget of the European Communities and recognizes two exceptions: when military operations are at issue and when the Council unanimously decides otherwise. If expenditure is not charged to the EC budget, it shall be charged to member states according to GNP. In case of a military operation decided with the constructive abstention of one or some member states, these shall not be obliged to contribute to its financing.

A draft interinstitutional agreement on CFSP financing was negotiated on the margins of the IGC and signed in July 1997. It considers CFSP expenditure as nonobligatory, which means that the European Parliament has the last word. It foresees that, on the basis of the Commission's proposal, the European Parliament and the Council shall annually secure agreement on the global amount of CFSP expenditure. This global amount will be allocated among new articles of the CFSP budgetary chapter (i.e., observation of elections, EU envoys, prevention of conflicts, disarmament, international conferences, and urgent actions). No funds will be entered into a reserve.

Security and defense. Article J(7) is the result of conflicting views of member states on the most difficult CFSP issue of the IGC negotiations: security and defense. Although the Amsterdam draft treaty did not go far enough on EU/WEU relations, it contains a number of improvements; for example:

- The eventual framing of a common defense policy becomes a progressive one;
- The inclusion in the treaty of the "Petersberg tasks" (humanitarian and rescue tasks, peacekeeping tasks, and tasks of combat forces in crisis management, including peacemaking);
- Agreement that the EU "will avail itself of the WEU to elaborate and implement decisions of the Union which have defense implications"

(Article J(7) Par. 3). When the EU avails itself of the WEU on the Petersberg tasks, all contributing member states will be able to participate fully and on an equal footing in planning and decisionmaking in the WEU.

On the link between the EU and the WEU, Amsterdam did not meet the expectations of a majority of member states. The idea of a draft protocol on WEU integration into the EU with a specific timetable was finally abandoned in the face of opposition from the UK and the three newest members of the Union. Nevertheless, Article J(7) Par. 1 still considers WEU as "an integral part of the development of the Union" and adds the idea that the WEU will provide the Union with access to an operational capability, notably for the "Petersberg tasks." In addition, the competence of the European Council to establish guidelines in accordance with Article J(3) shall also obtain in respect of the WEU for those matters for which the Union avails itself of the WEU (Art. J(7) Par. 3). According to a protocol to Article J(7), arrangements for enhanced cooperation between the EU and WEU are to be drawn up within a year from the entry into force of this protocol.

In relation to NATO, Article J(7) Par. 1 says that the policy of the Union "shall respect the obligations of certain member states, which see their common defense realized in NATO, under the North Atlantic Treaty." This amendment will have to be clarified.

Cooperation in the field of armaments "as Member States consider appropriate" (Article J(7) Par. 1) is not formulated in very strong terms.

Flexibility. The constructive abstention (Article J(13) Par. 1) is the form of flexibility that the draft treaty has finally adopted for CFSP. Member states making use of the constructive abstention shall not be obliged to apply the decision but shall accept that the decision commits the Union. The general clauses on closer cooperation/flexibility established in Section V apply to CFSP; therefore, the criteria for flexibility listed in Article 1 of this section apply. On the other hand, expenditure resulting from implementation of closer cooperation, other than administrative costs entailed for the institutions, shall be borne by the participating states, unless the Council decides otherwise by unanimity (Article 2 of Section V). Article J(18) Par. 3 also says that member states that have made use of the constructive abstention shall not be obliged to contribute to the financing of operations having military implications.

International agreements. The Amsterdam draft treaty has dropped the idea of recognizing the EU as a legal personality. Nevertheless the new Article J(14) (which was the logical consequence in CFSP of the EU legal personality) stands. This article foresees the possibility of international

agreements in CFSP without specifying who will be a party to it. It could
be interpreted in the future as recognizing an implicit legal personality for
the EU. Such agreements shall be negotiated by the presidency, "assisted
by the Commission as appropriate" (i.e., not on a regular basis) after authorization by the Council, acting unanimously. They will be concluded by
the Council, by unanimity, on a recommendation of the presidency. A declaration specifies that this article and the agreements resulting from it shall
not imply any transfer of competence from member states to the Union.

Article 113 (external economic relations) has not been extended to international negotiations and agreements on services and intellectual property. Nevertheless, it has been modified in order to allow its extension
without having to modify the treaty: a Council decision by unanimity on a
Commission's proposal and after consulting the European Parliament will
suffice.

Article 228(2) has been modified concerning the provisional application and the suspension of international Community agreements.

Assessment. The CFSP changes articulated in the Amsterdam treaty may
best be described as modest. It will, however, take some time to assess the
implications of the changes, as much will depend on their interpretation.
The Commission and Council will have to examine concrete forms of cooperation as requested in new Article C. Concrete steps to be taken include: arrangements for a good functioning of the new troika, strong coordination with the presidency and with the General Secretariat of the
Council, and participation in the new planning unit.

The tasks of the new troika remain to be defined. Under a minimalist
interpretation of the treaty, the presidency and the Secretary General of the
Council would be the principal actors, and the Commission would simply
be "fully associated." Another restrictive interpretation would limit the
scope of action of the troika to implementation and representation, thus
hindering policy formulation. Hence, it will be important to ensure that the
new troika is involved in all aspects of the CFSP process.

Article J(4) Par. 4 envisages the possibility that the Council requests
the Commission to submit proposals relating to CFSP to ensure the implementation of a joint action. The exact meaning of this new provision will
depend on the content of the joint actions—which might encompass, for
example, special envoys, observation of elections, or financial contributions to international organizations—but could cover both first and second
pillars. This new provision should allow enhanced consistency between the
first and the second pillars, but it also risks restricting the Commission's
freedom to maneuver. On the other hand, the Commission's proposals could
also cover the member states' contributions if the Council so decides.

The interinstitutional agreement will have important consequences for the
Commission's role in CFSP financing. These could involve the Commission

in preparing a preliminary draft budget containing a CFSP budget chapter with specific budgetary lines reflecting CFSP priorities. On the basis of a Council decision, the Commission will have autonomous authority to make credit transfers between articles of the CFSP budget chapter. The respective roles of the Council and the Commission concerning the "fiche financière" will have to be clarified. The Commission shall inform the budgetary authority (Council/Parliament) on the execution of CFSP actions and the financial forecasts for the remaining period of the year on a quarterly basis.

In a declaration on the organization and functioning of the Commission, the conference noted the Commission's intention to prepare a reorganization of tasks within the College in good time for the new Commission of the year 2000; considered that the president of the Commission must enjoy broad discretion on allocating and reshuffling of tasks within the College; and noted the Commission's intention to undertake a reorganization of its departments, in particular those dealing with external relations, and the intention of appointing a vice-president for external affairs.

CFSP and Enlargement

With the publication of "Agenda 2000" on 16 July 1997,[31] the Commission set out its views on the EU's priorities for the coming decade and recommended, on the basis of individual opinions on the candidate countries, that accession negotiations commence early in 1998 with five countries (Poland, Hungary, Estonia, the Czech Republic, and Slovenia) as well as with Cyprus, which received a positive avis in 1993. It recommended that the remaining five candidates (Latvia, Lithuania, Slovakia, Romania, and Bulgaria) be subjected to an annual review, with the possibility of joining those already at the negotiating table when sufficient progress was made. At Luxembourg in December 1997 the European Council broadly endorsed the Commission's proposals in Agenda 2000 concerning the enlargement process. The heads of state and government agreed that there should be (1) an enlargement process, (2) an accession process, and (3) a negotiating process.

In the CFSP chapters on the candidates, all received a positive assessment as they had been shadowing CFSP for some time and had demonstrated their general and specific support for CFSP declarations and actions. Given the predominantly declaratory nature of CFSP, one could argue that this was not a difficult hurdle for them to overcome. More challenging obstacles to accession might, however, be posed by their reaction to sharing sovereignty, by the increased difficulty of achieving consensus in a more numerous and heterogeneous Union, and by the small size and lack of experience of some new members' diplomatic services and armed forces.

Although all CEECs regained their national independence only a few years ago, their sensitivity regarding national sovereignty varies from country to country. This is partly due to their differing historical experiences and heritages, factors in which the public perception of sovereignty is deeply rooted. In addition, even during the period of Soviet domination they enjoyed differing levels of small freedoms, for example in the areas of political and economic reform. Moreover, in some cases, political independence resulted in the rebirth of nation-states, while in others, entirely new states were created. Czech independence dates back to 1618, Estonia has a record of only a few years of national independence, and Slovenia has never been an independent state. Thus, in many countries nation building (and state building) has to be carried out simultaneously with integration into EU and global structures. Sharing sovereignty in foreign and security policy could well pose domestic problems, but these could be eased with integration into NATO and WEU.

An enlarged EU stretching from Sweden to Cyprus and from Ireland to Estonia will clearly find it more difficult than previously to agree on common FSP interests, assuming that it is able to do so at all! The assumption of the presidency by one of the new small member states could also pose problems in terms of resources, experience, and credibility. Overall, however, enlargement should lead to greater security in Europe because the new members and continuing candidates will have to accept the strict political conditionality that EU membership necessitates. The challenge will be to expand the EU's own security community to the eastern half of the continent.

Conclusion

Despite the fact that reform of the CFSP was one of the main reasons for holding the IGC, and despite the large measure of agreement reached on the need to improve its operation, the outcome at Amsterdam was extremely modest. Past experience suggests that appropriate structures and procedures alone will not suffice to ensure a coherent and effective foreign and security policy. The political will to fully exploit them must exist if a real CFSP is to emerge. This will require deeper awareness among member states of the interests they share as EU members as well as recognition that many of their own national interests might be better served when pursued jointly. CFSP players on all levels will slowly have to learn to overcome the traditions and emotions of foreign policy and to look at themselves not only as national representatives but as participants in a common enterprise: the shaping of a genuine European foreign and security policy.

It is unrealistic to expect this transformation to happen quickly; CFSP touches on the most sensitive areas of national sovereignty. It is important to regard CFSP as a process in which the member states gradually pursue their external interests together rather than separately. Perhaps there is too much focus on the initials CFSP. The truth is that as far as the external relations of the Union are concerned, Europe has never been more united than it is today, and, given the changing nature of security in the post–Cold War era, the EU is well placed to deal with the new panoply of security risks that has arisen. After forty years in which security was largely seen in purely military terms—balance of power and deterrence—with the collapse of Communism, a range of new security risks have emerged that require a multifaceted response. The approach to security will encompass not only military but also political, economic, social, and environmental means. The EU, which is the very negation of the old balance of power approach to international relations, has a duty to take the lead in cooperation with other institutions dealing with European security.

The new European security system will need an anchor of stability that can only be provided by the European Union. To fulfill this role, the European Union will not only have to act in close partnership with the United States but also with countries such as Russia, the Ukraine, and Turkey. These partnerships will provide the foreign policy of the European Union with a vital transatlantic and all-European dimension, complemented by a strong Mediterranean component.

In the 1970s and 1980s West Germany was described as "an economic giant but a political dwarf." The same description could have been applied to the Union in the 1980s and 1990s. Just as the unification of Germany has given the Germans a stronger political voice, so too will the political weight of the Union increase in parallel course with its moves to deeper integration. This process will require a genuine commitment by the member states to ensure an effective CFSP if the Union is to take an active, as opposed to reactive, role in pursuing and defending its interests on the international stage. As the main provider of "soft" security, the EU is already performing an important stabilizing function, but it will also have to develop a "hard" security component if it is credibly to punch its weight on the world stage.

Notes

1. The views expressed are personal and do not commit the European Commission in any way.

2. Commission of the European Communities, "Speech by Mr. Jacques Santer to the Davos World Economic Forum," *Rapid*, 28 January 1995.

3. See Holbrooke's interview in the *Washington Post*, 23 February 1996; articles by Eizenstat and Gardner in the *International Herald Tribune*, 2 November 1995 and 30 January 1996, respectively.

4. Hill 1994.

5. Treaty establishing the European Coal and Steel Community Luxembourg: 1950.

6. Among the best texts analyzing the growth of EU external interests are Nuttall 1992; Hill 1983; and Lodge 1993.

7. All statistics are based on figures provided by *Eurostat*.

8. Ibid.

9. See Babarinde's examination in Chapter 7.

10. See Herrberg's discussion, Chapter 5, of EU-Russian relations, where this change has been particularly evident.

11. Commission of the European Communities, "ECHO: Ufficio per gli aiuti umanitari della comunita europea," *Rapid*, 16 November 1994.

12. Commission of the European Communities, "European Council in Lisbon 26–27 June 1992: Conclusions of the Presidency," *Rapid*, 27 June 1992.

13. PHARE and TACIS are the technical assistance programs for the CEEC and CIS respectively.

14. See Chapter 6 for an in-depth and somewhat more critical analysis.

15. For an assessment of the Europe agreements, see Center for Economic Policy Research London, 1992 report, "Is Bigger Better? The Economics of Enlargement."

16. Based on figures provided by *Eurostat*.

17. In a report from the Council to the Essen European Council found in *Euro-East*, 13 December 1994.

18. Commission of the European Communities, "European Council: 9–10 December 1994 in Essen Presidency Conclusions," *Rapid*, 10 December 1994.

19. Commission of the European Communities, "Enlargement: Questions and Answers," *Rapid*, 30 July 1996.

20. The conclusions at Madrid exceeded the expectations of the CEEC.

21. For an assessment of the Stability Pact, see unpublished paper by Fraser Cameron presented to the U.S. Defense Agency Conference on Regional Arms Control. Cameron 1995a.

22. The PCA with Russia was signed at the Corfu Council meeting, June 1994. For more information, see Commission of the European Communities, "European Council at Corfu 24–25 June 1994: Presidency Conclusions," *Rapid*, 25 June 1994.

23. There is a wide literature on the EU's role in ex-Yugoslavia. Cviic 1993 is one of the best reviews.

24. Commission of the European Communities, "Barcelona Euro-Mediterranean Conference 27–28 November 1995 Declaration and Work Programme," *Rapid*, 4 December 1995.

25. This is discussed at length in Chapter 8.

26. Transatlantic Declaration text in *Agence Europe*, 13 December 1995.

27. Ibid.

28. See conclusions of the Madrid summit, Krenzler and Schomaker 1996, p. 6.

29. Commission of the European Communities, "Strengthening the EU's Policy Towards Mercosur," *Rapid*, 25 October 1995.

30. The four commissioners involved were Sir Leon Brittan (DG I), Hans van den Broek (DG IA), Manuel Marin (DG IB), and João Pinheiro (DG VIII).

31. Commission of the European Communities, "Agenda 2000: For a Stronger and Wider Europe," 15 July 1997. Com (97) 2000; Supplement 5/97—*Bulletin of the European Communities*.

3

The European Union's Security Presence: Barrier, Facilitator, or Manager?

David Allen & Michael Smith

There can be no doubt that the role played by the European Union in the European security order is a key concern for both analysts and policymakers in the late 1990s. While the EU once could be seen as an epiphenomenon of the Cold War, reflecting, and at times magnifying, the overall level of tensions in a divided Europe, in the early 1990s discussions began to focus on both the attractions and the institutional limitations of the Union as a means of promoting or ensuring European security. In an era where the very definition of "Europe" and of "security" has become a matter of continuous speculation and political uncertainty, it is clearly important to ask analytical questions about the ways in which the EU "fits" within the emerging—or re-emerging—European security order.

Developments in 1995 and 1996 provided substantial evidence that the EU's position is both consequential and contentious. Despite the unclear relationship between the EU's security role and the European security order itself, fluctuating buildup to the Intergovernmental Conference security policy became a central issue involving further definition of the fate of the Union and of its international role. At the same time, specific security episodes, such as the Greek-Turkish flare-up in the Aegean, gave cause for concern over how the Union can, or should, respond to even relatively minor turbulence.[1] From an outside perspective, it appeared that the EU was often asleep on the job in the pursuit of European security.

The security role of the EU is an area of acute political sensitivity and complexity as well as academic interest. On one hand, observers might claim that the question is when, and not if, the EU will assume a major security role in the new Europe.[2] Indeed, it could be argued that the EU already has a major security position, and that the issue to be examined is how this position shall be discharged and transformed into a "European" policy. The basis for this assertion is that the EU clearly "matters" and, more importantly, that the significance of its security role has been fundamentally transformed by the cessation of the Cold War.[3] According to this view, the Union must move forward in order to maintain its credibility and leverage, and the way forward is to create an essentially state-like foreign and security policy.

The problem with this perspective is that the distinction between state-like and state is increasingly becoming critical for the EU. In the Treaty on European Union, the EU set for itself the ambitious objectives of creating an economic and monetary union, framing a common foreign and security policy, and enhancing cooperation in the fields of justice and home affairs. It is extremely difficult to conceive of an entity properly endowed with these capabilities that does not possess a central political authority, or government, capable of identifying, articulating, legitimizing, and pursuing common interests. From this vantage point, then, in the post-Maastricht EU, the centrality of the member states as regards national security issues will inexorably come under attack as the implications of the CFSP are confronted.

The institutional arrangements agreed upon at Maastricht and further developed at Amsterdam in 1997 certainly provide the basis for the EU becoming more state-like in the field of foreign and security policy. However, even though it was agreed at Amsterdam that the Secretary General of the Council would be appointed high representative for the CFSP, political authority in this realm remains diffused among the Council, the Council Presidency, the Political Committee, the European Council, the Council Secretariat, and the Commission. These arrangements, therefore, may not be sufficient to meet the challenges posed by the EU's stated foreign policy, security, and defense ambitions. If future demands require arrangements that go beyond the *state-like* to those we traditionally associate with *full statehood*, then the modest improvements incorporated into the Amsterdam treaty will prove inadequate.[4]

Unfortunately, the record of the past six years is far from encouraging for those who would wish to propel the EU toward statehood, particularly in security matters. While the EU may have a broadly diplomatic role, and a more tangible role in the provision of economic and social reconstruction, the harsh fact is that only states—and only certain states—can meet the most demanding challenges and take the ultimate risks.[5]

Perhaps it makes sense, then, to focus not on the EU, but on the fact that other, arguably more appropriate security structures are available to deal with the emerging European political-security order of the new millennium.[6] The anticipated demise of NATO has not occurred,[7] and in fact NATO has shown considerable political and institutional vigor. Its continued legitimacy and viability is reflected in the EU's recognition at Amsterdam that EU security cooperation "shall respect the obligations of certain Member States, which see their common defence recognized in NATO, under the North Atlantic Treaty and be compatible with the common security and defence policy established within that framework."[8]

The Organization for Security and Cooperation in Europe, on the other hand, has failed to find a significant role in the building of the wider Europe. It has, however, assumed important negotiating functions as well as provided a set of ideas for the prosecution of conflict management across the full breadth of the new Europe. In this context, the EU appears not to be unimportant, but to be important only in certain ways, which do not add up to a comprehensive framework for the pursuit of European security.

This chapter undertakes an analysis of the EU's security role in the new Europe, taking up and extending a number of themes raised by the authors in an article written during 1989, at the very moment that things were changing in ways not anticipated even six months before.[9] That article put forward a view of the (then) EC's role, which attempted to fill the gap between state-centric explanations and explanations that cast the EC as simply another organizational framework. This view, based upon the notion of "presence" in the international arena, has been widely used as a basis for argument by subsequent authors,[10] and it seems appropriate to revisit it briefly. This review is followed by a discussion of major new elements affecting the European security order during the 1990s, particularly as they might affect the EU's "presence."

This notion of "presence" needs to be accompanied by a more definite notion of purpose. Here, we contend that two developments of the "presence" framework can be used to focus argument about the EU in the 1990s: first, the notion of *making the EU's presence felt* in the European security order, and second, the notion of *taking responsibility*. These ideas are extended to explore three strands in the EU's presence: those of *barrier, facilitator,* and *manager.* Each of these contains a specific mix of the assumptions and insights generated by the extended "presence" framework. This chapter is thus an attempt to revisit, reassess, and extend the framework advanced in 1990, and to test it against empirical evidence from the post–Cold War European security order.

The Notion of "Presence"

Our original argument about "presence" arose from the perception that "concepts failed us" when we explored the international role of the EC. This failure took two specific forms: first, the identification of the EC with "Europe" or "Western Europe," and second, the adoption of a statist model for analysis of developments in the EC itself.[11] Both orientations proved inadequate when faced with the inherently ambiguous status and impact of the EC in the world arena. The sustained attention given by both politicians and academics to the development of "European foreign policy" and "European identity" during the late 1980s undoubtedly proved there was something going on, but its normative overtones prevented a rigorous analysis. For too many analysts, the institutional arrangements and their impact on the overall development of the EC itself were clearly more significant than the substantive policy that they produced (or failed to produce). The focus of their work was the state of the EC order itself, rather than the place of the EC in the wider European order.

Our central argument was that Western Europe was neither a fully fledged state-like actor nor a purely dependent phenomenon in the international arena. Rather, it was a "variable and multi-dimensional presence," playing an active role in some areas of international interaction and a less active one in others. "Presence," we argued, was a feature or quality of arenas, of issue areas, and of networks of activity, operating to influence the actions and expectations of participants.

In addition to providing the basis for a narrative of the EC's development during the late 1980s, this framework allowed us to draw some significant contrasts between issue areas. To be specific, in the political sphere, the presence of Western Europe could be seen as a "shaper" or "filter," molding the perceptions both of West European policymakers and of others, shaping collective action, and filtering out certain options. This was mainly an intangible process, but we discerned significant moves toward tangible impacts through the development of European Political Cooperation and other mechanisms and through the clear convergence of national foreign policy positions.

In the military sphere, the presence of Western Europe was also often intangible but powerful. The achievements of West European security cooperation during the 1980s were relatively modest, but the shaping power of ideas about a "European security identity" was consistent in the sense either that major EC members such as France or (West) Germany promoted such visions or that they were a matter of concern to powerful outsiders such as the United States. Such ideas, however, had to cope with powerful barriers put up both by individual countries and by NATO. Such were the inhibitions of the Cold War system that we tended to agree with the view that, after 1980, a true EC security identity was "always on the agenda but never in the cards."[12]

The most tangible West European presence was to be found in the economic sphere, but the effect of this presence was far from universally positive. In many ways the West European presence seemed to be an inhibiting factor, rationalizing or reinforcing defensive postures of national authorities, and forming a target for the attentions of other actors in the international arena.[13]

It is clear from this summary that in the late 1980s the EC had barely scratched the surface of the security *problematique*. Two elements in the challenge confronting the EC were crucial: first, national security remained a central part of national identity and a central rationale for state policies; and second, primary institutional channels for collective action in security were still those of the Cold War system, particularly NATO. For the EC, these factors were both a reflection and a cause of its inhibitions. On the one hand, the inherent qualities of the EC as a "civilian power" meant that the development of a tangible security presence was not given a high priority. On the other hand, the continuing assertion of national primacy in the area of security policy meant that even if EC institutions had conceived of a more active presence—and it is clear that Delors did harbor such ambitions[14]—the EC would have faced important obstacles.

It was logical to conclude that the EC did not have much of a track record in or many prospects for developing a more active and tangible security presence. Despite changes in the national security debate to encompass more explicitly notions of "economic security," the debate remained firmly entrenched in notions of statehood and state primacy. It appeared that the future would look, at least in the central areas of national security, rather like the past. By the end of 1990, however, it was clear not only that the future was more uncertain than we had ever imagined it might be, but also that the pressure on the EC in post–Cold War Europe was likely to be one of the dominating themes of the 1990s.

Change in the European Security Order

There is now a large and diverse literature about the nature and impact of change in post–Cold War Europe.[15] This transformation can be described as the central analytic theme of world politics and security studies since the turn of the decade. Essentially, it can be argued that the nature of change in the European arena has created new parameters for the expression of a West European presence, and specifically a presence in the changing security order. The institutional and functional development of the EU since 1990 makes it appropriate for the purposes of analysis to conflate the previously separate notions of "Western Europe" and the EC at this stage, although it is important to retain a sense of the nuances implicit in the earlier distinction.

What are the new parameters created by change in Europe, and how have they affected the ambiguous presence of the EU? It has often been noted that the EU expresses a number of paradoxes.[16] In the first place, it can be seen both as resting on a highly developed notion of the state and as challenging conventional notions of statehood. Second, it can be seen both as magnifying and as subverting the characteristics of interstate politics. Finally, it can be seen both as an emanation of the state system and as an agent of its transformation. In turn, these paradoxes, and the tensions they create, have led to uncertainty about the credentials of the EU as an international actor: the notions of "civilian power" and of the "capability-expectations gap" are two attempts to describe the boundaries of the EC/EU's presence.[17]

Many of these notions and paradoxes, however, were derived from settled assumptions about the context within which the EC/EU was located, about the character of the international arena, and about the qualities of statehood. For instance, the notion of civilian power, which could be seen positively as the expression of nonmilitaristic and noncoercive approaches to security, could also be seen negatively as a mere rationalization of military impotence in the face of superpower predominance, a fact of life in "Cold War Europe," where the lines of division and confrontation seemed to be set in concrete. It can, however, powerfully be argued that there is at present no settled definition of "Europe," and therefore that many of the traditional arguments about the EC/EU as an international actor are obsolete. During the late 1980s and early 1990s, there was a shift from change within a settled system to change of the system itself.[18]

This meant that at the level of European order, the assumed congruence between distributions of power, institutions, and ideologies of international politics dissolved. Where once a European order emerged from the superpower-dominated West European and East European orders, now Western Europe seemed on the verge of expansion to incorporate most but not all of Eastern Europe, while one superpower withdrew and the other imploded. The boundaries of Europe shifted not only territorially but also in the minds of political and other actors. While the Cold War system could be evaluated in terms of its rigidity and suppression of cross-European processes, what replaced it was a shifting mosaic of authority and actors, which some have described as neomedieval in character.[19] To anticipate part of the later argument in this chapter, the concept of "presence" has different meanings in such a milieu, and the question arises as to whether the concept can cope with the demands made upon it.

Furthermore, the notion of European security itself (and of national security broadly defined) has been challenged in many ways by the events of the 1990s. At one level, there is the tension between institutions designed to produce security in a Cold War system and the challenges posed by a mosaic form of security. As noted in Chapter 2, this can produce symptoms of institutional competition and institutional "overcrowding." At another level, there is the tension between essentially military concepts of security and the ever intensifying linkages between concepts and practices of security in the political, economic, and societal contexts, all of which have their own institutional expression. West Europeans, who for years lived in fear of the nuclear and conventional might of the Soviet Union, now find their way of life increasingly threatened by environmental and ecological challenges such as those posed by the Chernobyl disaster, or by the determination of millions of neighbors to the east and south who wish to live like they do—either by benefitting from opportunities Western Europe can offer their socieities or, if not, by migrating. Ecological dangers and the threat of mass migration give a very real security role to institutions like the European Union whose economic capability may be just as relevant as its military potential. A number of coinages have been developed to try and express some of the consequences of NATO's loss of "security exclusiveness": the notion of "institutional overcrowding," the linked notions of "organizational interlock" and "organizational gridlock," or the often nebulous ideas of "economic security" and "societal security."[20]

In this flux and uncertainty, it is not surprising that the EU has appeared to express important and desirable qualities, and that these qualities have been conceptualized in relation to security. Where there is political confusion, the EU appears to promise strong ideas of civic statehood and the rule of law. Where there is economic instability, the EU appears to promise strong mechanisms of governance and regulation. Where there is the potential for movement from diplomatic friction to military confrontation, the EU, along with the revived and revitalized WEU, appears to be a vehicle for European order. Such perceptions are current both within and outside the EU, and one of their clearest expressions is the widespread desire to be included in the EU itself. Another such expression is the desire on the part of EU member states to extend the mechanisms of governance into new areas, most particularly the areas of foreign and security policy and, more ambitiously, defense policy. Such a desire is a reflection of perceptions about the importance of the EU to the establishment of a viable European order.

This is only the starting point of new ambiguities, which take us to the heart of our enquiry in this chapter. In the first place, it is clear that the EU expresses a strong and tangible presence in the changing European order. It is uncertain, however, whether this presence is likely to contribute to pan-European forms of integration, through the generation of a "politics of inclusion," or whether it will be characterized by the "politics of exclusion."[21] Such uncertainty potentially produces considerable tension between the "EU order" and the broader European order (the extent of which is still under much debate—a European order that extends from the Atlantic to the Urals is rather different from one that extends from Poland to Portugal or, yet again, from Vancouver to Vladivostok). Furthermore, given the tension between challenges to the European order and the existing institutional framework, it is inevitable that new patterns of incentives and expectations will arise for members of the order. There will be a demand for presence, so to speak, in new areas, both spatially and politically defined. This was clearly demonstrated by the "spotlight" that fell on the EC as the iron curtain came down. George Bush considered the EC to be the central focus of a Europe "whole and free," and Mikhail Gorbachev clearly identified the EC as the major expression of a "common European home." But the problem for the EU is whether this presence can effectively be supplied through the existing institutions and mechanisms of the "EU order."

This means that the EU order is now of direct relevance to our enquiry, and in particular that the relationship between the EU and statehood is thrown into sharp relief. Much of the argument so far has left implicit the relationship between European integration and the persistence of state power, which has been a continuous thread in the evolution, and the limitations, of integration. The focus on security gives a particular cast to this debate, since it sets the most demanding test possible for the integration process. In addition, it could be argued that the safety of the EU order itself, as both an institutional and a normative expression of the progress of integration, may be challenged by the circumstances that now exist in post–Cold War Europe. Much of the current work on the EU, whether it concentrates on its potential "widening" or "deepening," tends to take the achievements of the past for granted and assume that they are "safe." The problem is then seen to be one of finding a way to extend the current EU order to new members or to new areas of activity without frustrating its continued development.

The safety of the EU order is taken for granted because, unlike most other European organizations, it was not perceived to be directly challenged by the end of the Cold War. Whereas NATO's central raison d'être could be said to have disappeared along with the Soviet challenge, it appeared that for the EC the time had arrived to come into its own. The end of the Cold War opened up the possibility of EC/EU membership for the neutral states of Western Europe and for the former Communist states of Central and Eastern Europe. The apparent end of reliance on U.S. superpower military capabilities suggested that it might be possible finally for the EU to emerge from under the protective and inhibiting wing of the United States and fully develop its own foreign policy and defense identity—thus taking a decisive step in establishing its security presence and in becoming a focus for the security needs and aspirations of its members.

Subsequent developments within the EU in general have underlined the fragility of its governance processes in conditions of political turbulence.[22] A critical analysis of CFSP itself could tend to suggest that, since the events of 1989, the national foreign and defense policies of the member states have begun to drift apart from one another after a long period of steady convergence during the Cold War.[23] It may well be the case that the Cold War provided some of the "glue" that held the EU states together. Once the glue is removed, the interplay of national security interests becomes more mercurial, and potentially more dangerous, a possibility discerned by some observers during the conflict in former Yugoslavia. If this is the trend, we may not be able to take entirely for granted the order that the EU's members both created and enjoyed, and there could be a process of "renationalization" in security policies with echoes of more traditional balance-of-power politics.[24] In speeches during 1995 and 1996, with an eye on the IGC, Chancellor Kohl alluded to this possibility, and argued strongly for the need to work to maintain, as well as extend, the established EU order. Indeed on one occasion he felt the need to remind his audience of the old European security order that the EC had replaced, and which some fear might return. The process in question is clearly neither well-defined nor unidirectional. That is, alongside evidence of continuing vitality for state-based national security needs and policies, expectations in a different direction and institutional innovations have both exerted continuous pressure toward an extension of the EU's security presence, particularly in the diplomatic domain. Thus, for example, the ability of the EU to initiate and develop the Balladur Pact during 1993 and 1994 contributed materially to the emerging European security framework, and EU members were able to coordinate their stances on a number of arms control issues—despite the turbulence caused by the French determination to complete their nuclear testing program during 1995 and 1996.

From Presence to Purpose

It is apparent that the 1990s context generates important questions about the ways in which EU presence can be given distinctive purposes. These questions focus on the tensions between a state-based conception of national security and a view that arises from the extension of integration processes into the changing security arena. Even if one hypothesizes a relatively untroubled extension of the EU's presence in the European security arena, this does not resolve all of the difficulties; historically, the area of most tangible EC presence, the world political economy, also generated the most overtly negative reaction to EC policies. Therefore, we are essentially confronted with two questions: First, what is possible? And second, once realized, what might its impact be on perceptions of the EU?

Making One's Presence Felt

The notion of "making one's presence felt" implies a concern with the more tangible aspects of presence. Evidence of the centrality of this concern for the EU in the 1990s can be found in the February 1996 Commission Opinion on the Intergovernmental Conference, which cited "making the EU's presence felt in the world" as one of its three core aims. To put it simply, the question is constituted by the mechanisms and procedures through which a shared perception of the need for action is translated into action and interaction: the relevant concerns are those of institutional capacity as much as of collective will. Thus, the issues for the EU are (1) to what extent institutional adaptation and reform can express the changing relationship between the EU and the changing European order; and (2) to what extent these institutional issues are matched by the collective will to act, interact, or intervene. Together these constitute a distinct area of inquiry. In the case of the EU and in the specific case of CFSP, the lack of institutional capacity, in particular central institutions, may well account for the lack of collective will. By focusing on this area, we become interested in three interrelated qualities of the EU as an institution, which could be summarized as its capacity to act.[25]

Learning capacity. First is the institution's learning capacity: the ability to absorb and adapt to information received, and to pick out the salient information from what might be a very "noisy" background. In areas of potential or actual conflict, or rapid and unpredictable change, the relating of presence to purpose is a crucial exercise, demanding the gathering and collation of information and the development of plausible scenarios for action. If this is not achieved, the presence can become that of the bystander rather than that of the shaper or the initiator; such was arguably the case for the EU in some of the faster-moving phases of the conflict in former Yugoslavia. For presence to be made effective, particularly in the security arena, it must be accompanied by the ability to pick up appropriate signals from the surroundings and to cast them into a plausible version of the situation that is distinct from the versions held by others.

In relation to "learning capacity," there is clearly a distinction between the demands of crisis or conflict situations and the generation of longer-term strategic responses to changes in the security arena. In this context one might cite the eventual response of the EU (in the face of considerable opposition from some member states) to the growing dissatisfaction of the states of Eastern and Central Europe with its enlargement strategy. Although it could be argued that the "Europe agreements" of the early 1990s functioned as part of an evolving security framework, this was recognized more in hindsight than at the time of their conception. At the Copenhagen European Council in 1993, and again at Essen in 1994, the EU did begin to evolve a more coherent long-term strategy for enlargement. This indicated that the Union had learned from the preceding years, which had been characterized by an unwillingness to contemplate enlargement in its broader security context.

Because the member states of the EU made relatively little progress during the early and mid-1990s with the Maastricht task of considering collective defense matters, it is hard to find examples of its learning capacity in the shape of emerging military or paramilitary strategies. Noise and the conflicting views of member states—for example, in relation to arms control or to "out-of-area" operations—combined to restrain learning capacity in the military sphere. While some member states argued that the lessons of the immediate past (e.g., the Gulf, Bosnia) suggested an urgent need for a collective defense identity with a sophisticated intelligence capacity, others argued that the same experience demonstrated why such an identity is impossible to achieve in the short term, whether it is desirable or not. Concomitantly, a welter of often conflicting communication came from the United States, Russia, and the applicant states, and the EU had little success in interpreting it.

Carrying capacity. The second element involved in capacity to act is the organization's carrying capacity: the ability to cope with the task of generating decisions, and to achieve coordination among decisions taken in different areas of activity. This is particularly important in situations of rapid flux, and where there are many uncertainties. Here the EU is clearly handicapped by its pillar structure, by the fact that the Maastricht arrangements assume the continuance of national foreign and defense policies, and by the severe coordination problems that both the EU as a whole and its individual institutions experience. Given the lack of strong central institutions, one might expect that, as in NATO, a hegemon or joint hegemons might emerge to insist on an ad hoc rationalization of the EU's carrying capacity. The problem is that the EU is specifically designed, unlike NATO, to prevent the emergence of a regional hegemon. Thus, in the defense area at the time of the TEU, Franco-German defense proposals were almost immediately countered by Anglo-Italian blueprints; similar signs were apparent in the run-up to the 1997 Amsterdam treaty. In general, the Maastricht arrangements concerning the Western European Union were indicative of a failure to generate decisions and coordinate ideas. WEU was thus left with the ambiguous role of being both the defense arm of the Union and the European arm of NATO. This ambiguity remains under the provisions of the Treaty of Amsterdam, despite language that stressed the WEU as "an integral part of the development of the Union providing the Union with access to an operational capability."[26] Furthermore, the unwillingness of member states to fully define the WEU's status within the Union is reflected in the treaty's postponement of substantive commitments to future negotiations.

Mobilization capacity. Finally, we can explore the organization's mobilization capacity: the ability to mobilize appropriate resources for the task at hand. Again, this capacity is significantly affected by the specific tasks in question, with the presence of rapid and multidimensional change a particular challenge. While it is clear that the EU has made some progress in the use of shared intelligence, it is difficult to point to tangible developments in the deployment of security resources in the narrower sense. The little progress that has been made has come essentially from U.S. leadership in NATO. WEU really made very little sense until the United States developed the notion, at the 1994 NATO Council, of Combined Joint Task Forces (CJTFs). Until then the WEU/EU collective defense future looked bleak, given that the EU states were clearly incapable, even if they had the will, of mounting any significant military operation without NATO's logistical and intelligence facilities—facilities that are predominantly owned and supplied by the United States.

The CJTF concept might in principle enable the EU/WEU to use European military resources in pursuit of European military objectives. Whether this potential mobilization capacity is capable of surviving either a U.S. veto or EU deadlock—through failure to achieve either unanimity or an acceptable majority—remains unclear at this stage, but a significant European deployment of military force seems extremely unlikely at present or in the near future. This assessment is borne out by the experience in former Yugoslavia in the wake of the 1995 Dayton Accords, where the driving force was NATO and the Partnership for Peace rather than the WEU and its associated mechanisms.

An analysis of mobilization capacity in a broader sense provides a more nuanced picture. Although much of the argument here has focused on the so-called second pillar of the EU, the CFSP, it is clear that a more comprehensive view of the security *problematique* brings into play not just "pillar one," the European Economic Community, but also "pillar three," the justice and home affairs domain. Attention has increasingly focused on the ways in which the interaction of the three pillars can be enhanced. Yet, the 1997 Amsterdam treaty was notably unambitious with regard to this concern.

The picture of the EU's potential presented here, in terms of learning capacity, carrying capacity, and mobilization capacity, is decidedly mixed, with areas of development balanced by areas of resistance or inertia. Nonetheless, it might appear that in discussing these aspects of presence, we have moved a considerable distance along the road to statist interpretations, forsaking the essentially multidimensional qualities of the concept. In other words, we could be arguing that only an entity that closely resembles a state (which the EU does not) can either make its presence felt or take responsibility. Is this the case? Clearly, if we take the logic of "making one's presence felt" to one extreme, we are faced with the growth of an essentially state apparatus, of foreign and defense policies, and of the appropriate institutional structures. This logic has an inescapably normative dimension: these are not only the logical structures; they are the desirable structures. As might be expected, our enquiry is rather different. For us, the question that matters is empirical in nature: Given the extensive focus on institutional reform and institutional capacities in the politics of the EU during the early 1990s, to what extent has the resulting set of structures afforded the EU the capacity to make its presence felt, in situations *where its presence is demanded precisely because it is not a state?*

Taking Responsibility

Implicit in the notion of presence are a number of qualities that are broadly intangible and essentially normative. In terms of the EU and the European security order, they focus on the extent to which the EU can be seen as a responsible participant. They are not identical with ideas of leadership, but they are strongly associated with notions of legitimacy, credibility, and reliability. Nor are they simply passive qualities, evoked in response or reaction to events: the notion of "taking responsibility" implies something proactive, involving some kind of collective will. Such qualities are particularly important where the international or European order is in flux, and where concepts and institutions are under challenge. Moreover, they imply something in terms of accepting costs, not only financial but also psychic, arising from the assumption of responsibility. Taking responsibility may also involve the forsaking of short-term gains for longer-term goals or for the pusuit of broader international goals even when they conflict with particular interests.

A range of highly significant questions arises from this broad set of generalizations. In terms of the EU, they concern the extent to which and the ways in which the EU is capable of mustering a normative and institutional consensus on paths of action, given the historically differing relationships of member states to the European order and the balance of power. Clearly, such issues also raise again the question of the model against which we are to judge the EU: Is a move toward taking responsibility to be seen as simply a confirmation of a basically statist model for EU policies, or can it be undertaken without the loss of the pluralistic and adaptable qualities that are not only part of the EU's heritage, but also arguably a better way of tackling the problems of the post–Cold War European order?

It is perhaps too soon to make conclusive judgements about EU/WEU attempts to take responsibility at the military end of the security spectrum. The EU's ability to make its presence felt here has developed to only a limited degree, matched by a lack of readiness to make collective commitments and exercise leadership. To date, the EU's role in the security sphere, as narrowly defined, has been extremely circumscribed and has been overshadowed by a continued U.S. inclination to take responsibility. This has been true even with regard to the former Soviet empire, where the EU's difficulty in steering a responsible and consistent course in respect to governmental change or the re-establishment of stability throughout the area is a key indicator of the limited extent to which it has developed its security presence. Both through its willingness to pressure the Russians (for example, on the decommissioning of nuclear weapons or withdrawal from the Baltic states) and through its support for the Yeltsin regime, the United States has demonstrated leadership and responsibility.[27] This contrast has been paralleled, it might be argued, by the asymmetry between EU and U.S. leadership roles in former Yugoslavia or in the Mediterranean. Even when it comes to security issues intimately linked to the EC or the EU, such as those relating to German unification, it appears that the United States has the initiative, not only because it can, but also because it will take the responsibility.

Still, the record suggests that the further one travels from the military end of the security spectrum, the more the EU finds it possible to muster a normative consensus and to translate this into diplomatic impact. The joint actions developed within the CFSP framework on security matters, such as deactivating antipersonnel mines, stabilizing relations between the states of Europe, and attending to the success of the 1995 review conference on the nuclear nonproliferation treaty, might be seen as small initial indications of a willingness to take responsibility as we have defined it. More substantially, it could be argued that the taking of responsibility—first through the Europe agreements and then through the enlargement strategy in relation to the CEEC—has given the EU a central leadership role in setting the political and economic framework for European security, while NATO remains paramount in the military domain.

It is equally possible, however, to see these processes as illustrations of the primarily halting nature of the EU's progress toward taking responsibility in the European security order. Does the EU provide support for the development of institutions and ideas at the strategic level, which might form the fabric of stable security arrangements in the new Europe? By our definition, in the late 1940s and early 1950s the United States, via the Marshall Plan and the Truman Doctrine, "took responsibility" for the West European security order by its pursuit of a long-term political objective that nevertheless entailed short-term economic costs. Many people argued at the start of the 1990s that the EU should adopt a similar role in the development of Eastern Europe, but this has clearly not happened. Although the EU has an enlargement plan of sorts for some states, it has made inconsistent offers of help to those it has apparently excluded from eventual membership.[28] There is clearly no coherent attempt to "design" or "manage" the general development of the European order. Seen in this light, the preparatory stages of the 1996 IGC suggest a fundamental unwillingness or inability to agree on either the institutional or substantive policy changes that would be needed if the EU's internal order is to be both preserved and extended to encompass the wider European order. This is a picture of paradox, in which the EU's presence in the European security order is demanded and often promoted, but in which crucial components are only partly developed and in which reversals or setbacks seem endemic. In order to explore this paradox further we would like to suggest three contrasting strands of the EU's presence in the European security order.

The EU: Barrier, Facilitator, or Manager?

The EU as Barrier

In taking responsibility and making its presence felt in the European security order, the EU would be acting to establish, maintain, and if necessary enhance the boundaries between itself and the broader European security order. Although this might be seen as dysfunctional for the broader order, it might be eminently functional in terms of the internal workings of the EU and relations among its member states. Here we return to the politics of inclusion and exclusion and to some fundamental concerns about the nature of the integrative "glue" that first bound the EC member states together. Related to this is concern about the "safety" of the original EC order and the extent to which it can survive recent developments. It may well be that for the first time in the history of the evolution of the EU a trade-off will have to be made between widening and deepening, or even just maintaining, the status quo. If this is perceived to be the case, then attempts to preserve the current EU order, and the EU's role in the broader European security arena, may well be at odds with attempts to extend that order eastward. Even a successful extension eastward may well prove divisive in the wider European order, particularly if that extension is incrementally drawn out.

The Council decisions taken in Copenhagen, Essen, and Madrid can be seen plausibly as attempts to forge a strategy for the EU in handling external demands and managing the EU's security environment. But this does not mean that they can be seen as the first stage in the rational and planned development of a new European security order. The impact of exclusion on states such as the Ukraine—and the handling of successive accession negotiations with those on the candidates' list—will have incalculable effects on the broader security milieu in Europe. The hasty EU offer to Russia of an eventual customs union in an attempt to blur the new divide that has arisen in Europe contrasted sharply with the sustained diplomacy surrounding the issue of NATO enlargement and the operation of the Partnership for Peace, developments that can, at least, be seen as a strategy for ordering security in the wider Europe.

A pessimistic view would stress the fact that the Partnership for Peace clearly evolved as a result of a major policy debate in Washington. It can be seen as the United States "taking responsibility," and it has had but little echo in European circles, even though a number of EU states in NATO have subsequently embraced the concept. By reconsidering its fundamental purpose, and shifting its focus from collective defense and deterrence to the support of peacekeeping and peacemaking, NATO has made some progress toward combining what is still an exclusive notion of enlargement (to eventually include Poland but not Russia) with a concern for the wider European order (involving Russian and other nonmembers in bilateral partnerships and multilateral action).

In its own enlargement, the EU has achieved little in the way of reconsidering its security role. Three new neutral members have joined Ireland and Denmark as "observers" in the WEU and are not therefore part of its collective security guarantee (although during the summer of 1996, Finland, Sweden, and Austria indicated willingness to join the WEU for certain purposes such as peacekeeping and related areas). They might all question the validity of the "ever closer Union" that they belong to were it not to come to their assistance in the event of an armed attack or extended military pressure. In practice, these states feel safer now that they are within the EU, and this would also clearly apply were states from Central and Eastern Europe to achieve membership. However, the EU has done little to date to recognize that reality. If the EU is not to be a barrier to the evolution of a stable European security order, then it must at a minimum seek to coordinate its own enlargement with that of NATO.[29]

The EU as Facilitator

Here, the EU might be seen as establishing rules, norms, and procedures enabling change to be accommodated and channeled in the broader order. There are obstacles to this role—not least the "investment" of EU members in existing institutional arrangements and allocations of resources—but there could be great benefits in enhancing cross-European linkages and a plurality of security relationships. This scenario is, of course, the idealistic view of enlargement, which assumes an almost endless continuum as the EU security order is extended until it is synonymous with the broader European order.

By involving nonmembers in structured dialogue and by making them associate partners of the WEU, the EU can perhaps be seen as facilitating the wider order. Progress within the structured dialogue is reported to be slow, however, and in many cases dialogue creates more frustrations than it resolves. Meanwhile, the WEU looks very strange indeed, either as a building on its own, or as a building block in the overall European security architecture. With its members, associate members, observers, and associate partners, the WEU both appears and is incoherent—uncertain of its central role and still unclear about its substantive relationship to both the EU and NATO. Far from facilitating clarity in the European order, attempts to extend and make sense of the Maastricht design have served only to create further confusion.

There is, though, a less tangible way in which the EU might be seen as facilitator. Notwithstanding its lack of institutional tidiness and development, it is apparent that the EU is facilitating a diffusion of ideas about European security, and generating crucial elements in a normative consensus about the future development of the European security order. This role is part of the value of initiatives such as the Balladur Pact, and of the extension of the structured dialogues to include the CFSP. Whether or not the EU provides the institutional fabric of a new European security order, establishing a presumption that that order is a subject of dialogue and negotiation can be seen as a crucial step forward.

The EU as Manager

Here, the EU's presence is clearly more tangible, exercising leverage to supply both channels and desired outcomes, managing both the agenda and the process. This type of presence blends normative and tangible elements, bringing together the taking of responsibility and the mechanisms through which the EU could make its presence felt. This extension of the EU's presence has been an aspiration of the EU institutions and some of its members during the past five years: witness Jacques Poos' declaration in July 1991 that this was "the hour of Europe" in Bosnia, and the determination that the 1996 IGC should have as a prime objective the creation of a new and greatly more tangible EU security identity. The problem is that almost as fast as such declarations can be made and determination expressed, evidence arises of continuing lacunae in the EU's capacity to act or take responsibility.

Nowhere has this been more apparent than in the former Yugoslavia. Initial euphoria rapidly dissipated when the need for a military presence became sharper during 1991. While the EU persisted with humanitarian action, with economic sanctions, and with diplomacy, these did not provide the leverage it needed to manage the central issues. Only when the use of force established a new field of play for diplomacy and economic reconstruction did the EU's management role re-emerge and its presence become more effective. The recently approved provisions of the Amsterdam treaty seem to demonstrate that both in the IGC and in the subsequent treaty negotiations as much time was spent devising ways of preserving the status quo as was spent facing up to the security aspects of the future agenda. This is at least as much of a failure to take responsibility as it is a shortfall in the EU's capacity to act.

Conclusion

Essentially, we have argued along two interconnected lines in this chapter: first, that in order to extend the empirical application of "presence" in post–Cold War Europe, we should investigate the notions of "making one's presence felt" and "taking responsibility"; and second, that as a result it is possible to develop empirically grounded images of the EU's impact on the European security order of the late 1990s.

Our conclusions are not encouraging to those who would wish the EU to take a giant leap forward and thus become a fully fledged manager of European security—including military—issues. They are significantly more positive if one adopts the position that the new European security order is likely to be multilayered and multifaceted, and thus significantly more subtle and nuanced than the remnants of the Cold War system.

Pessimists (or realists?) would argue that the EU is struggling to manage itself, let alone the future European security order, and that it is therefore in no position to take responsibility even in those areas where it clearly and increasingly makes its presence felt. They might in addition argue that this state of affairs reflects the continuing and unresolved tension between the forces of national statehood and security on one hand and those of European integration on the other, which tension lies behind the failure of the EU to translate presence into purpose. Some would argue that in the narrow issue of defense and the broader issue of security the EU currently is not even in a position to make its presence felt. After all, this implies more than just "being there," either as an observer or as a bystander. If one assumes that the acid test of a security presence is the capacity to act militarily or to influence military choices, then the EU has a long way to go.

Such arguments depend on an implied definition of security: the narrower it is, the less the EU's ability to make its presence felt; the broader it is, the more the EU's presence will have an impact, particularly through its economic weight. It is arguable that the further one moves away from the military end of the security spectrum, and the more one approaches security issues from an economic, social, and political perspective, the more the EU is in a position both to make its presence felt and to take responsibility. This line of argument leads to a more sanguine view of the EU's presence. It is not an unproblematical view, since it still does not resolve the tension between the national state and European integration. It does, however, put that tension into perspective and identify the areas in which it is likely under foreseeable conditions to be disabling.

At the beginning of the chapter we suggested that questions about the EU's presence were at least partly questions of "supply and demand": To what extent might the EU in the late 1990s reconcile the inevitability of demands for its presence with the equal inevitability of questions about how it can supply such a presence? What our framework enables us to do is to identify areas in which the disparity between supply and demand is most marked and most likely to create difficulties for the future development of the EU. It also relates these disparities to the broader development of concepts of security and of the European security order.

Notes

1. E. Wise, "IGC Goals Founder in the Aegean," *European Voice*, 29 February–6 March 1996, 12.
2. Kaiser 1996, 142.
3. Buzan et al. 1990.
4. Treaty of Amsterdam, Section 3, Article J.8, Para. 1–5.
5. Allen 1996a.

6. See Schirm's discussion in Chapter 4 of this volume.

7. McCalla 1996.

8. Treaty of Amsterdam, Section 3, Article J.7, Para. 1.

9. Allen and Smith 1990.

10. Hill 1994.

11. Allen and Smith 1990, 19–22.

12. McGeehan 1985.

13. See Smith 1994a for further discussion.

14. Ross 1995.

15. Carlsnaes and Smith 1994; Keohane, Nye, and Hoffman, 1993; Miall 1994.

16. Smith 1996.

17. Bull 1983; Hill 1994.

18. Smith 1994b.

19. Waever 1996.

20. See for example Smith and Woolcock 1993, Chapter 3; Rummel 1991–1992; and Waever et al., 1993.

21. Smith 1996.

22. Wallace 1992, 1994.

23. Allen 1996a.

24. Mearsheimer 1990.

25. Allen and Smith 1991–1992.

26. Treaty of Amsterdam, Section 3, Article J.7, Para. 2.

27. Allen 1992, 1996b.

28. See Mayhew's assessment in Chapter 6 of this volume.

29. Ruhle and Williams 1995.

4

Europe's Common Foreign and Security Policy: The Politics of Necessity, Viability, and Adequacy

Stefan A. Schirm

The Maastricht Treaty upgraded European Political Cooperation (EPC) in foreign relations and defined it as one of the three pillars of the European Union. In addition to the economic policy areas administered by the Commission and the agreements on justice/internal affairs, the Common Foreign and Security Policy (CFSP) became an integral part of the European Union. The 1991 decision to establish the CFSP can be explained by five factors:[1] (1) With the end of Cold War bipolarity, longstanding security structures vanished and supposedly left a policy vacuum that had to be filled with a new European approach. (2) The *Europeanization* of security policy also seemed necessary because of the selective withdrawal[2] of the United States from the European theater. (3) With the deepening of economic integration, the EU's international role as an economic giant but political "dwarf" in foreign policy and security matters became more accentuated. (4) In addition to these apparent policy requirements, EPC's vague legal status and the weakness of its institutional framework led to the demand for a stronger institutionalization and clearer definition of its purpose. (5) Spill-over effects from economic to political integration occurred as the dynamics of the single-market project stimulated political cooperation. These overlapping and mutually reinforcing reasons for creating a CFSP seemed to augur well for its development.

Six years after Maastricht, however, CFSP's performance is rather disappointing: the EU's role as an international actor in the foreign policy and security fields was not strengthened and, as Yugoslavia demonstrates, *decisive* conflict-resolution activities have not been achieved by CFSP. One of the main lessons from CFSP's performance is that it often duplicates functions better accomplished by NATO, the United States, or the United Nations. Thus the question arises as to whether an EU policy in the security field is necessary. Even if a European foreign policy proves to be meaningful, is the present CFSP an adequate response to such contemporary challenges as the stabilization of Eastern European countries? In light

65

of the widely acknowledged weakness of CFSP,[3] this chapter will discuss whether the EU needs a CFSP, and if so, what strategy and institutional features it should adopt to meet foreign policy and security challenges at the end of the twentieth century.[4] It is assumed here that the shaping of any policy has to start with an assessment of the actual needs and of strategies adequate to meet those challenges, and that needs and strategies can be agreed upon by EU members.

Analytical Framework: Necessity, Viability, and Adequacy

The successful development and implementation of any intergovernmental political cooperation requires that cooperation be: *necessary,* because other policy instruments do not perform sufficiently; *viable,* that is, able to be agreed upon by member states; and *adequate* to address the challenges it is supposed to meet. The framework that follows serves as an analytical tool to answer three questions: (1) Why has CFSP not strengthened the EU's role as a foreign and security policy actor? (2) Does the EU need a Common Foreign and Security Policy at all? (3) If so, what approach would be necessary, viable, and adequate? Presuming that actors in international relations are rational in *promoting* their interests, these three concepts can contribute toward an analysis of the policy performance and policy prospects of CFSP.

Necessity

When new international policy instruments are created by a group of states (as in the case of CFSP), their performance will depend on the existence or nonexistence of other policy instruments run by the same actors for dealing with the same issues. If other institutions and strategies do exist in the same policy field, and if their performance is seen as successful, then the states who created the new approach will have little reason to strengthen it. This applies only if the new mechanism does not provide any policy options and instruments that the older approaches cannot deliver. If the new policy offers desired options to the states, which other international mechanisms and the states cannot provide, only then does it become a necessary step, thus increasing its prospects for endorsement and promotion by the respective member states.

Viability

Obviously an international policy approach depends on the political will of the member states to agree on its activities. The performance of an intergovernmental mechanism such as CFSP depends on the national interests of its members. Though the relevant treaty text or the special interests of related bureaucracies (EU Commission, WEU) might advocate particular goals, actual performance will still reflect the perceived interest of the member states. The viability of joint international policies rests on common national interests and policy goals of the members. This causal link is only modified if international cooperation is institutionalized through a supranational actor with relative autonomy from its creators.

Adequacy

The success of international policy instruments also depends on whether they are appropriate for the challenges they are supposed to meet. If the strategy and instruments applied do not address adequately the problem at hand, they will fail. In addition, the support of member states depends on whether the joint initiative is *perceived* as appropriate (and therefore promising) vis-à-vis the issues at stake. Therefore, the conception of any policy depends on an evaluation of the challenges it is to meet. Inadequate strategies will not motivate member states to support a joint intergovernmental approach. The adequacy of a policy depends not only on appropriate strategies but on an efficient institutionalization of operational procedures and capabilities to execute the measures in question. Of course this sketch is an ideal scenario, because it assumes rational analysis and action to the extent that national interests (of whatever nature) predominantly shape intergovernmental cooperation; that duplication of existing policy instruments lowers the chances for success of the new approach; and that strategies that do not meet their respective challenges tend not to perform well.

CFSP:
Character, Performance, and Reasons for Its Weakness

The Common Foreign and Security Policy is an intergovernmental mechanism shaped and controlled by the governments of the member states in the European Council and the Council of Ministers. The Commission has only the right to propose initiatives to the Council in CFSP matters. Decisions on CFSP have to be taken unanimously in the Council. Only operational implementation can be voted by majority and only when the Council has unanimously so decided. Therefore national interests must be coordinated on every issue because every EU member has veto power. Divergent national interests of the fifteen member states often mean that only the lowest common policy denominator is achieved.[5]

CFSP goals were formulated vaguely in the Maastricht Treaty.[6] Article J (1) states that CFSP should "safeguard the common values, fundamental interests and independence of the Union," "strengthen the security of the Union and of its member states," and "develop and consolidate democracy, the rule of law and respect for human rights." With these aims the job description for CFSP is, to say the least, imprecise. At the same time, the Maastricht Treaty does not provide clear definitions of interests. Nor does it specify regulations about how and when to initiate which CFSP actions. Regarding the military dimension of security policy, the Maastricht Treaty provides that the execution of EU actions may be delegated to the Western European Union (WEU). Article J(4) expresses the aspiration for a European military policy by proclaiming "the eventual framing of a common defense policy which might in time lead to a common defense." Furthermore, a proposal by France and Germany was included, stating that CFSP decisions should not preclude any deeper cooperation between two or more member states, making possible a common foreign and security policy *inside* the EU-member group but *outside* CFSP. In addition to NATO, which includes eleven of the fifteen EU members, the Eurocorps (in which the Franco-German brigade is now joined by detachments from Belgium, Spain, and Luxemburg) is the most prominent example of a closer security cooperation of EU members outside CFSP.[7]

CFSP has officially existed since the Maastricht Treaty went into force in November 1993, but activities undertaken as early as 1991, when agreement on the treaty was reached, were shaped in light of the new regulations. However, apart from a dramatic increase in the number of meetings and declarations, no substantial improvement of the impact of the EU's foreign and security policy has occurred. The EU's role as an international actor in foreign and security policy matters continues to be that of a "dwarf"; *national* foreign and security policies remain the dominant feature.

The following activities have taken place under CFSP auspices:

- Creation of a Stability Pact to promote a negotiated settlement of minorities and border disputes among Eastern European countries.
- Support of the Gaza-Jericho Agreement by providing development aid for infrastructural projects.
- Monitoring elections in Russia and South Africa.
- Humanitarian aid to Bosnia and administration of the city of Mostar.
- Efforts to reach a negotiated peace in Bosnia.
- Agreements among EU members for restrictions on weapon exports.
- Promotion of the extension of the nuclear nonproliferation treaty.

Most EU activities were of microscopic significance and did not require the CFSP framework at all. The CFSP's work in regard to the Stability Pact and engagement in the Bosnian peace process was disappointing because these efforts produced no decisive results and even raised doubts about the necessity of a CFSP to promote such initiatives. The Stability Pact involved Eastern European countries (essentially the Visigrad group) that were interested in discussing their future membership in the EU. Minorities and border issues, however, were considered to be bilateral affairs not to be dealt with on a multilateral stage and as topics already settled by themselves in bilateral agreements.[8] Economic assistance and diplomatic pressures via the carrot of "future membership" did lead to communiqués stating common positions on the issues at stake. In 1995 the Stability Pact was handed over to the OSCE (the former CSCE), which has offered an institutional framework for such issues since the 1970s.

The performance of the EU in the peace negotiations in former Yugoslavia was disappointing because no breakthrough success was achieved. Numerous peace agreements were negotiated, in part agreed upon, and then broken by one of the warring parties. The main reason for failure was that the *decisive* and *visible* steps toward a peaceful settlement were undertaken by others: the United Nations provided the peacekeeping forces; NATO executed military monitoring and air strikes; and the United States promoted the peace agreement of Dayton (Ohio) in 1995. In order to implement the Dayton provisions, an international force (IFOR) was created by NATO. While the EU's activities can be considered as a contribution toward the Dayton agreement, they were not sufficient to reach a "European" settlement.[9]

In assessing the performance of CFSP toward third countries, it is important to look at instances of inaction as well as action. Examples are the conflicts in Rwanda, where France intervened militarily alone; the Iraq embargo, where different implementation was the rule; the ban on nuclear testing, where French national interests prevailed; and, most importantly, the policy toward Russia. Embedding Russia in an international security framework was not orchestrated by CFSP, but by NATO's Partnership for Peace. Russia's economic stabilization was largely organized and paid for unilaterally by Germany, because that country had a more imminent interest in Russia's continuing willingness to cooperate with the West and in preventing a definitive collapse of Russia's market reforms.

An evaluation of CFSP's—and EPC's—performance as disappointing makes sense only in light of the expectations created by far-reaching treaty declarations and political rhetoric of European politicians. Considering the EU's lack of experience in handling military conflicts as in Yugoslavia, it can be argued that "the Community has been doing rather well in this test."[10] Compared with the historical pattern of national diplomacy, the coordination of policies achieved by EPC and CFSP represents a significant departure from traditional foreign policy. As Christopher Hill has pointed out, EPC/CFSP is mainly perceived as weak and unsatisfying because of the "capability-expectations gap" between real resources/political will and "talked up" expectations.[11] Although weak in policy that addresses EU external problems, CFSP provisions can be thought of as a success regarding EU *internal* cohesion. Given significant differences in foreign policy attitudes between member states (for example France and Germany on Yugoslavia), it is surprising how few conflicts have emerged. Thus, CFSP seems to accomplish the important task of promoting internal EU coordination on an intergovernmental level.

The reasons for CFSP's weakness regarding its external activities can be traced to three factors.[12] First, national interests of the main EU players diverge on how "common" a foreign and security policy should be and on specific policy issues. Largely for historical reasons, Germany is thus reluctant to pursue national interests alone or to develop an autonomous security policy. Uneasy about acting independently in the international arena, Germany is the strongest advocate of a community approach toward CFSP and is willing to transfer sovereignty. France and Great Britain, on the other hand, show little willingness to give up any control over foreign and security matters. National capabilities are perceived as sufficient, while involvement in NATO is considered the only acceptable international coordination compatible with the preservation of national autonomy. This is true especially in the case of the United Kingdom. France is willing to make small concessions toward supranational EU power if those concessions would result in further control over Germany and a fostering of Europe's autonomy vis-à-vis the United States. Although most member states agree that they would gain international power by unifying their foreign policies, there is a "lack of political will to act decisively as a Union."[13] Member states other than the "Big Three" play only a minor role in shaping a foreign and security policy: some seem unable to cooperate in CFSP matters (Greece); others follow the "Big Ones" (such as Benelux, following France or Britain); some play a sound but weak cooperative role (Spain); and many adhere to most proposals as long as side payments from the core group are sufficient.

A second reason for CFSP weakness is a lack of strategic clarity. CFSP is missing any definition of common interests, precise goals, and operational provisions to achieve them. CFSP lacks a vision of *European* foreign and security interests that could prevail over specific national attitudes. Apparently, important member states such as the UK and France do not see the necessity of common strategies beyond national-level approaches and NATO. Given the virtual absence of the classical security threat—military attack—it becomes more difficult to define clearly what the EU considers a foreign and security policy challenge.

The third factor contributing to CFSP weakness is institutional. Decisionmaking by unanimity clearly does not provide flexibility or rapid reaction. Multiple veto points facilitate the mobilization of blocking coalitions by a minority. In addition, institutional weakness exists in CFSP's fragmented representation in the international theater, in its insufficient analytical capacity, and in indeterminate funding for joint actions. In addition, institutional rules not only affect operational efficiency but also shape the expectations and attitudes of member states. A weak, imprecise institutionalization of CFSP undermines the adhesion of EU members to common attitudes and rules.

Adequacy of Institutionalist and Military-Strategic Proposals for CFSP Reform

Proposals addressing these weaknesses in academic and policymaking realms focus mainly on two partly overlapping lines of argument, which are labeled here as the *institutionalist* approach and the *military-strategic* approach. The institutionalist approach addresses the deficits of CFSP discussed previously. Reform proposals range from the (still intergovernmental) introduction of majority vote procedures and creation of a planning capacity and unified external representation, to the institutionalization of a communitarian body for CFSP, to which member state sovereignty would be partly transferred. Both proposals point to the advantages of majority vote procedures. Nonetheless, advocates of majority vote have to acknowledge that a continuous overruling of certain member states, or groups of states, would lead to a de-Europeanization of CFSP. It would split the EU into a majority group that would be interested in CFSP and a minority whose integration into the development of the EU would slacken. A CFSP encompassing all EU members requires consensus. But since a CFSP depending on all member states will not work, given divergent national interests and uncooperative states such as Greece,[14] a core-group CFSP seems the only viable option. This concept refers to proposals of "multiple speed" or "concentric circles," where a core group around France and Germany would undertake activities that other member states could not prevent by veto, but would also not be forced to endorse.[15] A core-group lead is de facto already happening, as the Franco-German axis shapes most of the EU's activities.[16]

Proposals for a CFSP representation with relative autonomy from member state influence seem utopian in light of the strong nationalist stance taken by Britain and others. Similarly, the creation of a "New Western European Union" to which all CFSP activities would be transferred seems unlikely.[17] An intergovernmentally monitored "foreign minister" with the right to act autonomously on previously defined strategic lines appears to be more viable.

Common representation, planning capacity, and majority vote, however, all require a precise definition of the *contents of politics*—of common European interests and strategies—and these contents are not addressed by the institutional approach. The problem with the institutionalist proposals is thus twofold: they only partially offer realistic steps, and they do not address the *contents of politics.*

Political interests are at the core of the second approach to improve CFSP, the military-strategic. This line of reasoning calls for military capabilities for the EU. It assumes that powerful diplomacy needs military capacity as a tool for threat and implementation, that the United States might pull out of the European theater, and that any relevant security policy has to include military means in order to play the most important game of world politics—the game of "high politics."[18] Advocates of this approach argue that CFSP has to be strengthened by a European Security and Defense Identity (ESDI) and by a European military capacity to be built within the framework of the WEU.[19]

The military-strategic argument offers an interesting complement to the debate, but it too has drawbacks. Since it suggests that Europe needs a military organization *beyond* NATO, it assumes that NATO for some reasons cannot provide for sufficient security. This seems incomprehensible in light of NATO's recent "excellent health,"[20] its activities in Yugoslavia (1995 to the present), and its initiatives toward Eastern Europe, including Russia. In these arenas, for example, it is unclear what an EU-NATO could have accomplished that NATO could not. The main difference between a NATO-like WEU and NATO itself would be the exclusion of U.S. participation and thus enhanced autonomy for EU countries vis-à-vis the United States. Indeed, this reason sometimes put forth, because of the assumption that interests have grown more divergent since the end of the Cold War. Washington seems to be less concerned with European security and more with domestic, particularly economic, issues. Underlining this observation, President Clinton has actively advocated a stronger European engagement in the continent's security, but *inside* the transatlantic partnership (NATO).

The relevant question for Europe is whether to pursue security policy inside or outside of a framework that counts on the United States as a member. Creating a European NATO through an upgrading of WEU would doubtless imply further autonomy for the EU. At the same time, it would increase the probability of transatlantic tensions because it offers the possibility for a security policy without and against U.S. interests. Political conflicts with the United States are among the worst security scenarios one can think of for Western Europe. Comparing potential gains in autonomy with the potential increase in tensions, the EU has to make a very careful choice, as its most important international partnership in economic, diplomatic, cultural, and military affairs might be damaged. The dangers of an institutional split, furthermore, are magnified by the EU's inability—*and the unwillingness*—to achieve the leadership capacity that the United States offers, as Europe is not going to become a unified state like the United States. The EU will thus, for the foreseeable future, not be able to substitute for the United States in military and security affairs.[21]

Of course, security policy also has to take into account the unlikely possibility of a U.S. pullout from Europe. In this scenario a stronger European defense policy would become more necessary and more attractive to EU members. Even in this case, however, it is difficult to conceive reasons for the establishment of a *new* organization duplicating existing ones. Instead of an EU body copying NATO, a Europeanized NATO could provide the necessary organizing structure for defense *and* keep the transatlantic partnership involved in European security.

The military-strategic line of thought sometimes draws on the argument that the EU cannot continue to undertake only the "easy parts" of security, leaving the more "difficult" military portions involving casualties and heavy expenditure to the United States. This argument does not accord with the facts. In 1992 France, Germany, and Great Britain spent on average 3.3 percent of their GNP on defense, while the United States spent 5.3 percent and Japan 1 percent.[22] Considering that the three core EU countries are midrange powers and do not intend to perform a global security role like the U.S. "superpower," they actually devote a relatively large share of their domestic product to defense, 62 percent of the portion of its own GNP that the United States spent. Proposals for a European military capacity should also take into account that Europe does possess extensive military capacity when adding national forces. The latter include the large and modern French, German, and British armies, navies, and air forces, as well as Britain's and France's nuclear weapons. Except for Germany's, these military forces have been participating regularly in out-of-area deployments such as the Gulf War, Rwanda, Somalia, Yugoslavia, etc. The detachment suffering the most casualties in former Yugoslavia were French troops, not U.S. forces. Considering the strong military capacities of European countries and existing multilateral organizations, the demands for a new European defense capability are not convincing. Pursuing European security inside a *Europeanized* NATO does not preclude EU members from taking action without the United States and retains U.S. involvement in a transatlantic security framework.

The rapprochement of France toward NATO in December 1995 shows that even the country traditionally most preoccupied with keeping its distance from Washington has acknowledged the importance of NATO, and thus of the United States, for European security. As we have seen, maintaining NATO as the focal instrument of European security would prevent the risk of transatlantic tensions. Institutions cannot substitute for convergent national interests, but NATO should not be underestimated as it shapes member state expectations and policies that reinforce transatlantic cooperation.[23] Claims for the necessity of an EU military organization on the grounds of NATO's "paralysis" during 1991–1994 and of the EU's performance in ex-Yugoslavia do not seem convincing: What is often perceived as "weakness" in the Yugoslavia case did in fact reflect EU and

NATO member state preferences. If EU countries had wished to intervene militarily, they could have done so with combined national forces, under the existing political framework of WEU.

Both the institutionalist and the military-strategic proposals for reform of CFSP neglect the fundamental differences in attitudes among EU members regarding specific security challenges and degrees of willingness to transfer any control of their foreign and security policy to a common body. As mentioned earlier, only Germany would consider a "pooling of sovereignty" in CFSP matters.[24] Differing geographical interests also make it difficult to conceive a communitarian CFSP as a realistic option. Germany is mainly concerned with Eastern Europe; France is preoccupied with northern Africa and its former colonies; and Britain wavers between a global military vision of its former great-power status and the position of an observer, mildly interested in the balance of power on "the continent." In sum, no consensus exists for subordinating national defense policies and capabilities under a common EU policy.[25] On one hand, the institutional approach to reform seems insufficient because it neglects the *content* of policy (interests, challenges). The military-strategic approach, on the other hand, fails to convince when it is merely directed at a new organization, and appears unrealistic when directed toward a communitarian CFSP.

Challenges and Appropriate Strategies: Toward a Socioeconomic Approach to Security

In light of the political developments and analyses outlined so far, the reasons for the CFSP's establishment in 1991 must be reconsidered. Six years after Maastricht, some do not seem as convincing as they might have in 1991. The presence of the United States in Europe is still the most important security anchor for the continent, as shown in the Yugoslavia case and in the NATO initiatives toward Eastern Europe and Russia. The argument that the end of the Cold War left a security vacuum might have seemed accurate in 1991 but has been invalidated by NATO's performance since then. Furthermore, although institutional weaknesses of EPC must be acknowledged, member states were not willing to overcome them in the regulations for CFSP. Finally, the argument that the EU as an economic giant cannot continue to be a foreign and security policy "dwarf" must be examined.[26] This logic was never very compelling, as it rests on an automatic link between economic resources and military power. Why does an important economic actor have to be at the same time an important foreign and security policy actor? Unless there are challenges that cannot be met with existing policy instruments, there seems to be no convincing reason for a CFSP. So, does Europe need a CFSP at all?

Yes, it does. Europe needs a Common Foreign and Security Policy, but not necessarily the one established with the Maastricht Treaty and discussed in the institutionalist and military-strategic proposals for reform. An appraisal of the foreign policy and security problems Europe faces today, reveals challenges that cannot sufficiently be met by existing or proposed instruments. These problems pose immediate or potential threats to EU's core interests of economic development, democracy, the rule of law, peace, and regional stability.

First, the countries on the eastern border of the EU suffer from political and economic instability, which might result in an upsurge of new nationalism, economic crisis, weak enforcement of law, and internal conflicts. These could spill over to the EU in the form of illegal migration, the spread of organized crime, the breakdown of trade, and the loss of investment, to name a few examples. Second, Russia presents an unconsolidated state in political and economic terms. Economic hardship and political unrest could lead to a weakening of democratic development and market reforms. Nationalists might—if they seize power—feel tempted to turn to old imperial attitudes in order to distract attention from socioeconomic hardships. As a consequence, the EU's economic interests might be harmed, and even a renewed military threat could become possible. Third, the countries in northern Africa face severe domestic cleavages as a result of socioeconomic disparities and Islamic fundamentalism.

Last, but definitely not least, in the absence of the unifying force of the Cold War, and in the presence of growing domestic economic problems, member states of the EU face an increased possibility for tensions among themselves. As resources grow scarce, distributional disputes might increase within and among the EU states. A more egoistic pursuit of national interests might damage European integration. EU internal divergencies will probably become more accentuated with the upcoming enlargement to the east.

The common characteristic of all of these challenges is that they cannot be addressed by military means. They *might* develop into conflicts that would appropriately call for EU or NATO military intervention, but until then it is in the interest of Western European countries to *prevent* their militarization. Insofar as preventive security policy involves "cold" military action such as surveillance, peacekeeping, and deterrence, NATO, the United Nations, and the WEU offer a widely experienced and ready-to-deploy arsenal of policy instruments.

Europe however does not face any threat of military attack as it did during the Cold War. For this reason, military organizations do not provide sufficient answers to *today's* security challenges. The present security landscape requires a reorientation of security policy away from traditional military concerns and toward a focus on nonmilitary problems as well as the means to handle them. A report by DG I-A of the European Commission and the University of Munich states: "Rather than relying primarily on defence and deterrence, European security now requires a multifaceted approach in which a variety of instruments are used together to reduce the risks of instability and insecurity on Europe's frontiers and in its neighbouring states."[27] In dealing with illegal migration, crime, and a socioeconomically unstable neighbor, U.S. policy vis-à-vis Mexico (erecting physical walls and establishing a special police force for border control) has not offered an efficient model. By creating NAFTA, the United States acknowledged that economic policy might be the better security policy.[28]

What Europe needs is a foreign and security policy to address non-military challenges by *civil* means and to prevent the escalation of tensions into military conflicts. To stabilize the countries of Eastern Europe or northern Africa, additional military capability would be inadequate, and enhanced institutional efficiency would be insufficient. Political, economic, and social stability in these regions requires, foremost, economic development and the development of legal as well as political institutions.[29] In order to stabilize Eastern Europe, CFSP has to foster participative political systems, economic development perceived as providing equal opportunities, and the rule of law. The European Union is prepared for these purposes, as it acts on the same lines internally and because it possesses a forty-year experience in mediating and integrating economic and social policies. Promoting international relations along an economic logic lies within the very nature of the European Union. This is best exemplified by its leading role in the world political economy and its abilities to shape global politics—for example, in the Uruguay Round of GATT, in North-South relations, and in monetary policy. With the end of the Cold War, the essence of international relations revolves more around technological, developmental, trade, and currency issues, therefore magnifying Europe's specific role. Because the EU's international "power" is of an economic nature, and because EU members do not agree on a common military security policy, a socioeconomic approach to CFSP is the more appropriate option.[30] Europe can thus focus on its specific strength as a *civil power* in order to promote a "stability transfer" as a preventive security policy.[31] Obviously such a mechanism must complement conventional military security; it cannot substitute for it. The question is one of emphasis.

To some extent a socioeconomic approach to foreign and security policy is already in place. Present activities are insufficient, however, as they are only loosely coordinated and not incorporated into a strategically directed CFSP framework. Several activities of the Commission contribute toward a stabilization of other countries. The PHARE and TACIS programs provide technical assistance to Eastern Europe; development aid is given to LDCs; the Lomé agreements on trade benefit former French and British colonies; energy cooperation with Eastern Europe includes improvement of safety standards in nuclear power plants; etc. At the *intergovernmental* level the most effective civil means is probably the "carrot" strategy of offering the Visigrad countries full EU membership—largely perceived by

their populations as offering a better future—and in that context supporting market reforms and democratic political procedures. The Europe
agreements on trade provide economic opportunities and thus support for
stability in the associated countries.[32] The "Stability Pact" of 1994 was a
diplomatic attempt for preventive security policy as it envisioned the
peaceful settlement of tensions before they developed into open conflicts.

To reach a comprehensive and powerful civil CFSP—adequate to the
actual challenges Europe faces—coordination of these activities and the development of new tools is as necessary as a clear definition of policy objectives, strategies, and instruments. Therefore, a socioeconomic CFSP goes
far beyond the present status quo but also builds upon it. In order to deepen
and strengthen CFSP's civil, socioeconomic reach, the EU has to undergo
several levels of definition. The first is a definition of interests following
DG I-A priorities and the security scenario outlined above.[33] Second, geographic priorities have to be set, acknowledging, for example, that Rwanda,
Somalia, or Chechnya do not possess the same intrinsic relevance to the EU
as the Visigrad countries. Third, policy instruments must be identified and
assessed, to determine which tools are to remain at the national level, which
should be handled at the intergovernmental EU level, and which are best
transferred to the EU Commission. The task is to reduce the fragmentation
of instruments and to bring them together under a common strategy and implementation plan. In light of the economic needs of neighboring countries
and the EU's character as a "trading model," one of the most effective tools
for a civil CFSP is commerce.[34] Enlarged trading opportunities can contribute to economic development and provide a precondition to stability. As
liberalized trade also benefits EU member countries, a socioeconomic
CFSP is also *more cost efficient* than military-institutional options. The
buildup of an EU-NATO organization would imply heavy financial burdens
without stimulating economic development inside the EU.

Several factors argue for the pursuit by EU member states of a common civil foreign and security policy. First of all, a common approach is
more efficient than individual policies because it avoids duplication of activities, thus reducing financial *and* political costs (in the form of contra-
dictory national policies). Second, CFSP facilitates mobilization of domestic support for long-term foreign and security measures that are often
resisted. Using European commitments as their rationale, national governments can better justify long-term policies that do not show immediate re-
turns.[35] Third, a European approach provides member states with a tool to
block special interests of private business, by defining certain economic
policies as "European security issues." The same blocking mechanism can
be thought of vis-à-vis the traditional defense establishment (military,
industry, bureaucracies), whose special interests in a strategy of deterrence
can be thwarted by defining "European security" as a strategy focusing on
stabilization of neighbors. Fourth, a common approach will be perceived
by third countries as more powerful than national policy, if it follows a

clear strategy to which all important EU members agree, and if it possesses an effective operational institutionalization. Joint EU actions leave third countries no alternative West European partners. In this context, exploitation by third countries of divergences between national policies in Europe becomes unviable.

In its respect for national divergences on the military-defense side and for existing organizations, the socioeconomic concept is more *realistic* in terms of chances for implementation than the proposals for a militarization of CFSP. Furthermore, it serves the "last but not least" security challenge mentioned above. That is, it fosters EU internal cohesion by providing a common European interest and strategy. It also does not rely on policy realms in which differences remain fundamental, as in the area of traditional defense policy. Avoiding EU internal tensions in foreign and security policy issues is an important task for CFSP, not only because of deepening economic integration but also because of the radical changes in the international system since 1989. With the demise of the Soviet Union, the external impetus for integration has ceased to exist, thus increasing the probability of national divergences among EU members. These could be prevented by participation in a CFSP that aims at identifying common interests and means and resists duplicating existing organizations and playing with sovereignty-intense issues such as military policy. To those preoccupied with potential German "hegemony," NATO—as the sole central defense institution in Europe—represents a better means to embed Germany than would a purely European defense alliance.

Moreover, a civil CFSP is more plausible than a military policy because it builds on values and traditions of European integration that have evolved over the last four decades. It follows the functionalist logic of much of EC/EU's achievements in that it is directed at issues requiring improved political tools (stabilization of neighbors), and in that it follows the path of socioeconomic integration in Western Europe already forged in the past decade. The political values guiding European integration encourage achieving economic development and creating a "security community"[36] through deepening international ties as well as strengthening and managing international interdependence. Projecting these concepts on neighboring countries provides the values any political order or continent-wide European security order needs to reach consensus.

Conclusion:
Toward a Necessary, Viable, and Adequate CFSP

Looking at the actual CFSP, proposals for its reform, and its potential future activities, this chapter has focused on three questions: Which kind of CFSP is *necessary,* considering existing institutions? Which concept is *vi-*

able regarding member state interests? Which form is *adequate* to meet actual security challenges? The argument developed here is that present policy and proposals do not fully satisfy the criteria of necessity, viability, and adequacy. These criteria can instead best be met with a socioeconomic approach that builds upon existing instruments, experience, and consensus.

Necessity

Considering NATO's recent performance and the continuing leadership and military presence of the United States in Europe, a new European military organization seems superfluous. The main effect of an EU-NATO would be the exclusion of the United States and thus a higher probability of transatlantic tensions, potentially damaging European security instead of improving it. A continuing effort to coordinate policies between the United States and the EU *inside a common institution* can provide a mechanism to handle tensions.

Viability

Because two of the three "big players" in the EU (Britain and France) and several "small players" as well are unwilling to transfer to any kind of common European body sovereignty in foreign and security policy (much less in military matters), a CFSP along traditional defense policy lines is not realistic. Therefore, institutionalist proposals that envisage a community approach toward traditional foreign and security policy are not viable. Instead, a socioeconomic approach to CFSP is viable because (1) it reflects the character of the Union as an organization promoting stability and wealth through the management of interdependence; (2) it affects policy areas in which member states traditionally have agreed to pursue common activities; and (3) it is already practiced, albeit in a fragmented way, by the Commission and the Council.

Adequacy

To make sense, a Common Foreign and Security Policy should meet the actual security challenges Europe faces today. As these challenges are not military in nature, an enhanced military capacity and an institutional deepening of traditional security means are not adequate. A socioeconomic approach would be the most effective policy to stabilize neighboring countries economically and politically and thus to enhance the EU's own security and economic interests. This approach would also promote democracy, the rule of law, and peaceful settlement of disputes.

Operating along these lines, the European Union is best situated to become a more important global player. It would concentrate on its strengths instead of duplicating existing and functioning organizations, and would focus on policy areas in which its members can achieve agreement. Most important, it would meet the challenges the post–Cold War world faces instead of sticking to inadequate parameters and instruments. If the widespread observation proves to be true—that today's international system is shaped more by economic logic than by military capabilities—then the EU can best attain a powerful international role through the economic means, experience, and consensus that the Union represents. When socioeconomic and political instability is the main threat to security, the traditional notion of defense changes: Military power becomes an instrument of last resort and socioeconomic policy becomes the first priority.

Notes

This article was written at the Center for European Studies, Harvard University. I would like to thank CES for the J. F. Kennedy Fellowship in 1995–1996 and for an intellectually creative environment. For comments on earlier drafts, I am indebted to Laurent Goetschel, Jeff Kopstein, Andrew Moravcsik, Carolyn Rhodes, Elmar Rieger, and to the participants of the CES European Integration Study Group and of the ECSA Workshop.
    1. On the grounds for CFSP, see Rummel 1992, 112–123; Morgan 1994, 413–423.
    2. This refers to the reduction of troops and closing of bases (while keeping only those considered indispensable in post–Cold War Europe).
    3. Burghardt 1994a.
    4. For a theoretical contribution on European foreign policy see Smith 1994b, 21–44, and Wessels 1993, 9–29.
    5. Compared to the previous EPC, CFSP represents integrative progress: security was incorporated as an issue area of common policy, the Commission was given the right to initiate cooperation, and a light possibility of majority vote was established. For an assessment of EPC see Regelsberger 1993, 270–291.
    6. Title V, Article J(1)-J(11) of the Treaty on European Union.
    7. On NATO and European security see Kelleher 1995.
    8. "EU's Struggle to Form Foreign Policy Shows Scant Sign of Abating," *Wall Street Journal*, 22 February 1994.
    9. On the reasons for EU's weak performance in the Yugoslavia case, Rummel states that "it was first of all the lack of preventive diplomacy that reduced the influence of the Community, not the lack of economic or military leverage." Rummel 1994, 122.
    10. Rummel 1992, 29.
    11. Hill 1994, 103–126.
    12. See Schirm 1996, 263–270, and Cameron 1995b.
    13. Cameron 1995b, 3.
    14. The negotiation of side payments for every decision on CFSP matters would turn CFSP into a bazaar.
    15. See Jopp 1995b, 134–139, and Tourlemon 1995, 61–67.
    16. On the Franco-German axis see Deubner 1994.
    17. See Sawers 1996.
    18. On arguments for a military-strategic approach, see "Hard Choices Ahead: European States Need to be Prepared to Pay for Military Independence," *Financial*

Times, 14 December 1994, 12; Jopp 1992, 397–404. For a critique of the military-strategic argument, see Becher 1994, 400–401.

19. See Martin and Roper 1995.

20. Zelikow 1996, 11.

21. "Europeans, in turn, should do all they can to ensure that the Americans remain involved—while preparing for the inevitable occasions when US commitment will not be as strong as Europe would like." Gordon 1996, 51.

22. See United Nations Development Programme (UNDP) 1995, 182.

23. On the policy shaping power of institutions see Keohane 1989.

24. Keohane and Hoffmann 1990, 277.

25. See Gnesotto 1996, 21.

26. This argument was, for example, stated by the CFSP Commissioner Hans van den Broek, asking the IGC 1996 to define "if Europe's political influence in the world is to match its economic power," in *Agence Europe*, No. 6342, 22 October 1994.

27. Bertelsmann Stiftung 1995, 8. The report continues, stating: "For security policy to be successful, it needs to be well resourced, swift and flexible. In current circumstances, it is more likely to be about the soft security provided by instruments such as human rights monitoring, trade policy, economic and technical assistance than about the hard security provided by military defence."

28. On the foreign policy and security grounds for NAFTA, see Schirm 1994, 103–120 and Krugmann 1993, 13–19.

29. On a civil "Peace Concept" for Europe, see Senghaas 1993, 654–666.

30. Morgan takes a pragmatic view: "If, then, the 'high road' to world power status for Europe—the road of politico-military 'high politics' along which the proposed CFSP points—is strewn with obstacles of varying shapes and sizes, the EC's leaders might be well advised to take another look at the 'low road,' that of commercial and monetary affairs, and of Europe's weight in the global political economy rather than in the politico-military balance of power." Morgan 1994, 422.

31. See Becher 1994, 401 and Goetschel 1995, 56–59.

32. See Kramer 1993, 226.

33. The Director General of DG I-A mentions six "interests and priorities": consolidation of the EU following enlargement; integration of Central and Eastern European countries into the Union; developing an ESDI as the European pillar of a reinforced North Atlantic alliance; promoting a stable immediate neighborhood; maintaining close political and economic ties with the United States and Japan; and safeguarding the security of energy supplies and raw materials. Burghardt 1994b.

34. Rosecrance 1993, 127.

35. I would like to thank Andrew Moravcsik for suggesting this argument.

36. On the concept of "Security Community" see Deutsch 1957, 5.

5

The European Union and Russia: Toward a New *Ostpolitik?*

Antje Herrberg

The EU-Russian relationship is central to an understanding of the European Union's external capabilities and relations. During the Cold War, the bipolar competition between the United States and the Soviet Union drove the European internal integration processes. Now the post–Cold War era contains economic and political imperatives to integrate the new Europe into the international system. Given the immediate integration agenda of the European Union, its association with Eastern European countries, and its planned enlargement, a consistent and constructive relationship with Russia is of crucial importance. This became particularly true when Finland acceded to the Union, giving the EU a border with Russia.

The purpose of this chapter is to demonstrate that the development of EU-Russian relations has been shaped by Russia's and the EU's perceptions of each other, and that systemic change following the end of the Cold War created an unprecedented opportunity to develop a new relationship. Seeing the opportunity before them, EU member states granted the Commission the authority to deal proactively with the former Soviet republics. Concrete actions in the process of rapprochement between the European Union and Russia are tangible indicators of the emergence of a genuine EU foreign policy toward this region, or, in other words, a new European *Ostpolitik.*

This discussion is divided into three parts. The first part highlights conceptual issues regarding the European Union as an entity in the international system. The second part focuses largely on an empirical record of the EU-Russian relationship. The aim of the third and final part of the chapter is to come to some tentative conclusions about the character of this relationship and about the development of EU foreign policy toward this important region.

Conceptual Issues

Foreign and External Policies in Flux

While the European Union's relationship with Russia must be given importance equal to the transatlantic relationship, it clearly differs in its nature and content. An assessment of the relationship must take into account the changing character of both Russian and European foreign policy. It must be understood that Russian foreign policy has, until at least 1993, reflected the internal turbulence and uncertainty that govern its society and government.[1] The domestic difficulties associated with the political and economic transformations taking place in Russia have produced a high degree of uncertainty in the conduct of both domestic and foreign policies. It can be argued that a relatively ambiguous and changing Russian foreign policy over the last five years is a reflection of the domestic search for a post-Soviet identity. This important process has followed many currents, often swinging from one extreme to the other, from total openness toward the West to overt nationalism.[2] These processes of identity formation and the corresponding visions and definitions of Russia's position in the world have decisive influences on the shaping of its foreign policy.

Institutional weaknesses of the Russian foreign policymaking system, particularly prior to 1993, provided little direction or means to assess the success or failure of foreign policies. This allowed multiple ideas about the international environment to permeate Russian foreign policy debates. The perception of the external environment has acted as a powerful influence in determining and shaping Russian foreign policy, especially when uncertainty and instability remain high within Russia.[3] Therefore, any assessment of EU foreign policy toward Russia must consider Russia's own view of its relationship with the rest of Europe. How Russia views the EU as an international actor is a crucial factor in determining the relationship that develops, as well as influencing how EU foreign policy will proceed.

It must also be remembered that genuine European foreign policy, as it was initially formulated by the European Union, has not yet come into existence. The character of the European Union's relationship with third states remains sui generis in nature and cannot be compared either to national foreign policies or to the role that multilateral institutions traditionally assume in the international environment. Scholarly inquiry thus faces an important predicament in this area of European integration. An additional caveat is that Article J(5) in the Treaty on the European Union (TEU) is presently not a clear reflection of the diversity of approaches by which member states would like to see the European Union act.

Ambiguities such as these have not restrained students and practitioners of European integration from attempting to assess where the barriers to a genuine Common Foreign and Security Policy (CFSP) lie. It is difficult to ascertain whether the fact that member states do coordinate their foreign policy has a significant impact on third states. For example, Christopher Hill's work has established a framework that has spurred considerable case research.[4] His framework explores actorlike characteristics of the European Union by outlining the gap between capabilities of the European Union as a foreign policy actor on the one hand and expectations of potential recipient states on the other. In mapping out *which* capabilities a foreign policy actor *should* possess, he comes to the worthwhile conclusion that there is a fundamental gap between capabilities and expectations, and prefers to label the dialogue between the EU and the world as a "system of external relations."[5]

Such a framework raises a pivotal question about Europe and its institutional core in regard to third actors. The fact that the EU is often seen not as a series of ad hoc mechanisms but rather as a seamless web of "Europeanness" was addressed by Allen and Smith in 1990.[6] In recognizing specific problems in the evaluation of the European Union in a statist perspective, these authors have shifted the definition of the European Union from that of an international actor to that of a "variable and multidimensional presence," which might have more important roles to play in some issues than in others. Their work is significant since it implies that the EU is not only an institutional phenomenon but also an economic and cultural one. The way in which the new Europe defines and legitimizes its presence within these dimensions has a fundamental impact on the shaping of its relation with "Others."

Definitions of "Self" and "Other" in Europe

The issue concerning self-(re)definition of Europe provokes the controversial question of how and where to set Europe's boundaries.[7] This exercise can be roughly translated into the practice of the politics of inclusion and exclusion between itself and significant "Others." Specifically in reference to Russia, the denotation of Europe as a way of describing Europe's cultural boundary (the idea of Europe), the EU's institutional boundary (the EU as an actor), and where Europe's security boundaries are to be drawn has given rise to misunderstandings and confusion for both policymakers and scholars alike.

From its side, the Russian search for identity has not rested in its own easily identifiable cultural traits but in relations with other nations;[8] hence, questions of where and how borders toward "the Other" should be drawn become crucial. In fact, Russian self-definition and its relevance to Europe has been a focus of debate for centuries. The Western "Other" has been a volatile concept in Russian identity constructions. The meanings of "Europe" are used to distinguish it from the "West," notably from the United States and NATO. The way in which Russia will interpret the "Other" is closely related to the difficulty it has in coming to terms with the challenges of a changing concept of Russian identity and with the way it integrates the idea of Europe in that process. This is not because there is no "Russian idea" but rather because there are many of them. Russia's identity crisis has thus tended to reactivate an age-old Russian ambiguity toward Europe and the West at large.[9]

The Issue of Identity

"Collective Identity," according to Bill McSweeney, "is first a matter of perception, just as security and insecurity also begin in our perception of vulnerability."[10] From a general historical viewpoint, the very idea of Europe and its identity has been defined by and large through images of foes. The present post–Cold War readjustment of countries in Western, Eastern, and Central Europe signifies an attempt to surmount the former "frontiers" of Europe, including the division between the East and the West. European "Others" have changed over time; the present political processes might well be conducive to further changes or manifestations of the imagined borders within which Europe lies.

In addition, any thinking about European identity has both political and cultural dimensions that are difficult to define in a quantitative way. It is essential to recognize that European identities center on the idea of the "Other," where the European "We" is mirrored in the "Them," which from any national perspective makes up the larger part of the world.[11] This is important because it is here where the European Union as a *presence* will find the major part of its justification and its claim for existence. In the context of interpreting the European Union's external relations, the images about "Otherness" might drive, but also inhibit, collaborative behavior between the East and the West, between Russia and the European Union.

European identity and European international identity. The integration of the idea of Europe in Russia's search for identity forms an important basis for a consciousness of common interests and common values between the European Union and Russia. This might well promote the establishment of common frameworks and institutions.[12] In this vein, it is not merely sufficient to view European external relations as a totality of individual policies, nor as a diffuse idea of what Europe represents. Rather, the European Union needs to be analyzed as a distinct unit of identity that represents discrete capabilities, outputs, and strategy formulations. It is for this reason that it is useful to view the European Union as possessing both a "European identity" and a "European international identity." The first term relates to how Europe is interpreted by its citizens and reflects a value system, as well as a largely cultural and historical concept.[13] The latter is a more exclusive concept, namely establishing how the presence of the European Union in the development of a system of relations is received by others. The term "European international identity" reflects perceptions regarding the European Union in the international system that might or might not overlap with those of Europe at large. The prime reason why it is employed here is to assess to what extent the European Union—analyzed as an institution—possesses a distinct presence, and accordingly how its interests are perceived by others.

External capacity from within. No conclusions can be drawn about the EU-Russian relationship if we cannot distinguish the role of the EU Commission in fulfilling an autonomous, executive function for policies and strategies that might develop either from pillar one issues or genuine CFSP issues. As Jupille and Caporaso point out in Chapter 11 of this volume, it is the "corporate" rather than the "collective" identity that matters. One example here refers to the association of the sole will and actions of Germany,[14] or those interests defined by the European contingent of the G-7. One might assume that the EU's internal institutional capabilities may slowly adapt to new realities, which will give it a greater capacity to deal with them. Such an assumption reflects a neoliberal institutionalist approach that accepts a learning capacity for institutions.[15] As a result, in this view, internal integration might provide a greater incentive for cohesive integration of the foreign policies of each member state. Accordingly, it could be argued that individual interests represented within the European Union are influenced by feedback relating to the EU's international identity in the world provided by third actors.[16]

A case in point refers to the dense network of interests and sectors the EU-Russian relationship exhibits. This network has resulted from agreements and commitments concluded not solely by the Commission's Directorate General for External Relations (DG I), as one would expect, but also under the competence of other dictorates dealing with issues such as nuclear energy, the environment, or scientific cooperation. As such, competence on certain matters regarding the EU-Russian relationship is not always entirely clear, and might be a source of portfolio competition within the Commission. In addition, multiple competencies produce a certain level of confusion to third actors about where to find suitable interlocutors. The Commission initially responded to this issue by recruiting functionaries from DG VIII (Development) to deal with all issues on technical assistance to the former USSR. Given the increasing scope of the EU-Russian relationship, this reflects only a short-term solution.

Upgrading its external presence. A third conceptual imperative in viewing the EU's international identity refers to how the European Union–Russian relationship has contributed to the EU's role in the international multilateral scene. This imperative supposes that contextual factors have a powerful influence in upgrading the credibility and international identity of the European Union. "Procedural and output cohesion," as addressed by Jupille and Caporaso in Chapter 11, is relevant here as is the internal competence and efficiency of Community institutions to deal with new policy issues. These factors bear on how the European Union might be seen as an actor in its own right, not only in this case of Russia, but in the case of any other actor responding to the EU's capacity to deal with it. Reception can act as an influence to both strengthen (if seen as a capable actor) or weaken (if seen as an incompetent actor) the EU's autonomy.

Viewing the European Union as an autonomous entity, possessing both distinct competencies or capabilities, necessitates a consideration of its internal dynamics. As will be shown in the case study below, levels of internal competence and willingness on the part of Community institutions other than the Commission (such as the European Parliament or the European Court of Auditors) may function as either barriers to or catalysts in the European Union's role in the world community. Inadequacies on the external level—for example, slow implementation of technical assistance—could arise from internal inefficiency, lack of dialogue, or a slow interaction process among the responsible Community institutions. In this way, the EU's presence in the world derives from a complex set of internal and external dimensions and interactions, which are taken into account in the case study below.

The Record of EU *Ostpolitik*

It would be difficult to argue that the European Union has taken a passive stance toward those states that belonged to the former USSR. In fact, there are some who argue that abrupt changes in the international system have catapulted the EU into a leadership role, especially in Eastern Europe.[17] The following description focuses on the process of rapprochement developed by the EU. This has been largely executed from DG I, and gives reason to argue that the European Union is in the process of developing a new European *ostpolitik.*

The Cold War: From Ignorance to Adaptation in the New Europe

Not long after the signing of the Treaty of Rome, the European Community was soon confronted with strong opposition from the USSR. U.S. support for European integration was seen as an effort to create a counterweight to the Soviet threat, as an "annihilation of the internal communist threat"[18] in Europe. As such, the construction of the EC could only be seen as an economic arm of NATO. In other words, the attitude of the USSR was that in bipolar competition, Europe should not have a sphere of influence.

The creation of an internal market, as well as the attraction of the EC to its neighbors, posed the threat of total exclusion to the USSR. It destroyed any hope of creating pan-European cooperation and harmonious development of international relations, which had been a major objectives initially pursued by the USSR.[19] It was not by coincidence that the creation of the Warsaw Pact was complemented in 1966 by an encompassing plan on economic cooperation. The creation and subsequent reinforcement of the Council for Mutual Economic Assistance (CMEA) was a clear sign that the Soviet Union felt the imperatives of European integration and recognized the first signs of the EC's international identity. The EC, for its part, did little to counter the bloc image and reinforced its boundaries with the East by instigating the Common Commercial Policy (Article 113).[20]

The successive enlargements of the European Economic Community in the 1970s and the creation of the European Parliament convinced the Soviet Union that a more functional approach in its foreign policy conduct was required. The only way for the Soviet Union to reintegrate into the international system was to take a multidimensional approach.[21] It was believed that formal bilateral relations with Europe could reinforce both the USSR and the EC and could thus weaken the Atlantic alliance.

Although initial efforts toward a commercial agreement between the Soviet Union and the EC were well received, resulting in meetings between the Commission and the USSR,[22] they soon failed because the EC would not recognize the CMEA. The CMEA was seen as a promoter of separate bilateral cooperation with each of the individual member states, rather than as a promoter of relations between the two trade blocs. The EC acted accordingly in suspending its official contacts with the Soviet Union until October 1980.[23]

The USSR's strategy, on the other hand, was to disregard the realities of the EC, circumvent negotiation with it directly, and seek cooperation in the multilateral scene. The Soviet Union attempted to use the basket II negotiations as a forum for commercial questions.[24] In reaction, however, the EC forced the Soviet Union to recognize its presence, by acting on behalf of its six and later nine member states on basket II issues. This undoubtedly contributed to the realization that the EC had an agenda-setting role and a given mandate provided by its member states.

Seen in retrospect, it appears that the Soviet Union's desire to reintegrate into the international system required that it accept the realities of the EC. A policy of cooperation, which could potentially promote the status of the USSR in the increasingly tense bipolar system, would have to include recognition by the USSR of the EC, not only as an economic but also as a political entity. Gradually the Soviets perceived the European integration process less in terms of imperial tendencies than as a peace-building system with economic benefits.

New Thinking and Rapprochement: The Return to Europe

Soviet "new thinking" in the 1980s can be viewed as a reaction to the realities of the international system and the Soviet Union's increasing interdependence. These circumstances demanded either a policy of forced retreat or an attempt to assert influence in the world by changing its domestic situation. It is clear that the return to the world economy was one of the most important interests of the Soviet Union in order to avoid economic collapse. Taking these interests into account, the EC had to be regarded as an entity with common, or complementary rather than hostile, interests. This perspective led the Soviet Union to view the EC as a partner in mutual accommodation, which stance, in turn, evoked expressions of European cultural integration: the notion of the "common European house." This was intended to reflect common historical experiences, cultural traditions, economic rationale, and new geographic realities, all of which became a cornerstone for the Soviet Union's post-1985 foreign policy attitude. In addition, the Soviet Union appeared to focus increasing attention on its close neighbors, and the EC was seen as an obvious partner.

It is here where we can observe the beginnings of a dual perception problem that persists today: The EU can be seen as a logical enhancement of a notion integrated in the "new thinking," but it can also be viewed as a barrier to the return to "civilization," and the opening between the East and the West. From the Atlanticists's perspective, and to the minds of some decisionmakers within the European Union, the policy most favorable to Russia's own interests seems to be the pursuit of integration, entailing a respect for political and economic international standards. Such a strategy would allow Russia to deepen its dialogue with its Western neighbors. In the mid-1980s the "new thinking" was in fact reinforced by a period of intensive preoccupation with the European question by the *mezhdunarodni;*[25] Lukin remarked at that time that "the bloc image had been overtaken by events."[26] It was then that the idea of Europe and European identity returned as a priority in the public and official debate within the USSR. While Europe was still regarded as a part of the capitalist West, it was also seen as a potentially important political partner for USSR foreign policy.

To signify its desire "to rejoin Europe" and to show its cultural roots, the USSR labeled the year 1987 the "Year of Europe," and made a point of displaying and professing its European identity. Multiple thinkers were brought together to reflect strategically on which position the USSR should take toward the European Community. This rapprochement was based on the conviction that glasnost needed to co-construct with the European Community a system of international security in order to survive.[27] In this way the best method to deal with an enemy was to turn him into a friend.[28] Such domestic debates help to explain some of the first elements of the European *ostpolitik,* which included invitations to Brezhnev and later Gorbachev to visit Brussels, with the latter visiting the European Parliament in 1985.

Ideological relaxation and consequences of the "new thinking" were felt as well in 1985 after a visit to Moscow by Italian Premier Bettino Craxi. It was then that Gorbachev officially recognized both the political and economic consequence of Europe's communitarian construction.[29] This loosening of tension and ideological boundaries resulted in the proposal by CMEA Secretary General Sytchov to re-establish official relations between the CMEA and the Community. Dialogue continued between the Commission and the State Commission of the USSR until February 1989, allowing for a strategy to embark on an exploratory phase in bilateral relations.

As a consequence the Commission submitted a set of directives for commercial and business relations to the Council for consideration, the content of which had yet to be decided.[30] The Commission also accommodated the interests of the Soviet Union in tolerating specific agreements that recognized the bilateral relations already existing between CMEA member states and EC member states. This strategy allowed the Community a certain bargaining space in which to conduct negotiations with Eastern Europe without being severely constrained by Moscow. By 1989, during the period of perestroika, the first agreement with the USSR on trade and economic cooperation was signed, forming a foundation for future agreements.[31] Cooperation with the EC was seen by the Soviets as an attractive foreign policy option that posed no immediate dangers: the EC's relatively weak political cooperation structure and its largely civilian nature prevented a potential military threat. However, a security identity in which the United States remained involved in Europe was seen as a serious impediment to opening dialogue on any new security schemes based on a pan-European structure.

Certainly, a clear bifurcation of opinions was evident in the debate on Europe within Russia, accompanied by increasing criticism of Russia's unequivocal attachment to Western values. In this context the question reverted to Russia's place in the structure of the European "Other," namely the European Community. The processes of glasnost and perestroika, which led to the collapse of the Soviet and the Communist empire, only deepened the debate about how the former USSR, particularly Russia, should "fit itself in" with Europe.

Disintegration and Integration in the Reshaping of Europe

The period between 1990 and 1993 in the evolving EU-Russian relationship saw the first outputs and indicated a rapprochement by way of an *Ostpolitik*. It signified an era of change both for the EU—which responded to the new realities by preparing and ratifying the Treaty on European Union and subsequently formulating a Common Foreign and Security Policy—and for the Russian Federation, which established a policy of openness. At the same time, this period signified both internal and external institutional adaptation to new realities.

In 1990, after sending a group of economic experts from the European Community to Russia, the European Community decided that economic reform would be one of the ways to stabilize the transition period for the former USSR. Following visits from President Gorbachev's advisors to the European Commission, Brussels began to see opportunities to make its international identity felt. The fact that the USSR was trying to cope with multiple changes in the international system offered the European Community a leadership niche if it could respond adequately to the changing political situation in Moscow.[32] The EC therefore took the initiative to work toward a new cooperation agreement and establish a joint committee consisting of both EC and USSR officials. In addition, the Commission decided to open an official EC delegation in Moscow in the spring of 1991.[33]

In setting up its diplomatic representation, the European Community made sure to communicate what the ideas of Europe and of cooperation—both in the European and in the international context—entailed. As Michael Emerson, head of the EC delegation in Moscow, remarked, "Institutions matter." Moreover, he noted that "openness and diversity combined with increasingly intense integration require a sufficient common force to avert either hegemonies or centrifugal tendencies."[34] In some ways the European Community was considered a model for the Soviet Union in transformation. This was stressed first in visits by Gorbachev and later by President Yeltsin, during his visit to the socialist group of the European Parliament in Strasbourg. Particularly during the August 1991 coup in Moscow, interest in "copies of the Treaty of Rome became intense."[35]

Parallel to increased Community efforts to negotiate with Russia, Russian interest in the deepening process of European integration intensified, particularly regarding ratification of the Maastricht Treaty. As Kozyrev stated, "the prospects of ratification directly affect our external political and economic interest. Internal stability and peace, and the dynamism of the Community's development, will, to a great extent, determine the nature, depth and real possibilities of our cooperation and joint action with the EC."[36]

First responses, outputs, and new assertiveness. Following the conclusions of the Rome European Council in December 1991, the European Community and its member states increased their efforts to strengthen and establish a working relationship with Moscow, while at the same time supporting a dissolution of the USSR. It was the EC's support for independence for the Baltic countries that created the first friction between Brussels and Moscow.[37] One can also see in this issue the first contours of a policy line taken by the Commission.

In order to determine how Europe could assist in the peaceful transformation of the former Soviet Union, an active shuttle diplomacy evolved that included visits to the Baltics, Ukraine, and Russia by the Community troika, members of the European Parliament, and many European heads of state. At first the Moscow leadership reacted cautiously to the European Community's support for—and interest in associating with—independent states in the Baltic region and in Eastern and Central Europe. Cooperation continued, however, in exploratory talks. The creation of a system of triangular operations in order to establish credit guarantees—amounting to US$10.2 billion for the export of agricultural and food products—was a method of aid welcomed by Moscow.[38] On the other hand, funds for emergency food aid, technical assistance, as well as short- and medium-term loans amounting to roughly ECU 1 billion, could only be released after considerable delay.[39] The reason was largely resistance in Moscow to the movements toward independence of the Baltic States. By December 1991, the European Council pledged substantial funds for food aid and technical assistance for temporary relief, granting ECU 200 million worth of food and medical supplies as a response to appeals for emergency help from the mayors of St. Petersburg and Moscow.

The EC remained firm in exerting influence by attaching political objectives to its aid, and Soviet military pressure in the Baltics resulted in an initial suspension of food aid and technical assistance programs.[40] Vice President Yananev remarked that the Soviet-European relationship had cooled as a result of such unfriendly gestures;[41] President Gorbachev, however, succeeded in persuading the West that events in the Baltic did not represent a reversion to old ways but were only a passing disturbance in his pursuit of reform. The European Community suspended its help for the second time during the August coup in 1991, when the political future of the Soviet Union became so uncertain.

The twelve member states of the EC produced by the end of 1991 a declaration on guidelines for recognition of new states in Eastern Europe and the Soviet Union, with the objective of providing a foundation for its future relationship with the dissolving USSR. In this way the EC was prepared to adopt a statement indicating its readiness to recognize eight republics of the CIS by the time the Soviet Union officially ceased to exist. In 1992 Russia took over the former Soviet mission to the European Community in Brussels. The significance Yeltsin attached to this post is exemplified by his appointment of Ivan Siliayev, the Soviet prime minister after the August coup, as a permanent representative to the European Community.[42]

In sum, the uncertainty of the political scene during 1991 and 1992 in Russia made it difficult for the European Commission to work on a set of strategies regarding Russia. Furthermore, the Community soon realized that technical cooperation needed to be complemented by political dialogue. It pursued this under the umbrella of, and in preparation for, the Partnership and Cooperation Agreement.

Post–Cold War Europe and Russia: Toward Partnership

Deepened and ambitious cooperation strategies within a rapidly changing international political environment entailed for the EC institutional adaptation and learning, but also capacity and credibility building in the multilateral fora. For Russia, the EC was its prime ally in its effort to integrate into the international political system. Indeed, the new EC-Russian rapprochement provided important frames of reference in which state building was pursued for Russia and integration furthered for the European Union. The EU ambassador to Russia, Michael Emerson, remarked in 1994:

> Thus the twin magnetic poles of Europe—centered in the EU and Russia—began also to see their powers and attraction tidy up the geographic organization of post Cold War Europe. Increasingly more countries formerly part of the USSR now look to Europe. Russia desires to play a full part in European civilization, as well as to reverse much of the recent disintegration of its links with other CIS countries, and the EU had important interests in building deeper links with Russia, in addition to pursuing its own integration.[43]

Internal and external institutional adaptation. Commission Vice President Andriessen, in reference to implementing goals with the changing Soviet Union, noted that "we must start again from zero . . . we had a structure and it is not working."[44] The collapse of the Soviet Union gave rise to frustration in the Commission since, as Andriessen put it, one had to work on the basis of "bricolage."[45] It was repeatedly noted that the Commission's human resources were inadequate for working with such an enlarged and complex portfolio. Ill-prepared functionaries with little diplomatic experience faced the problem of finding appropriate mechanisms for establishing a dialogue and implementing the decision of the Council of Rome.[46]

Despite these shortcomings, however, it appeared that the EC's capacity to act was soon recognized by other actors. The European Community was increasingly seen as a capable interlocutor, not only in continued and heavy interaction between Moscow and the Commission, but also in multilateral settings such as the G-7 and the World Bank. Within the G-7 framework, member states of the Community (most notably Germany and the United Kingdom) and Commission President Delors stressed the need for the international community to integrate Russia and to enlarge the G-7 to a G-8, at least on the political level. The G-7 took an active role and cooperated with the Community in the assessment and coordination of aid and loans given to the former USSR. The financial commitment made by the European Community, amounting to 80 percent of total humanitarian aid to Russia, gave the Community a certain kind of recognition, as this commitment also represented the interests of those member states who were not formally included in the G-7 negotiations. In addition, the European contingent of the G-7 used agreements with other states, notably the United States, to show its presence. By calling on the spirit of the Transatlantic Declaration, it promoted the European Community's international identity, while also making clear that as a partner the United States as well had some responsibilities to fulfill toward the Soviet successor states.

In recognizing the European Community's capacity to act, the Commission received the mandate to organize a follow-up conference on aid in Lisbon the same year, in which the Russian side expressed its wish to be included in the preparatory work.[47] Furthermore, the Community was included in the workings of the World Bank to ensure efficiency in the coordination of international aid. Particularly during 1992, when quick reactions by the international community to market changes within Russia were needed, the Commission received the mandate to consolidate the Community's program for technical assistance.

Toward partnership and cooperation. With the aim of conducting a political dialogue, the post-Maastricht European Union instigated negotiations for the Partnership and Cooperation Agreement (PCA) by the fall of 1992.[48] The EU came to realize that Russia could offer immense opportunities. The EU-15 is Russia's main trading partner, with a trade volume of over US$31 billion as compared to China, the United States, and Japan taken together, amounting to just under US$11 billion.[49] Building the PCA however, proved to be a difficult enterprise, not least because it was very ambitious in content and scope. In the second round of bilateral negotiations, it was accepted that the new relations between the European Union and Russia needed to be based on common values.[50] While both parties reaffirmed consistently their willingness to conclude negotiations, differences between the European Union and Russia persisted, in particular over the clause regarding human rights and the provisions applying to the exchange of goods in sensitive sectors.

Russia viewed the Partnership and Cooperation Agreement as a way to integrate into the international political system, in particular in reference to trade issues. Russia stressed the need no longer to be considered as a centralized state-planned economy but as an equal partner, and demanded from the EU that it be treated on equal footing with GATT countries. The EU was not willing at that time to grant complete access to GATT-type trade policy rules to Russia, whose cost and price structures were not transparent enough and whose industries could in some cases inflict severe damage on EU producers. In the end the bargaining focused primarily on economic issues, and in June 1994, after two years of negotiation, the PCA was signed in Corfu. It was here that Yeltsin made the grand statement, "Our country has made a strategic choice in favor of integration into the world community, and, in the first instance, with the European Union."[51]

While the agreement is still pending ratification of the national parliaments of the member states of the European Union,[52] the PCA (valid for an initial period of ten years) sets important rules of trade and business with Russian principal economic partners. It creates a body of trade and business law that binds Russia to a combination of EU international market law and the international trading system (GATT/WTO), with enough flex-ibility for future negotiation of a free trade area (planned to start in 1998). It is also an agreement on political integration, in the sense that it includes a human rights premise, expressed through its suspension clause (Article 170). In fact, this suspension clause has already been invoked in the con-text of the Russian military response to the Chechnyan crisis.

Parallel to negotiations for the Partnership and Cooperation Agree-ment, the European Commission implemented the TACIS program toward the former Soviet Union, with the main purpose of directing EU economic competence and expertise toward improving market mechanisms. The Commission sees TACIS as an "inseparable part of western Europe's pre-sent and future strategy towards the emerging democracies" whose main aim is "to build bridges" between the East and the West, and to provide "collective response to a collective lesson learned from history."[53] In its first year the TACIS program alone amounted to ECU 400 million, even though implementation was severely backlogged by coordination prob-lems. Russia is by far the main recipient, receiving 60 percent of the an-nual ECU 450 million awarded. In justifying this aid, the European Par-liament stressed maintenance of "European" values regarding human rights and democracy.

New integrative efforts. With the European Union as its prime advocate, Russia became increasingly interested in participating in European Cooper-ation. Results of this were its participation in the EU's Stability Pact con-ference in Paris in May 1994, its application to GATT in March 1994, its application to the Council of Europe in 1992 (of which it became a member in early 1996), and its active membership in the European Bank for Recon-struction and Development (EBRD), the International Bank for Recon-struction and Development (IBRD), and the International Monetary Fund (IMF). Cooperative participation with the European Energy Charter and conclusion of the cooperation agreement with the OECD in June 1994 are also signs that Russia wants to be seen as a normal state and equal partner in international political forums. Russia has also participated in several re-gional efforts aimed at integrating complicated border areas, such as the Barents and Baltic Sea Regional Cooperation Council, an endeavor seen by the EU as important in ensuring that future enlargements of the European Union will not create a bloc mentality. In the security and foreign policy field, Russia pushed for an upgrading of the Conference for Security and Cooperation in Europe (CSCE) into the Organization for Security and Co-operation (OSCE) in 1994.

Action and support in uncertainty. The European Union, for its part, showed its political character in supporting the status quo of the political leadership in Russia. For example, when the Russian parliament attempted to strip Yeltsin of his powers, the EU continued, in the framework of Political Co-operation, to support him. While the political climate slowed diplomacy and postponed meetings between Delors and Yeltsin, the Union continued to offer its support and was even willing to accelerate negotiations of the partnership agreement.[54] As a recognition of its efforts and also as a gesture of openness and commitment to Western values, Foreign Minister Kozyrev invited EU observers for the 1993 elections. The European Parliament subsequently approved funding for technical support for the elections. The first EU joint action (under J(3), Title V of the TEU) was taken on EU election observation in the winter of 1993, at a time when Russia's political situation was dangerously unstable.

By 1995 the initial international integration of Russia was seriously undermined, both by domestic problems, exemplified by numerous banking scandals, and by the massive military force used in response to the ethnic conflict in Chechnya. Fronts increasingly hardened between the East and the West. The war in Chechnya had wide-ranging international repercussions. After a visit to Chechnya by a delegation led by Hungarian Prime Minister Kovacs, the OSCE protested in Moscow against the violation of human rights, and the Assembly of the Council of Europe postponed its decision about Russia's membership. The response of the European Union, which was backing the OSCE in its fact-finding missions, was harshest in its suspension of procedures for signing the interim agreement, an action that was supported by the European Parliament.

Toward security concerns. Multiple signs that the Russian tendency toward an open foreign policy had abated were also evidenced in the 1993 Russian foreign policy doctrine, which reflected the re-emergence of a hardened political will toward a strongly nationalistic policy. This became particularly evident in the concept course, "Strategy for Russia," published by the non-governmental Russian Council for Foreign and Defense Policy in March 1994, affirming that Russia must pursue a policy of balancing between the centers of power and of establishing a new security system in Europe.[55]

In a press conference following the first Russian-EU meeting after the signing of the interim agreement, Commission President Santer stressed that the EU did not seek to "establish a new frontier" in Europe and maintained the importance of Russia's role in the construction of a new European security architecture.[56] Thus, despite frictions, the EU ministers saw the need to strengthen the relationship with Russia further. This became particularly evident when EU ministers met informally in Carcassone in the spring of 1995 and discussed in depth events in Russia. As a consequence of that meeting, an EU strategy exercise was launched in order to provide an analysis of EU-Russian interests, to generate guidelines for policy, and to identify future areas of cooperation in all pillars of the TEU.[57] The strategy exercise was important in that it ensured EU member states' commitment vis-à-vis Rusia and resulted in a decision to upgrade the political dialogue with Russia already foreseen in the Partnership Agreement.

The Commission subsequently produced a Communication to the Council titled "The European Union and Russia: The Future Relationship." In doing so, it made use for the first time of the rights of initiative it holds with member states in CFSP under J(8) of the TEU. The paper recommends that a political dialogue be established on issues of security, "comprising such questions as NATO enlargement, Partnership for Peace, OSCE strengthening and the development of relations between the Russian Federation and the Western European Union."[58] It emphasizes in particular a rapprochement and intensified dialogue between Russia and NATO in the context of Partnership for Peace and the North Atlantic Cooperation Council (NACC).

Russian authorities welcomed this initiative but regretted that they weren't consulted in the preparation of the document, which in their view was at times lacking in "clarity, substance and comprehension for certain Russian realities."[59] They thus proposed that the Commission and the Council include Russian experts in the work for concrete and practical implementation of the new Union policy toward Russia. The Russian delegation complained, furthermore, that Russia was still not considered a market economy by the EU, and also that it was not able to benefit from loans from the European Investment Bank. On the political side, greater involvement with the EU on questions affecting security and stability in Europe was demanded. It can be argued, however, that overall, the instigation of the "action plan exercise" has injected an important degree of momentum and dynamism in EU-Russian relations, since it aims to implement a concrete working policy with identifiable and achievable actions, the first proposals of which were adopted by the General Affairs Council on 13 May 1995.

Throughout 1995 and 1996 the European Union maintained its technical assistance programs. It also coordinated with the OSCE international observations for the State Duma and presidential elections, while taking a cautious approach in awaiting their outcome. Perhaps because of the Communist victory in the Duma elections, the Commission and most member states strongly vocalized their support for Yeltsin's candidacy in the presidential elections, with a view to maintaining the relations established. During this time, preparing a strategy toward Russia was a major preoccupation in the political unit in Brussels, and technical assistance and support for reform continued to flow into the Russian Federation.

However, Russian actions such as discriminatory legislation toward foreigners, which were in contradiction to the basic principles set down in the PCA, gave rise to frustration in Brussels and in the EU member states. Given its relatively limited capabilities in influencing Russian domestic policy, as well as the desire of member states to take a "wait and see" approach in the prevailing context of fluidity and instability, the European Union was both incapacitated and somewhat less than willing to take a more proactive position toward Russia.

Three "Pillars" of the New European Ostpolitik

After reviewing the complex dynamics of the EU-Russian relationship, it is useful to outline the loci of competence, autonomy, and internal capacity within the EU with reference to the three main elements undergirding the European Union's conduct toward the Russian Federation. The first element concerns the Partnership and Cooperation Agreement. On a fundamental level, negotiations for the agreement allowed the European Union and Russia to reflect on each other's priorities toward the other. It is evident that the agreement has not, as Delors noted, "the same physiognomy as an agreement with the U.S.," as long as the reform process in Russia has not advanced more. Nonetheless, the EU has recognized that "Russia is a great power, and we want agreements with her on the same political intensity as with the United States and Japan."[60]

The agreement is of importance because it marks a vital change, bringing together key political and economic issues previously held separate. Its significance lies in the instigation of a political dialogue on the presidential level at least twice a year, a procedure that the EU formerly shared only with the G-7 countries. Furthermore, on Russia's part, the agreement demonstrates willingness to move toward European standards and toward rapprochement with the GATT system. The agreement might be seen as a landmark in the relationship between the West (and in particular the European Union) and Russia because many of the provisions set out in the PCA have far-reaching implications for domestic legislation entailing legally binding obligations. As such, it brings together the desires of two "actors" representing the first part of the new mosaic of European and Russian integration of the international system.

On the institutional level, the agreement also signifies the capability of the Commission to act as a competent interlocutor with a third state. Because of its increased interaction with Russian Federation authorities, the Commission acquired increasing autonomy in negotiating this agreement. During the period between 1991 and 1995, it received mandates to balance the agreement between the desires of the member states and Russia. These include authorization from the Council to negotiate a clause concerning the establishment of a free trade zone, the content of the democracy clause, and also the way in which the Russian economy should be treated by the European Union. Other important mandates include specific negotiations in reference to trade and cooperation in nuclear materials and issues concerning the banking sector.

The second element concerns the EU's role as an advocate for Russia in the international political system, as a way to promote its own international identity. Both the Partnership and Cooperation Agreement and the Communication of the Commission to the Council demonstrate that the European Union can be seen as Russia's closest advocate in integrating more fully into the international political-economic system. In return, Russia's demands to upgrade the CSCE promoted and strengthened the role of the European Union in the security arena. The European Union has relied on and cooperated with the OSCE, both in the Russian parliamentary elections in 1995 and also in the presidential elections in 1996. In addition, the European Union has strongly supported the accession of Russia to the World Trade Organization.

While the European Union and its member states can be seen as the closest allies Russia has in its integration with the international system, this process has also afforded the European Union an opportunity to promote its own role in the international arena. Moreover, the increasing competence of the Commission, which gradually evolved into a regular set of interactions with the Russian Federation, has given the European Union a profile to allow it to participate more closely in the negotiation, preparation, and policy formulation of international institutions to support the transformation of Russia.

The establishment in 1991 economic assistance programs for the Russian reform process served both as an important policy tool and as a significant catalyst in promoting cooperation among Community institutions, in particular between the European Parliament and the European Commission. The European Parliament since the 1980s has been very supportive of democratic and economic reform in the former USSR. As a result, having established a delegation for relations with Russia, it was able to engage in a constructive dialogue with the deputies of the Russian State Duma, and as such it was better informed about current political events and trends than was the Commission. The European Parliament had a considerable interest in the humanitarian aspects of Community aid and called for increasing EC financial support from early 1991.[61] As such, it was an important influence in ensuring that EU cooperation with Russia reflected and communicated a set of European values. The insistence of the European Parliament on maintaining European practices regarding human rights and democracy provided for the rationale under which the TACIS Democracy Program was founded. The wish to support the political nature of transition and to provide the expertise and know-how necessary to support the development of democratic practices in the Russian Federation represented a qualitative enlargement of the scope of technical assistance. As a "watchdog" of the expenditures of the EU's budget, and thus also of technical assistance, the European Parliament was able to influence the content and the outlook of TACIS.[62]

The expenditure of TACIS funds and the program's management has received a certain degree of criticism not only from the parliament, but also from the Court of Auditors and from some of its beneficiaries as well. Reference has been made in particular to the slow rate at which commitments and payments have been made, the poor liaison between the Commission and contractors in executing technical assistance, poor coordination with other donors, and poor assessment of the needs of the recipient country. The slow implementation of and unrealistic rule setting for projects point to serious shortcomings within the Commission regarding its coordination efforts. Overall, some of these problems are due to very limited staff resources; they also, however, indicate the low priority given by the Commission to follow-up, control, and evaluation of TACIS funds.[63]

In reaction to criticism from the European Parliament, Court of Auditors, and some beneficiaries, the Commission has made efforts to improve its performance in this program. The fact that it had to develop distinct working methods and the relevant expertise in a short time frame points to a learning effect, and to the possibility of more realistic and adequate implementation of funds in the future. Two important improvements made are an increasing emphasis on horizontal themes (i.e., technical assistance given to sectors and not only to specific regions) and a considerable increase of staff. Additionally, the inclusion of town-twinning programs between the European Union and Newly Independent States (NIS) has promoted cultural rapprochement, providing incentives to build cooperative networks that reach beyond technical assistance.

Conclusion

This chapter emphasizes that both the content and the quality of the EU-Russian relationship has contributed to the role of the European Union in the world. As we have seen, this relationship has been strongly influenced by historical as well as powerful cultural imperatives. As such Russia was, is, and will remain Europe's most significant "Other." In the evolution of the EU-Russian relationship, it appears that the European Union had an opportunity to strengthen its international identity when both the Russian foreign policy system and the structure of the international system showed most flexibility and openness. This was particularly evident from 1987 to about 1993. During this time frame, images of the unsettled "Other" tended to drive collaborative behavior because the European Union could be seen as an independent presence within the newly shaping structure of international relations. However, opportunities for proactive European Union dialogue with Russia entailed new approaches that in turn challenged the EU's foreign policy capability. This case study shows that external capability requires internal competence. The international changes in the political system were coupled with a reshaping of the European integration agenda. This provided the European Union with a "competitive advantage" for restructuring its internal competencies, allowing the Commission to initiate important strategies toward EU-Russian rapprochement. But at the same time its initial lack of experience in dealing with a complex external relationship slowed the dialogue to a considerable extent. This difficulty could be attributed in part to the extremely uncertain political situation following the breakup of the Soviet Union, but the initial lack of interinstitutional cooperation among the European Parliament, the European Commission, and the Council also exacerbated the problem.

Still, the conclusion of the Partnership and Cooperation Agreement provided the European Union with both a strategy and a rationale on which it could work. Progressively more bargaining mandates were granted the Commission to bring the negotiations to a close. In using these mandates the member states (despite some minor drawbacks) invested a certain degree of trust in the Commission's role as a "diplomatic interface." This process gained the European Union respect within multilateral forums and also, very importantly, with its partner Russia. Consequently, even though criticism has been leveled at the EU's foreign policy capability, this case has shown that where the historical imperative is strong and when member states agree, the European Union can be a highly influential actor in the world community.

Notes

I would like to thank the participants of the ECSA workshop held on 16–19 May 1996 in Jackson Hole for their critical remarks, in particular Michael Smith, David Allen, Carl Lankowski, Jonathan Davidson, Fraser Cameron, and Pierre-Henri Laurent. Special thanks for reading, commenting, and editing on earlier drafts to Brian Whitmore, Olivier Allais, Henrik Plaschke, and particularly to Carolyn Rhodes.

1. Wallander 1996.
2. See for example, Carlton, Ingram, and Tenaglia 1996.
3. Wallander 1996, 215.
4. See, for example, Holland 1995b.
5. Hill 1994.
6. Allen and Smith 1990.
7. Smith 1996.
8. Neumann 1996.
9. See Lester 1995; Malcolm 1994; Mommsen 1996; Neumann 1996.
10. McSweeney 1996, 87.
11. Hedetoft 1995.
12. Bull 1977, 1983.
13. Anderson 1983; Allen and Smith 1990; Hedetoft 1995; Smith 1991; McSweeney 1996.
14. Herrberg 1996b.

15. Keohane 1989, 158-179
16. Herrberg 1996a.
17. Pelkmans and Murphy 1991.
18. Quoted in Neumann 1996.
19. De la Serre 1994, 13.
20. The Common Commercial Policy (CCP) was named in Article 3 of the Treaty of Rome as one of the activities of the EC. As a customs union, it was essential for the member states to draw up common policies with respect to their trading relations with the rest of the world. Article 113 EC required the need for "uniform principles to underpin the CCP with regard to tariff rates, the conclusion of trade agreements, liberalization measures, the promotion of exports and instruments of commercial defence against dumping and subsidies."
21. Baranovsky 1994.
22. Most notably, from the Directorate General of External Relations, Mr. Wallerstein in 1974 met to prepare a formal meeting with President of the Commission Ortoli.
23. The result was an initial doctrinal hostility, especially from the Soviet Union, which nonetheless did not impede Poland, Romania, and Hungary from concluding between 1965 and 1980 sectoral agreements on agricultural imports and exports, which could be interpreted as the first signs of the so called socialist realism.
24. The CSCE (now OSCE) divides its work into three baskets. Basket II refers to recommendations to cooperate in economics, science, and environmental protection.
25. The term *mezdhunarodnik* refers to foreign affairs specialists but also to a wider range of leading intellectuals engaged in the discourse concerning the USSR's and Russia's integration in the international system.
26. Lukin 1994.
27. Neumann 1996; Hedetoft and Herrberg 1996.
28. Shakhnazarov 1995.
29. Baranovsky 1994.
30. De la Serre 1994.
31. Ibid.
32. Emerson 1994.
33. Today the staff in the delegation in Moscow numbers about sixty-five. Author's interview with Catherine Magnant, Public Information Division, Delegation of the European Communities, Moscow, August 1996.
34. Emerson 1994, 5.
35. Ibid.
36. *Agence Europe,* 5 August 1992.
37. Emerson 1994.
38. Triangular operations constitutes a form of aid given in loans that, for example, allowed the former Soviet Union states to purchase food and agricultural produce from each other. The advantage of this operation was that it provided the states of the former CMEA an export incentive to continue production.
39. *Agence Europe,* 8 October 1991.
40. Emerson 1994.
41. Ibid.
42. *Agence Europe,* 20 December 1991.
43. Emerson 1994.
44. *Agence Europe,* 20 September 1991. Andriessen gave this comment at a meeting with the enlarged bureau of the European Parliament Foreign Affairs Committee.

45. *Agence Europe,* 19 December 1991.

46. *Agence Europe,* 29 August 1991; *Agence Europe,* 19 September 1991.

47. *Agence Europe,* 12 March 1992.

48. Russia was the first country to engage in negotiations for a partnership agreement since it took over the rights and obligations of the former agreements concluded with the Soviet Union.

49. Out of a total $70 billion in 1993 figures. Illarionov quoted in Emerson 1994.

50. *Agence Europe,* 28 November 1992.

51. Partnership and Cooperation Agreement 1994.

52. The interim agreement entered into force on 1 February 1996.

53. "Brittan Pledges EU Support for Russia Post-Privatization Measures." *Europe Information Services,* 19 July 1994.

54. *Agence Europe,* 16 July 1993, 23 September 1993.

55. Krause and Jahr 1995, 16; *Nezavisimaha Gazeta,* 27 May 1994.

56. *Agence Europe,* 8 September 1995.

57. European Commission, Directorate General I-A, Directorate C. "Main Facts on EU/Russian Relations." No date given.

58. Commission Communication to the Council 1995a. (Com [95]: 9).

59. *Agence Europe,* 11 July 1995.

60. *Agence Europe,* 31 October 1993.

61. *Agence Europe,* 14 March 1991.

62. Author's interview with Joseph Dunne, desk officer for Russia, European Parliament Directorate General for Committees and Delegations, 1996.

63. Author's interview with Olivier Allais, head of the Technical Office of the European Commission, St. Petersburg, Russia, on the occasion of the mission of the European Court of Auditors to St. Petersburg, June 1995.

6

The European Union's Policy Toward Central Europe: Design or Drift?

Alan Mayhew

As an influential actor in the international arena, the European Union must be capable of not only initiating, but also implementing, a coherent foreign policy. The European Union's reaction to the triumph of democracy in the countries of Central and Eastern Europe underlines many of its problems in developing consistent foreign policy. This chapter addresses the question of whether there has been any clear overall strategy governing this policy and whether there is any clear policy today. It argues that despite key initiatives by the Council and ongoing efforts on the part of the Commission, the nationalistic economic interests of member states have dampened enthusiasm for enlargement eastward. These divergent interests will continue to interfere with the development and implementation of EU initiatives toward this region as long as crises in EU employment levels, institutional capabilities, and policy revision are not resolved.

The countries of Central and Eastern Europe freed themselves completely from Soviet domination and in most cases from the rule of the Communist Party between 1989 and 1992. The triumph of democracy over dictatorship came with almost no help from the West in general or the European Community. In fact many senior politicians within the EC appeared quite happy to live in a divided Europe that guaranteed peace and stability but denied freedom and prosperity to those behind the iron curtain.

This is perhaps not astonishing given the history in Western Europe over recent decades of promoting perceived self-interest. What is astonishing is that the member states of the Community and the Community institutions appeared unprepared and without any well-developed strategy for tackling the results of the collapse of Communism. It had been obvious since the end of the 1970s that the centrally planned economies of Central and Eastern Europe were in a terminal decline that could only be arrested by fundamental market reforms. Since the triumph of Gorbachev, change had also become possible on the political level. This chapter shows that even though the whole world was impressed at the speed with which an empire self-destructed, the unpreparedness of the Community was astonishing. *This underlines a major problem for EU foreign policy: that there is no real capacity to predict crises and no forward contingency planning for crises.*

When the peoples of the region took power from the Communists, the reaction of Community politicians was extremely enthusiastic. The Community's leading politicians queued up to visit the countries of the region and gave speeches welcoming the new democracies into the European family of nations. Especially in Central Europe, which had been unwillingly separated from Western Europe by the Yalta agreements, these speeches were interpreted as promises of rapid integration into the Western European structures and markets.

However, as it became clear that integration into the structures of the EU was the objective of the countries of Central Europe, the enthusiasm of the member states rapidly declined. There were various reasons for this, including fear of a dilution of the existing level of integration in the EU, fear of a slowing of integration in the future, uncertainties over the course of reform to the east, and preoccupations with other problems such as the reunification of Germany. Most likely the main reason was that enthusiasm (which is costless) rapidly gave rise to the need for economic concessions, as trade within the former Council for Mutual Economic Assistance (CMEA) broke down. This is a reminder that the European Union today still remains essentially an economic union based upon the assumption that it is in each member state's economic interest to be a member. Member states consistently oppose foreign policy measures that they consider will not bring them additional economic advantage; even minimal trade concessions at the Copenhagen European Council, for example, were opposed far more strongly than the political declaration on the common objective of accession for these countries.

The EU's relations with Central and Eastern Europe also illustrate the difficulty of constructing consistent policy when the traditional spheres of interest of the members differ so largely. Both geography and history play roles in complicating foreign policy development. The most consistent supporters of enlargement to the east are the countries that are geographically close to the region: Germany, Austria, and the Nordic countries. These are also the countries historically most closely linked with Central Europe. The peripheral, and especially the Mediterranean, member states are at best neutral to enlargement and would rather focus on other issues.

Geography and history also play a role in the importance given to Russia in determining the relationship with Central Europe. There has been a long tradition in German foreign policy (and indeed in U.S. policy and to a lesser extent that of the other EU member states) of allowing Russia to exert a major influence on the EU's relations toward this region. There is nothing strange in this influence, but a question arises about the degree to which it may be used to slow down or prevent the integration of certain democratic and independent countries (e.g., the three Baltic nation-states) into the EU.

Relations with the Central and Eastern European Countries (CEEC) have also revealed fault lines in the European Union between countries that have a liberal approach to economic policy—such as the Netherlands and the United Kingdom (and on some issues, Germany)—and those such as France and Spain that have a more protectionist policy, giving the state a larger role. These differences have been particularly obvious in the retention by the EU of an extremely high level of protectionism in agriculture in the face of large trade surpluses with the CEEC; they are also evident in more obscure areas such as rules of origin or rules on establishment. These differences will re-emerge in the negotiations for accession.

While the European Union's relations with the associated countries in Central and Eastern Europe raise a number of questions about the formulation and execution of EU foreign policy, the course of relations over the coming decade will also be affected strongly by the crises afflicting the Union at the present moment. At least three crises can be easily identified: (1) the employment crisis; (2) the institutional crisis; and (3) the policy crisis.

Most fundamentally, the member states of the Union must find solutions to their unemployment problem. With current policies there is no prospect of the core countries of the Union (France, Germany, Italy, Spain, Belgium) reducing their unacceptably high levels of unemployment. It appears that governments in these countries do not have the courage to pursue appropriate economic policies to reduce unemployment (liberalizing markets, reducing the cost of labor, etc.). If these governments cannot push through adequate reforms, there will always be a danger that they will choose the way of protection. This may temporarily help but will lead to further decline in the long run and endanger the very existence of the Union itself. Above all, it will mean that enlargement of the Union to the associated countries will be delayed or abandoned.

Institutionally, the Union is also in crisis, as it appears that there is little chance of achieving a major breakthrough in finding institutional solutions for a Union that may include up to twenty-seven countries in the near future. Failure to achieve any thorough reform will certainly lead to a change in the scope for enlargement, probably limiting it to three, or at most four, countries in the first instance.

The policy crisis results from the fact that several policies must be adjusted before enlargement can take place. The common agricultural policy is an obvious example, but reform will also be required in the redistributionary policies (the structural funds) and in many other areas. There appears today to be little enthusiasm for any meaningful reform in these policies. Monetary union is the only policy area in which leading politicians appear willing to move forward.

First EU Reactions to the CEEC: Assistance

The great historic changes that culminated in the year of peaceful revolution, 1989, came as a surprise to many politicians and policymakers in Western Europe and the United States. During the events of 1989 and 1990, and indeed through to the independence of the Baltic countries in 1992, Western leaders were always slightly behind events, at least in terms of understanding their real significance.

Even so, the reaction of the Community was relatively rapid, especially in the area of assistance to reform. The first coordinated Western response came in the G-7 summit meeting in Paris in July 1989. In the declaration on East-West relations, the G-7 leaders pledged themselves to encourage economic reform and provide better trade opportunities, stating, "We recognize that the political changes taking place in these countries will be difficult to sustain without economic progress."[1] On assistance in particular the summit agreed to call a meeting of all interested countries to support the reforms in Poland and Hungary and asked the Commission of the European Communities to take over responsibility for this coordination; this marked the birth of the G-24 process in which twenty-four donor countries agreed to coordinate their assistance.

As far as the European Community itself was concerned, an informal summit of heads of government was called by the French presidency in Paris in November 1989 to consider the Community's response to the challenge of revolution in the East. The summit agreed to look at a series of further measures to support reform, including the creation of the European Bank for Reconstruction and Development (EBRD) and the opening to the east of Community programs in education, training, and technology. It underlined the importance of the Polish stabilization fund and balance-of-payments support for Hungary, subject to agreements between these two countries and the International Monetary Fund.[2]

By December, at the summit in Strasbourg, the European Council was already able to welcome progress toward the reunification of Germany, and could also point to an impressive series of measures taken to support reform in Poland, Hungary, and the Czech and Slovak Republics.[3] The Council reported on the creation of the European Bank for Reconstruction and Development, which was destined to play a significant role in the transition in Central and Eastern Europe. It also confirmed that the Community's member states were to contribute over half of the US$1 billion stabilization fund to support internal convertibility in Poland and that it was necessary to make a balance-of-payments loan of the same magnitude available to support reform in Hungary. Furthermore, it reinforced its commitment to the coordination of assistance through the G-24 process.[4]

In a special declaration on Central and Eastern Europe, the heads of state and government noted again that developments in the region meant that "the division in Europe can be overcome . . . whether in the security area, in economic and technical co-operation or in the human dimension."[5] In the same declaration the Council looked forward to the reunification of Germany, in the context of East-West dialogue and cooperation and in the perspective of European integration. It also stated that it was "ready to develop richer and closer relationships based on an intensification of the political dialogue and co-operation in all areas with the USSR, and the other countries of Central and Eastern Europe and with Yugoslavia," once it was clear that these countries had embarked on a reform course.[6]

The declaration was followed immediately by the creation of the PHARE program (the French acronym for Poland and Hungary Assistance to Economic Restructuring) adopted by the Council on 18 December 1992.[7] This grant program was intended to implement economic aid measures "primarily to support the process of reform in Poland and Hungary, in particular by financing or participating in the financing of projects aimed at economic restructuring."[8] With an immediate allocation of ECU 300 million, this was a significant response by the Community to the challenges of reform. Not only were funds made available by the Community, but the member states also responded with major allocations. Germany, the United Kingdom, France, the Netherlands, and the Nordic countries especially made an effort to make knowledge transfer available for the transition.

By the end of 1989 the assistance effort was in full swing, and a structure for the coordination of assistance was established. Through 1990 this effort continued as more countries were added to the list of states receiving help from the G-24. G-24 assistance was extended to the DDR, Czechoslovakia, Yugoslavia, and Bulgaria at the G-24 ministers meeting in July 1990; Romania had to wait another six months before being admitted, owing to the unclear situation of reform following the elections in May 1990. In September 1990, the European Community extended the PHARE program to cover Bulgaria, Czechoslovakia, the DDR, Romania, and Yugoslavia. An additional ECU 200 million was also added to PHARE's 1990 budget, bringing total spending up to ECU 500 million.

The first response was therefore an assistance response, as was to be expected and which was indeed required. Poland's first Solidarity government inherited a catastrophic economic situation with rampant inflation and food shortages and was determined to introduce a radical reform program. Hungary, while in a less precarious situation because it had been reforming steadily since 1968, nevertheless required support for the necessary transformation of the economy. Romania and Bulgaria were in very difficult situations and required immediate help.

On balance, the aid effort for Central Europe has been less generous than the donors pretend, although sometimes better than some of the governments in the region have charged. It is clearly not through aid, however, that the countries of Central and Eastern Europe will succeed in their reforms and achieve eventual accession to the European Union. Such success will come through trade and other economic relations and through appropriate macroeconomic policies.

Trade and Economic Cooperation

From the beginning it was clear that financial assistance was not going to be of sufficient volume to make a significant difference to economic recovery in the countries of Central and Eastern Europe, though it could effectively support the process of reform. Far more important were the macro- and microeconomic policies applied by the CEEC governments and the development of trade and other economic relations with the West. The end of the 1980s saw a series of negotiations between the Community and individual CMEA countries to establish stronger trade relations. These negotiations led to the signing of agreements on trade and economic cooperation between the Community and Hungary (September 1988), Poland (September 1989), Czechoslovakia and Bulgaria (May 1990), and Romania (October 1990).

These agreements reaffirmed the commitment to grant each other most-favored-nation treatment in accordance with the General Agreement on Tariffs and Trade (GATT). These CEEC governments abolished, over a period of four years, the quantitative restrictions that had governed trade under their respective protocols of accession to the GATT. The agreements included strong safeguard clauses for the EC, and these countries were still treated as state-trading countries under the Community anti-dumping regulation.

The EC also rapidly improved the terms of these trade agreements by offering better import access for agricultural produce and textiles via the GATT's Generalized System of Preferences (GSP). Furthermore, the transition period for abolition of quantitative restrictions was removed, so that from early 1990 no quantitative restrictions remained, at least as far as Hungary and Poland were concerned. In 1990, Polish exports to the Community rose by over a third in nominal ECU terms, while Hungarian exports rose by 16 percent over the previous year. Thus, in the earliest phase of relations between the Community and the Central European democracies (1989 and 1990), the response of the European Community can be considered to have been adequate to support the immediate needs of reform both in terms of aid and market access.

German Reunification

German policy toward the Central European countries was affected at least in four ways by the problems of reunification, and this has had a significant effect on EC policy. First, reunification naturally absorbed an enormous proportion of the energies of political and economic actors in Germany. There are many indicators of this. German investment in the Central European countries was lower than that of other third countries, even though Germany is a direct neighbor and through its trade links dominates the regional economy. Germany also was often only barely represented in discussions on the development of the relationship between the European Community and Central Europe. Germans were likewise greatly underrepresented among service providers flocking to the region. Because of the enormous amount of work that was available in the New Bundesländer, Central Europe held less appeal for German advisers and consultants.

Second, reunification absorbed enormous financial resources, and indeed is still doing so today. While Germany consistently contributed more to G-24 assistance than the other eleven member states together, the financial strain of reunification has set a clear limit to German financing of Central European development and will continue to do so for years to come.

Third, potential competition with the New Bundesländer from the Central European countries made the German government less ready to open markets than might otherwise have been the case. In 1992, for instance, the German government resisted an increase in the tariff quota for imports of television tubes from Poland (produced by Thomson, the French company, in one of their investments near Warsaw), in order to protect a Samsung plant that had just been attracted to the former DDR. Despite this marginal effect, however, Germany remained consistently one of the most liberal countries with respect to imports from Central Europe.

Fourth, and perhaps most importantly, reunification once again reinforced the natural German predilection to negotiate with Russia over the heads of all the countries lying between. Reunification was only possible because of the success of a consistent *ostpolitik,* which was always privileging relationships between the two major powers. The negative side of this is that Germany has frequently been prepared to neglect the interests of the Central European countries for the sake of its relationship with Moscow.

The Association (Europe) Agreements

Superficial facts do not appear to support the claim that through 1990 the member states of the Community became less positive about their relationship with Central Europe than they had been after the first enthusiasm of the revolution. For it was in 1990 that the foundations for the association agreements with these countries were laid; and it is these agreements that form the fundamental legal basis of the relationship today. Nevertheless, in the negotiation of these agreements a different tone crept in, compared to the welcoming declarations of 1989.

The idea of offering associated status to the newly emerging democracies in Central Europe emerged at the end of 1989. A further deepening of institutional relations had already been mentioned at the Strasbourg European Council in December 1989. It was next considered by foreign ministers meeting in Dublin at the end of January 1990, where it appears that the British government introduced the point in the discussion leading up to the Council meeting. At the Council meeting Frans Andriessen, the commissioner in charge of foreign relations, could already present an outline of the contents of such an agreement. The idea had also been discussed between President Delors and the Polish prime minister, Tadeusz Mazowiecki, early in 1990.

The offer to Czechoslovakia, Hungary, and Poland was indeed a major step forward in the quality of relations between the Community and these countries. Association meant not only that there would be a formal legal basis for a close relationship between the partners, but also that a process of political dialogue would be started that would lead to ministers from both sides regularly discussing matters of common interest. It would also establish common institutions, notably the Association Council, Association Committee, and the Association Parliamentary Committee. These would ensure close cooperation between the Community and these states. For the three countries concerned, association was an important way of locking into the Community and was a clear step on the road to accession.

Following the adoption of the negotiating mandate by the Council on 18 December 1990, it took a year to finalize the negotiation and sign these agreements—the signature taking place on 13 December 1991. During the negotiations it became clear to the negotiators from the three partner countries that they were experiencing a different quality of negotiation compared to that to which they were accustomed with the World Bank or even the IMF. The relatively rapid negotiation of the association agreements shifted to a hard-nosed trade negotiation, in which the Community sought clear objectives. The impact on the negotiators from the Central European states, some of whom had no previous experience dealing with the Community, was quite marked. They found themselves under pressure to get a relatively quick agreement because of the precarious economic and strategic position of their countries. Their populations had also been led to expect a rapid conclusion to the negotiations. While from one perspective the Community was offering an asymmetric agreement, with faster import liberalization on the Community side than on the Central European side, the degree of market liberalization on offer in agriculture, iron and steel, textiles, and certain other "sensitive" goods was considered unsatisfactory. The problem of agriculture led to a virtual breakdown of negotiations over the summer of 1991; the coup attempt in Moscow did not promote greater flexibility on the Community side in its relations with Central Europe. The refusal by the Community to agree to include a statement in the agreement that it was the *joint objective of both parties to work toward accession* made many people in these countries wonder if they were following a mirage in their determination to join the Community.

The association agreements, which were called "Europe Agreements" in order to underline their importance, mark a turning point in relations between the Community and Central and Eastern Europe in several respects. They represent a significant move forward in formalizing relations and creating the institutional framework within which it has been possible to deepen these relations further. They were an important step on the road to trade liberalization in industrial products, and they imposed Community competition and state aid rules on the three countries as far as trade was affected. Perhaps the most important role of the agreements was to make sure that the associated countries did not turn to massive protection once the initial euphoria over liberalization ebbed. In ensuring a reasonably liberal trade policy and in laying down some of the fundamental building blocks of the market economy, the agreements have certainly been valuable.

They did, however, also have severely negative impacts on relations. They clearly mark the end of the phase in which the response of the Community to the needs of Central Europe was invariably positive. By the end of 1991, with deep recession in the Community and difficulties over ratification of the Maastricht Treaty evident, it was already clear to the Czechs, Hungarians, and Poles that they were now in a different world— one where they could no longer assume that the Community was acting in their favor and where they would have to defend their rights vigorously.

The Copenhagen European Council, June 1993: The Common Objective of Accession

The signing of the association agreements at the end of 1991 was the beginning of a very long ratification process in the twelve member state parliaments. For Hungary and Poland this process was concluded exactly two years later on 13 December 1993. The agreement with the Czech and Slovak Federal Republic was never ratified, as a result of the peaceful breakup of the country on 1 January 1993. Those parts of the agreements that were of Community responsibility (essentially the trade aspects) were, however, immediately put into effect with all three countries in March 1992. The interim agreements established joint committees, which were responsible for their implementation until ratification of the association agreements. The joint committee meetings immediately led to an increase in contacts between the three countries' respective institutions and those of the Community, which had an important impact on the quality of relations that were under development. These growing contacts also allowed difficult trade problems to be resolved in quiet and constructive ways out of the glare of publicity.

With the signing of the three agreements with the Visigrad group of countries, attention turned to Romania and Bulgaria, which had also started on their own reform programs. The negotiations with these countries were concluded very rapidly, partly because the countries themselves wanted to conclude quickly and partly because the agreements with the Visigrad countries had become a model. The agreement with Romania was signed at the beginning of February 1993 and that with Bulgaria in March 1993.

The decision to offer association agreements to these two countries was an important step. On one hand, it underlined the Union's policy of offering association agreements to all the countries of Central Europe that set upon the course of reform—for Romania and Bulgaria it was an important part of government strategy to pursue reformist policies. Each country would receive the same opening deal from Brussels, and each would then make its own way toward deeper integration depending on its own democratic and market progress. On the other hand, by broadening the potential coverage of the association agreements the EC removed the possibility of immediate accession for everyone. For the Visigrad countries, then, the agreements with Romania and Bulgaria marked the end of their special relationship with the Community, a relationship which they had assumed would lead to rapid accession. For the Union too, the fast track to accession, which had seemed to exist for the Visigrad countries, and which seemed to have been supported by the more liberal member states, was no longer open. The decision to open negotiations with Romania and Bulgaria opened the road later to agreements with the three Baltic countries, with Slovenia, perhaps in the future with Albania, and perhaps even in the more distant future with the Ukraine. The association agreements lost their very special meaning and became important but standard agreements with the Union's European partners in Central and Eastern Europe.

An enormous amount of thought was given at this time to the question of the future European architecture. The negotiations that led to the Maastricht Treaty in December 1991, and the questions that emerged in the process of reflecting seriously about the construction of Europe over the longer term, gave rise to many diverse proposals regarding enlargement. The idea of a European confederation was proposed by President Mitterand. Various arrangements of concentric circles with different degrees of integration were considered. The relationship between the Community and the European Free Trade Association (EFTA) countries seemed to some to be an interesting model for the Central Europeans.

One of the most conclusive statements on the European architecture was made by the EFTA states themselves, when five of them—Austria in 1989, Sweden in July 1991, Finland in March 1992, Switzerland in May 1992, and Norway in November 1992—applied for membership in spite of having all the advantages of the European Economic Area Agreement. For these countries it was clear (though apparently afterwards not for the Norwegian or Swiss electorates) that close economic integration without membership, and thus without the power to influence decisions, was second-best to membership itself. This message was not lost on the associated countries in Central Europe, all of which persisted in proclaiming accession as one of the most important elements of their reform policies.

Following the far-reaching discussion on enlargement at the European Council in Lisbon in June 1992, the Commission presented a report to the next European Council in Edinburgh in December 1992.[9] This document (which was barely discussed at a summit overshadowed by the question of Community finance) stated that "the European Council should now confirm that it accepts the goal of eventual membership in the European Union for the countries of Central and Eastern Europe when they are able to satisfy the conditions required."[10] The document went on to underline the real significance of such a declaration: "By offering this perspective, the Community will provide encouragement to those pursuing reform and make the short-term economic and social consequences of adjustment easier to bear. This perspective will also provide a stimulus to investment and discourage excessive nationalism."[11] The document then indicated certain conditions that would have to be met by acceding countries and suggested that it was, however, impossible to give a timetable for accession.

The paper concentrated on the idea of moving toward a "European Political Area." Here the idea that later became known as the "structured dialogue" was launched. Dialogue would not be limited to the Association Councils, but there should be a multilateral structured dialogue, where ministers from the associated countries would be invited, not only to European Councils and Foreign Affairs Councils, but also to sectoral councils such as transport or agriculture. The paper also raised the possibility that countries in Central and Eastern Europe could be associated with particular policies and could thus have the right to participate in the relevant Council or Commission meetings. Although in many areas this paper was somewhat vague, it marked an important advance in Commission thinking. The Edinburgh European Council asked the Council of Ministers to give early consideration to the Commission's proposals, with a view to taking decisions at the Copenhagen summit in June 1993.

The tenure of the Danish presidency was obviously a favorable moment for pushing through the Council additional advances in the Union's relationship with the associated countries. The Commission prepared a proposal for the Council, which took up several of the elements of the Edinburgh summit paper but went further in specifying concrete trade concessions to be made to the associated countries. This paper contained four chapters of measures: (1) toward a European Political Area; (2) improving market access; (3) making assistance more effective; and (4) furthering economic integration.

The most important proposal was contained in the first part on moving toward a European Political Area: that "the European Council should confirm in a clear political message, its commitment to membership of the Union for Europe agreement signatories when they are able to satisfy the conditions required."[12] This was the great achievement of Copenhagen. Interestingly, it was hardly discussed by the member states and certainly not disputed in the many hours of discussion and negotiation leading up to the summit. The explanation for this demonstration of unanimity is difficult, given that a majority of countries were probably not totally in favor of accession, at least in the near term. On the other hand, once the conditions for membership in the Union are met, the Treaty of Rome is clear that countries can become members of the Union. Further resistance to such a general statement on accession was therefore not only bad politics but was also not in the spirit of the Treaty.

The Commission's proposal also included the creation of the structured relationship, which had already been advanced in the Edinburgh paper, with the proposal to hold joint Council meetings and to expand cooperation in the area of justice and home affairs. There was also the proposal "to establish an Action Committee for Central and Eastern Europe to make recommendations on other means to create a structured relationship between partners in Central and Eastern Europe and the European Union."[13] Although this last proposal was not accepted by the Council, agreement on the remaining proposals was accomplished with remarkably little resistance.

The proposals on improving market access were, however, contested strongly. European political cooperation was not perceived to cost member states much money, but market opening could lose votes! The Commission's arguments for its rather modest proposals were that trade opening was vital to support the reforms in Central Europe, that the Union was already running a large trade surplus with the region (understandable in the context of rapid economic growth in the region), and that improving market access to Central Europe would also help EU producers.

By this time trade relations between the Union and several of the associated countries were becoming very difficult and causing major political friction. This was particularly so in agricultural trade, where measures that were seen as minor in the Union were making headline news in Poland and Hungary. The imposition of minimum prices on cherries from Hungary and Poland, considered in the Union to be a trivial and entirely political measure, led to massive ill feeling in Central Europe, where such protectionism was considered to be the real response of the Union to the needs of these countries, as opposed to the nice words of the declarations of European summits.

The total value to the associated countries of the measures proposed by the Commission was negligible, but politically the additional unilateral concessions were significant. They were consciously intended to limit damage in the political relationship between the partners caused by disagreements in areas such as agriculture and antidumping. Nevertheless, the negotiation of these measures in the Council proved to be extremely difficult, and several of the Commission's proposals were lost in the negotiation, weakening the whole packet.

The Commission also proposed to improve the allocation of assistance to Central Europe, to intensify work on the approximation of laws to those of the Union, and to open up certain Union programs to the participation by the Central Europeans. An important decision was taken at Copenhagen to use PHARE resources to financially support the development of infrastructure in Central Europe, part of the general move to shift assistance toward investment. Agreement on these proposals was achieved in slightly amended form by the Copenhagen European Council.

Copenhagen marks an important logical step in the development of relations between the Union and the associated countries of Central and Eastern Europe. However, the practical economic and trade stance of the Union was rather negative—in spite of the overall rapid movement toward free trade in industrial products—essentially because of its attachment to agricultural protection and antidumping and safeguard measures. In Central Europe and among many nonpartisan observers in Western Europe, the perception was growing that the Union was very reluctant to open its markets in any areas that could remotely be called sensitive, or to agree to anything whose implementation would require real financial resources. Progress in the political area, this view maintained, could be attributed to the fact that political cooperation is a relatively costless activity and that negotiations on accession can be delayed a very long time (e.g. Turkey).

The proliferation of small trade disputes was beginning to undermine the political approach. It was also becoming clear that the driving force in the Community was the European Union and that several member states were being dragged along rather unwillingly. With the difficult debate over Maastricht still in full swing, significant reticence on the part of certain member states signaled an important warning for the future.

A Strategy for the Preparation of Accession: The Essen European Council

While the associated countries approved of the decisions of the Copenhagen summit, the offer of accession lacked credibility for two principal reasons. First, the offer mentioned no timetable for membership and it only mentioned general criteria, which could not easily be turned into concrete policy objectives for the countries of Central Europe. Second, the attitude of the Union on trade issues indicated that there were powerful forces within it that were protectionist and against accession.

In order to keep some dynamism in the process of integration with the associated countries, it quickly became clear within the Commission that new steps would have to be taken to reinforce the credibility of the common objective of accession. These next major steps were therefore outlined for the German presidency at the end of 1994, a presidency that could be expected to be particularly favorable to the eastward enlargement of the Union.

The logical first step was to attempt to point the way from Copenhagen to accession. This would not only be important for policy planning in both the Union and the associated countries, but it would also add considerably to the credibility of the accession pledge. There were four main elements that the Essen European summit, scheduled for December 1994, needed to tackle in any realistic accession strategy: (1) how to implement properly the structured relationship decided upon in Copenhagen; (2) how to support the acceleration of economic growth rates in Central and Eastern Europe; (3) how to help the associated countries to prepare to adopt the EU *acquis;* and, finally, (4) how to change existing Union policies to make accession possible.[14]

Potential proposals were discussed first among Commissioners at the instigation of President Delors in a seminar held in March 1994. Next they were discussed informally with the associated countries, and at a very early stage with the German government. In addition, they were circulated among a large number of experts in areas such as trade policy. Nevertheless, as the *Financial Times* noticed, it was difficult to get the Commission to reach a consensus on proposals in all these areas. There was considerable resistance to any decrease in agricultural protectionism and to reductions in protection afforded by the trade instruments of the Union. Even the very idea of helping to bring these countries into the internal market of the EU met with considerable resistance. The same fate befell the proposal for turning the assistance program PHARE into a type of structural fund, where the countries receiving the assistance would be responsible for its implementation and where the assistance could be used for investment purposes.

At the end of a long battle, the Commission forwarded two proposals to the Council in July, which were then discussed over the six-month period leading up to the Essen summit in December 1994. Many of the original proposals were lost in the negotiation, and more would have been lost but for the powerful leadership of the German presidency. The Essen strategy, as it has become known, was certainly a major step forward in preparation for accession, but it was almost as important for what it did not include as for what it included.

Essen marks an important phase in the development of the political logic followed by the EU after 1989. The association agreements laid down the essential legal relationship; Copenhagen underwrote the objective of accession to the Union; and Essen designed a strategy for the associated countries to follow in achieving this goal. The Essen strategy can be measured against the four elements necessary to promote accession listed above. Essen did indeed lay down in considerable detail the way in which the structured relationship should function. A strict annual timetabling of enlarged Councils to be approved by the Council presidency at the beginning of each year was established. It was agreed that the heads of government of the associated countries would be invited once a year to European Council meetings and twice a year to Foreign Affairs Councils.

However, with regard to fostering economic growth in Central Europe, and notably in terms of trade liberalization, Essen was a failure. In agriculture, for instance, many improvements could have been made without hurting Union producers. That it was not possible at Essen to agree on improved access for producers in associated countries to the EU market was a failure of significant proportions and gave support to those who maintain that the Union operates as an exclusive club rather than a potential community of European nations.

Little progress was made in the area of commercial policy instruments as well. There is no doubt that the Union antidumping regulation is sometimes used as a mechanism to achieve protection by the industrial interest groups in the EU. Commercial policy instruments have been blatantly misused, and regulatory capture is a phenomenon not limited to the European Union's regulators. These practices have been a target of considerable criticism by CEEC exporters, yet here again only minor improvements in the regulatory process were agreed to by the Council in Essen. The Council also sidestepped the formulation of a clear policy on rules of origin, putting off consideration of this matter to the distant future. The only gleam of light in Essen's otherwise gloomy chapter was that it was decided that up to 25 percent of the PHARE program could be used for infrastructure investment. This decision meant that well over 50 percent of the program could be used for all forms of investment.

Essen was considerably more productive in helping the associated countries prepare for accession. The essential part of the strategy consisted of steps to prepare the associated countries to enter the internal market of the Union. Three areas are important: competition policy, control of state aids, and the *acqui communautaire* in the internal market area. The Union promised assistance in the first two areas; this is already forthcoming through the provision of technical assistance by the PHARE program and in the form of close consultation between the competition and state aid authorities in Brussels and in the associated countries. In the third area, the Essen strategy promised a white paper to assist the associated countries in adopting the necessary *acquis*. This form of assistance was a somewhat dangerous element for an accession strategy, in the sense that the compilation of a list of regulations in order to provide guidance to the governments of the associated countries could easily be used by the opponents of enlargement as new criteria for accession. The white paper exercise was, however, carried out exceedingly efficiently and with great professionalism by the European Commission and sent to the European Council meeting in Cannes in June 1995.

The final criterion for a realistic accession strategy, that of considering how Union policies might change to prepare for accession, is almost totally absent from Essen. There is once again a simple request for the Commission to submit "a detailed analysis . . . on the impact of enlargement in the context of the current policies of the Union and their development."[15] Indeed there was considerable resistance amongst member states to the very notion that Union policies might have to be changed.

The Essen strategy marked a logical extension of European Union policy towards the Central and East European countries and an additional important step on the route to accession. Once again, however, the credibility of the common objective of accession was not fully established, largely because of the inability of the Union to take further concrete steps in the trade area, notably in agriculture, and also because of its failure to produce a timetable or series of objective criteria by which the associated countries can judge themselves or be judged.

The Cannes and Madrid European Councils

The Essen strategy and the GATT agreement provided a major work program for the Union in 1995. Perhaps the most important task was the writing of the white paper on the preparation of the associated countries to enter the internal market of the EU. This was approved by the European Council meeting in Cannes in June 1995. In outlining an overview of the most important Union legislation that the associated countries should adopt into their own legislation, the white paper provided an important new guide for future work. It also provided a shock to many associated countries by making clearer the obvious complexity of the task before them.

Many of the other proposals emanating from the Essen strategy were implemented—or at least a start was made on their implementation—during the year. However, the whole process suffered a loss of momentum as the two southern presidencies concentrated more on the Mediterranean area than on Central and Eastern Europe, and as implementation in Bosnia of the Dayton peace agreement grabbed headlines and resources at the end of the year.

The most important revelation of the Madrid European Council in December 1995 was that leadership in the accession process had moved from the Commission to the member states. As noted earlier, such a move is not necessarily a positive sign for enlargement; nonetheless, because of the initiative taken by Chancellor Helmut Kohl, progress was made. It was Chancellor Kohl who pushed the Madrid summit into making concrete and important decisions on the preparation for enlargement. While his proposals to treat enlargement in stages, starting with the Visigrad countries, were resisted by the other member states, the pressure exerted by Germany led the Council to ask the Commission to prepare opinions on the membership applications of all the applicant countries. This important step kept the process of preparing enlargement on track for the rest of 1996. The Commission opinions (generally referred to by the French term "avis") offer advice to the Council of Ministers on whether to open negotiations for accession with an applicant state, based on a thorough technical assessment of the country's economy and democracy and human rights performance. The "avis" can be rejected (as in the case of Greece) by the Council of Ministers. Madrid also asked for papers to be prepared on the overall impact of enlargement on the Union and particularly on the financial perspective of the Union post-1999. It finally expressed hope that the preliminary stage of negotiations for membership of CEEC countries could be accomplished when negotiations begin with Cyprus and Malta (six months after the end of the IGC).

On agriculture, the change of Commission brought a new approach to the joint problems of preparing the Common Agricultural Policy (CAP) for the next century and of preparing for accession. The Commission's proposals to the Madrid European Council marked a clear step forward in strategic thinking. These proposals make it clear that further reform of the Common Agricultural Policy is necessary with or without enlargement. The CAP is unsustainable both in financial efficiency terms and in the context of progressive world trade liberalization within the World Trade Organization. A move from price and export subsidies to income subsidies in the CAP will clearly make enlargement less costly.

After Madrid

On the Union side, 1996 was taken up largely with preparation of the Commission's opinions on membership applications of the associated countries. This exercise allowed politicans in the Union to push Central European accession and its challenges to the back of their agenda. Instead of reflecting on strategies for enlargement, politicians were able to plead that there was little that could be done until the Commission had completed its opinions. With major crises in the economy, the preparation of monetary union, and the lack of progress in the IGC, this meant that enlargement had slipped out of view of many governments.

The completion of the opinions in July 1997 and their publication in the Commission document Agenda 2000, together with an analysis of the impact of enlargement on EU politics, has brought the politicians back into play.[16] Agenda 2000 has laid out, in a very professional way, part of a strategy to tackle the problems of enlargement. Whether this strategy will get the support of all member states and whether it is sufficiently robust to withstand all the shocks that will hit the Union over the coming years are open questions. The worry is that the member states themselves have given inadequate attention to the questions posed by enlargement (reform of the Common Agricultural Policy among them) and have no real strategy for completing the process.

The Luxembourg European Council decided in December 1997 on the opening of negotiations with six countries (Czech Republic, Cyprus, Estonia, Hungary, Poland, and Slovenia) and these negotiations began on 31 March 1998. The other applicant countries will join the negotiations as they become ready. However with still unresolved economic and political problems inside the existing Union and very little serious preparation at the member state level, governments in the Union may push for delays in the accession process. The impact of differentiating between the applicants on the opening of negotiations is also not clear. Unless the interested member states exert clear and strong leadership in the Union, enlargement may not happen, and the Union will have committed an immense breach of faith and turned its back on an opportunity to enhance prosperity, peace, and stability on the European continent.

In the associated countries, the preparation of accession continues to be a major objective of government. The policy distance that most countries must travel to reach the Union is large, and up until now the populations of these countries have not really been told what the consequences of accession will be. The amount of work still to be completed was underlined by the replies to the Commission questionnaire for the "avis" in summer 1996 and by the Commission "Opinions" in July 1997. Accession remains at the top of the list of most countries' foreign policy but there are signs of a first fatigue in the realization of this objective, especially given waning enthusiasm in the Union. On the other hand, the most promising signs are that economic development is progressing well in many of the associated countries to the point where the Czech Republic, Hungary, and Poland have already become members of the OECD. Output growth in several countries is two or three times that of the Union itself and there is little sign of a break in this trend or of macroeconomic instability.

Credibility of EU Policy

It is clear that, while far from perfect, Union policy has not been marked by pure drift. Policy has evolved over the last six years in a consistent and relatively clear way. Progress has been marked by compromise, but sufficient core policy has been saved at each step to take the integration process forward. The main problem has been the discrepancy between policy development on the one hand and concrete steps in the economic area, notably in trade policy, on the other. Currently, however, faced by numerous internal crises, the Union appears to have no clear policy on enlargement and indeed to be drifting toward crisis.

Conclusions are difficult to draw, but some observations on the credibility of EU policy can be made. First, Union policy has evolved relatively consistently: from association to the Essen strategy for preparation for accession, to the Council request to the Commission to prepare its opinions on membership applications, and to the Luxenboug decision to open neogtiations. Policy development has led to a widespread feeling in the Union that accession is already accepted as a fact, though the timing and the "how" are vague.

Second, the common objective of accession proclaimed at Copenhagen nevertheless still lacks credibility, and therefore cannot play the role it should in helping associated country governments adhere to a reform course in their domestic policy.

This credibility is lacking for three reasons: (1) No timetable or clear criteria for accession have been established in spite of the Copenhagen, Essen, Madrid, and Luxembourg European Council conclusions; (2) the opposition to accession in the Community is growing, and there is apparently no clear majority for rapid accession in the Council; and (3) the revealed performance on agriculture and trade policy and the reluctance even to consider changes in Community common policies have indicated a reluctance on the Union side to make concrete efforts to support reform in the region. This may seem strange given that the Union has opened up its markets in industrial goods more or less completely, but such opening is conditioned by the selective use of trade policy instruments and by the exclusion of certain important sectors.

The assistance effort has not been a major factor in the success of reform in these countries, though it has been useful in specific areas. Compared to the Marshall Fund Program, Western assistance has been ineffective. Moreover, the most difficult part of policy development is still to come. The challenges posed by institutional reform within the EU, the agricultural problem (and the budgetary problem associated with agriculture), and the structural funds are all exceptionally difficult to handle. The problem of differentiating between associated countries in the context of accession will be another major test for policy.

The situation after the Luxembourg Council remained unclear. The major uncertainties lie not in the associated countries themselves but in the Union. There the crisis engendered by the discussions on monetary union and institutional reform have led to serious doubts about the future of the Union itself. Unless serious proposals are produced on the new European architecture, adequate to serve a Community of twenty or more member states, the future of enlargement looks fraught with difficulty. Such proposals are on the table, but there appears to be a lack of enthusiasm and political will to grasp them. If short-term political opportunism causes the preparations for enlargement to stall, the very future of the Community will be put in doubt, and the warnings of disintegration sounded by Chancellor Kohl in a speech at Leuven University in February 1996 may become reality.

Conclusion

This consideration of the European Union's policy toward the new democracies in Central Europe suggests a certain number of conclusions about the EU's ability to define and sustain coherent and consistent foreign policy goals. Strong national interests still override Union interests. These national interests are determined by history, geography, fundamental economic policy convictions, and calculation of financial interest at the national level.

One of the reasons for the domination of Union interests by national interests is the lack of serious redistribution mechanisms at the Union level to compensate for costs incurred asymmetrically by member states. This makes the pursuit of national interest in the Union particularly keen. A specific gain to one country from a foreign policy action does not have to be shared with other member states, and there is no financial compensation mechanism for direct losses incurred by one nation. In the context of eastward enlargement, the existence of a win-win situation for the EU will not persuade those member states who are little affected to vote for enlargement, as they will receive none of the gain. Moreover, when direct costs might result, member states will be motivated to actively resist enlargement. This lack of automatic distribution of gains and losses throughout the whole EU leads to a situation wherein member states agree to foreign policy actions only when they can negotiate specific deals for themselves in other areas. This slows decisionmaking and leads to "second best" decisions.

The present rule of unanimity in foreign policy issues obviously makes it difficult to obtain clear and appropriate decisions. This has been evident in many of the issues relating to the Central European associated countries. The Copenhagen and Essen Council decisions and the association agreements themselves might all have been a little clearer and given more support to transition in Central and Eastern Europe if majority voting had been the rule. It is, however, inconceivable that the large countries in the EU will allow themselves to be outvoted by a host of smaller countries, which have overproportional weight in Council of Ministers voting. A solution to this problem requires, therefore, not simply acceptance by the member states of majority voting in foreign affairs issues, but—even more difficult to achieve—agreement on reform of the voting system in the Council, with a loss of influence of the smaller member states. Several of these issues are being addressed by the IGC. The issue is so complex, however, that it will surely take another decade or more to achieve real improvement in the credibility and efficiency of Union foreign policy.

Notes

1. "Seven Nation Summit Held in Paris; Environment Heads Agenda," *Facts on File World News Digest*, 21 July 1989, 521 A1.
2. "EC to Study Setting Up Bank to Aid Eastern Europe," *Reuters Financial Service*, 19 November 1989.
3. "Britain Retreats as Europe Votes on Closer Union," *The Daily Telegraph*, 19 December 1989, 1.
4. Council Regulation 3906/89 of 18 December 1989 on economic aid to the Republic of Hungary and the Polish People's Republic, Official Journal L 375, 23.12.1989.
5. Ibid.
6. Ibid.
7. Council. Conclusions of the Presidency, Edinburgh, December 1992, and the Commission paper "Towards a New Association with the Countries of Central and Eastern Europe" submitted to it. Text contained in Commission of the European Communities, "European Council in Edinburgh—11 and 12 December 1992—Conclusions of the Presidency," *Rapid*, 13 December 1992.
8. Ibid.
9. Ibid.
10. Ibid.
11. Ibid.
12. Council. Conclusions of the Presidency, Copenhagen, June 1993. Text contained in Commission of the European Communities, "European Council in Copenhagen—21 and 22 June 1993—Conclusions of the Presidency," *Rapid*, 22 June 1993.
13. Ibid.
14. Council. Conclusions of the Presidency, Essen, December 1994. Text contained in Commission of the European Communities, "European Council in Essen—9 and 10 December 1994, Conclusions of the Presidency," *Rapid*, 10 December 1994.
15. Commission of the European Communities 1995B. White paper on the Preparation of the Associated Countries of Central and Eastern Europe for Integration into the Internal Market of the Union. (COM 95), 163.
16. Commission of the European Communities, Agenda 2000, 15 July 1997. Com (97) 2000; Supplement 5/97—Bulletin of the European Communities.

7

The European Union's Relations with the South: A Commitment to Development?

Olufemi Babarinde

The European Union's relations with the countries of the South are of particular relevance to scholars interested in the role of the EU in the international community. As the world's largest trading and economic entity, it trades extensively with lesser-developed countries (LDCs). Moreover, its development assistance by far surpasses that of other actors, and its role in humanitarian aid is the largest in the world. These distinctions are especially noteworthy given the circumstances that characterize North-South relations. As this millennium hastens to its end, the gulf that separates the affluent "haves" of the world and the impoverished "have nots" is getting wider. According to the World Bank and the United Nations Development Programme, the inequity characterizing the world's income distribution resembles the shape of a champagne glass. An estimated one-fifth of the world's population dwell in the wealthiest countries, accounting for about 85 percent of global income. At the polar opposite is the one-fifth of the world who reside in the poorest countries and account for less than 2 percent of global income. According to current estimates, there is a 60:1 ratio in the amount of wealth controlled by the wealthiest and poorest 20 percent of the world's peoples.

Most of the poorest peoples of the world can be found in the southern hemisphere. The South is comprised of more than one hundred countries, in which an estimated three-fourths of the world's population reside. Most of the countries in question are in Africa, the Middle East, Asia, and Latin America, where privation is rampant. In these countries, food shortages and hunger abound, literacy and per capita income are low, sanitation and health care facilities are poor, and political stability is highly suspect. The disparities between North and South remain bleak reminders that no scheme has successfully been implemented to bridge the North-South gap. However, the European Union's policy toward the South has been distinctive in its commitment to an agenda of economic empowerment of the South.

During its more than forty years of uninterrupted longevity and remarkable achievements in the realms of regional integration, the EU's contributions to international development are not only unsurpassed but have become the standard against which the rest of the world measures itself and is judged. It has consistently committed twice as much economic assistance to the South as the other major global economic powers, the United States and Japan. The EU has not only increased its economic assistance for development projects, but it has also become the largest donor of humanitarian aid and the quickest provider of relief to distressed communities and victims around the world. Furthermore, over the years the EU has become the largest trading partner for the LDCs, absorbing roughly $300 billion of their annual exports in the 1990s, in return for which the South has accounted for about 20 percent of EU exports. Since its inception in the 1950s, the EU has remained a reliable and important partner for countries of the South.

The purpose of this chapter is to analyze the degree to which the EU has, through its myriad policies, acted as a cohesive factor in alleviating poverty and in promoting development in the LDCs. To that end, we will first chronicle the progression of the EU's presence in the South. The second section will then explore the rationale for the EU-South dialogue. A discourse on the endogenous and exogenous factors influencing relations between the EU and the South will follow, and the final section will review the degree to which the European Union has acted as a bona fide international actor in the realm of economic development.

A Review of the EU's External Relations with the South: An Increasing Visibility?

The European Union has, since its inception, maintained an assortment of external economic relations with the LDCs. These interactions have been both bilateral and multilateral in nature. They have also varied in breadth, substance, concessions, size, and duration. Using these elements, existing EU-LDC relations can be broadly categorized into three discrete clusters relative to the layer they occupy on the EU's pyramid of privileges. The first cluster of countries consists primarily of sub-Saharan Africa, Caribbean, and Pacific (ACP) countries, which, until recently, occupied an unrivaled position atop the EU's pyramid of privileges. By most accounts, the second cluster of countries refers to those states around which the EU's Mediterranean policy has been developed. The group has historically included southern European countries, Middle Eastern and North African countries, and the erstwhile Republic of Yugoslavia. A third cluster encompasses Asian and Latin American (ALA) countries, which, historically, have enjoyed the least concessions from the EU among the LDCs. The three categories will now be briefly summarized in that order.

The ACP Group[1]

Broadly, relations between the EU and the South have derived from two formidable sources: historical and legal. Historically, European countries have long had close economic and political relations with the LDCs, dating to the colonial era. European adventurism, imperialism, and colonialism that began in the fifteenth century brought Europe into contact with the peoples of Asia, Latin America, the Middle East, the Caribbean and Pacific islands, and Africa. The relationship continued, although it underwent some transformation, following the decolonization exercise commencing in the late 1940s with British India. The decolonization exercise coincided with the commencement of European integration and with the creation of the European Coal and Steel Community in 1952. It was not until the Treaty of Rome, which established the European Atomic Energy Community and the European Economic Community (EEC), entered into force in 1958, that the foundations of a "new" postcolonial relationship between the EU and the LDCs were laid down.

During the negotiation of the Treaty of Rome, the French government insisted that the treaty define a relationship with the (ex)colonies of member states; and the other five founding member states, especially Belgium and Italy, agreed. The French government's insistence was driven by a perception that the creation of a Common Market posed a threat to arrangements with its former colonies. A French proposal to automatically extend the EEC Treaty to the colonies and territories of member states was blocked by Germany. Instead, a compromise was made to incorporate the overseas possessions through an "association" arrangement. Accordingly, Part Four of the EEC Treaty contained provisions that automatically bound to the EC the former colonies of its member states via an Association of the Overseas Countries and Territories. Specifically, Article 131 of the Treaty stipulated that the purpose of the association was:

> To promote the economic and social development of the countries and territories and to establish close economic relations between them and the Community as a whole . . . (and) to further the interests of prosperity of the inhabitants of these countries and territories in order to lead them to the economic, social, and cultural development to which they aspire.[2]

The remainder of the provisions stipulated the nature and instruments (Articles 132–135) as well as the duration (Article 136) of the relationship. In accordance with Article 132.3 of the Treaty, the EC inaugurated the first European Development Fund (EDF), to which member states contributed ECU 580 million, largely from Germany and France. This fund aimed purposely at financing basic infrastructure developments and at facilitating "the progressive development of these countries and territories."[3]

By the early 1960s, virtually all of the associated countries and territories had gained political independence, thus necessitating a negotiated relationship with the EU, in accordance with international law. A new agreement, negotiated by the European Commission, was signed in 1963 but did not enter into force until 1964. It was signed in Yaoundé (the capital of Cameroon) between the EC and eighteen Francophone African countries, otherwise known as the Association of African States and Madagascar (AASM). The 1963 Yaoundé convention was thus the first negotiated comprehensive agreement between the EU and any group of developing sovereign countries. Essentially, the Yaoundé convention retained the generous provisions of the 1958 association agreement, such as duty- and quota-free entry of exports from the eighteen AASM countries into the EC market, reciprocal trade preferences, and an elaborated second EDF (ECU 800 million), most of which came from the coffers of member states. Later, in 1969, the Yaoundé convention was renegotiated, signed, and entered into force for a period of five years. Other than the replenishment of the third EDF (ECU 1 billion), the structure, instruments, and duration of the Yaoundé II convention were changed very little from those defined by its precursor.

The first enlargement of the Union in 1973, especially the accession of the UK, meant the EU had to consider an arrangement for the British Commonwealth's LDCs similar to that for the eighteen AASM group. A byproduct of the British accession was the formulation of a coherent and comprehensive external economic relationship with British Commonwealth African, Caribbean, Pacific, and Asian nations, which, until then, had existed haphazardly and piecemeal. Meanwhile, the expiration of Yaoundé II was fast approaching. Following a meeting convened by the Commission in mid-1973 and attended by several African, Caribbean, and Pacific states, negotiations in Brussels were undertaken that year between the EC and the ACP group, under the leadership of Nigeria. Early agreements at a mid-1974 Kingston, Jamaica, conference eventually led to a comprehensive agreement, which was signed in Lomé, the capital of Togo, in February 1975. The pact, otherwise known as the Lomé convention, was signed by the nine EC countries and forty-six ACP countries; it became operative in 1976.

Intended to be a sui generis model for North-South dialogue, the 1975 Lomé convention was renegotiated and renewed in 1980 (Lomé II), in 1985 (Lomé III), and in 1990 (Lomé IV), with each renewal entailing only marginal modifications and improvements over the precursor convention. A summary of the key ingredients of the conventions follows.

First, most ACP products were accorded nonreciprocal, duty-free, and quota-free access to the EU market, purposely to encourage ACP exports as a stimulus for development.[4] According to Table 7.1, and using the exports of the African continent as a surrogate measure, the volume of exports to the EU jumped by almost 250 percent between 1976 and 1980, and by almost 300 percent between 1976 and 1995 (in nominal terms).

Second, the conventions provided for industrial and technical cooperation between the EU and the ACP countries, the purpose of which was to foster the industrial and technological development of the ACP states. To this end, an Industrial Cooperation Board and a Center for Industrial Development were created in 1975.

Third, all four conventions thus far have contemporaneously been accompanied by economic assistance under the EDF scheme, which was to enable direct financial and technical support for ACP societies. Accordingly, Lomé I was granted ECU 3.5 billion under the fourth EDF program, Lomé II was granted ECU 5.5 billion under the fifth EDF program, and Lomé III was allocated ECU 8.5 billion under the sixth EDF program. In view of Lomé IV's ten-year duration, the seventh and eighth EDFs were replenished respectively by ECU 12 billion and ECU 13 billion, corresponding with the first and second five-year periods of the convention.[5]

Fourth, the conventions provided for two unique insurance compensatory schemes designed to ameliorate the adverse effects of natural calamities and vagaries of the market on ACP countries that finance domestic expenditures with revenues from the export of primary products. Thus, a Stabilization of Exports (STABEX) scheme was launched under Lomé I to benefit ACP countries that rely on agricultural exports, and under Lomé II, a System for Mineral Products (SYSMIN) was inaugurated for ACP exporters of mineral products. Finally, the conventions created a host of institutions (e.g., a Council of Ministers, the Committee of Ambassadors, and a Consultative Assembly) purposely to facilitate regular political dialogue between the two entities.

The MENA Group[6]

Included in this rubric of the Middle Eastern and North African (MENA) group of countries are the Maghreb countries (Algeria, Tunisia, and Morocco); the Mashreq countries (Egypt, Jordan, Lebanon, and Syria); the Gulf states (Bahrain, Kuwait, Oman, Qatar, Saudi Arabia, and the United

Table 7.1   Imports to the European Union (US$ million)

	1976	1980	1985	1990	1995
Africa[a]	12,434	43,403	39,247	48,342	49,378
Middle East[a]	2,703	90,214	38,786	47,021	39,986
Asia[a]	10,212	25,781	25,723	81,723	143,465
Latin America[a]	9,520	26,117	24,861	36,566	43,988
LDCs	90,040	201,791	144,236	281,016	387,932
World	350,748	772,518	660,800	1,416,200	1,901,500

Source: Direction of Trade Statistics, Washington: IMF, various years.
a. Excludes oil exporting countries for 1976.

Arab Emirates); Yemen; and Israel. If, as argued above, historical and
legal factors were responsible for making the ACP group the centerpiece
of the EU's external economic relations since its inception, history and geography explain why the MENA group occupies the second layer of the
EU's pyramid of privileges. As is typical of virtually all external relations
of the Union, the Mediterranean policy steadily and incrementally evolved.
It was initially begun in the early 1960s to accommodate the needs of primarily "European" countries in the Mediterranean basin, notably Greece,
Turkey, Cyprus, Malta, and Spain, out of the growing realization that they
constituted an "extension of Europe." Since they were geographically located in the "backyard" of the EC, the economic development of these
countries could thus not be neglected or taken for granted. Therefore, in
response to their separate requests for an agreement in 1959, the EC concluded association agreements with Greece in November 1962 and with
Turkey in September 1963. Both agreements provided for the strengthening of economic and commercial relations with the EC via the creation of
customs unions, the harmonization of economic policies, and the creation
of implementing institutions (e.g., a Council of Association). Moreover,
the agreements acknowledged the eventual accession of Greece and
Turkey to the EC as long-term aspirations. Spain and Malta separately
reached agreements with the EC in 1970, and Cyprus concluded its association agreement with the EC in 1972.

By the early 1970s, in light of the history between member states of
the EU and the MENA group and in view of the proximity of the group to
Europe, the Mediterranean policy was broadened to encompass the MENA
group. A classic illustration of this was French Algeria, which, until its independence in 1962, was considered an extension of France and was thus
included in the EEC Treaty. As early as 1963, independent Algeria, Morocco, and Tunisia approached the EU to request an association agreement.
The talks between the EC and the Maghreb states encountered a host of
problems, not the least of which were the special relationship between
France and Algeria and the competitive problems that many Maghreb agricultural exports—for example, olives and olive oil—would pose for Italian
producers. The EU finally signed a commercial agreement with Morocco
and Tunisia in March 1969, which became operative in September of that
year. The five-year agreement granted preferential treatment to most exports from Morocco and Tunisia, including industrial products.

Meanwhile, Algeria's negotiation with the EU had not resulted in any
tangible agreement. When it was time to renegotiate the association agreement with Morocco and Tunisia in 1974, the Commission decided to include Algeria in a comprehensive strategy for the Maghreb states, which
would constitute a part of an evolving Mediterranean policy. Subsequently,
the EU concluded cooperation agreements with Tunisia (25 April 1976),
Algeria (26 April 1976), and Morocco (27 April 1976). These agreements,

which included some trade concessions, have formed the bases of subsequent pacts and continued relations between the EU and the Maghreb states to date.

With regard to the other countries in the MENA group, Israel and Lebanon expressed the earliest interests in reaching agreements with the EU, which were concluded in 1964 and 1965, respectively.[7] Both agreements were nonpreferential trade pacts, but the Commission later received a Council mandate in 1969 to negotiate a preferential trade agreement with Israel, even though Israel preferred an association agreement. A preferential trade agreement with the EU was finally signed and became operative in 1970 and was renewed in 1975 under the comprehensive Mediterranean strategy. Subsequently, like the agreements with the Maghreb states, the EU-Israeli agreement has been revisited a few times to take stock of the Union's enlargement exercises and other developments in the international political economy. In 1977, the EU concluded cooperation agreements with the Mashreq countries under the aegis of its Mediterranean strategy. In all of the aforementioned bilateral agreements that the EU has concluded with the MENA group, financial provisions have also been made, usually in the form of grants and EIB loans.

Unlike other linkages with the South, however, the initiative to establish relations with the Gulf states came from the EU, specifically in a European Parliament resolution in September 1981. Subsequently, the EU signed a cooperation agreement with Yemen in 1984, which entered into force on 1 February 1985. The remaining six Gulf states, which had formed a Gulf Cooperation Council (GCC) in 1981, signed a cooperation agreement with the EC in June 1988. Understandably, given Europe's appetite for petroleum, the agreement with the relatively affluent, oil-rich GCC countries, called for cooperation in the spheres of energy and investment promotion, although both groups remained strong partners. The EU has indeed assimilated quite a lot of exports from the Middle East. According to Table 7.1, the Middle East's share of EU imports from the South jumped from 3 percent in 1976 to 45 percent in 1980. In the 1990s it hovered around 13 percent. Similarly, the volume of Middle Eastern imports from the EU (Table 7.2) increased, in nominal terms, from around $6 million in 1976 to $60 million in 1995.

ALA Group[8]

This group is known, in EU jargon, as the "nonassociated" countries, basically because of an agreement reached at the time of the first enlargement that these countries would not qualify for associated status with the Union. Until recently, this group has occupied the unenviable bottom layer of the EU's pyramid of privileges, meaning that agreements with the ALA countries have tended to be nonpreferential. That is, the bulk of the benefits

Table 7.2   Exports from the European Union (US$ million)

	1976	1980	1985	1990	1995
Africa[a]	13,117	41,996	28,147	43,383	50,331
Middle East[a]	5,584	46,512	37,155	47,215	59,659
Asia[a]	7,842	20,982	27,535	66,110	135,999
Latin America[a]	8,409	21,489	13,926	27,097	51,456
LDCs	74,859	157,124	123,893	215,064	422,719
World	331,376	691,208	647,500	1,370,900	1,911,400

Source: Direction of Trade Statistics, Washington: IMF, various years.
a. Excludes Oil Exporting countries for 1976.

these countries receive from their relationships with the EU is derived from the Union's Generalized System of Preferences (GSP), humanitarian aid, and food aid, all of which are also available to other LDCs. Recently, however, the EU has become the ALA group's largest provider of official development assistance (ODA) and one of its largest trading partners. As with all EU relations with the South, agreements with this group have steadily grown over the years. Beginning in the 1960s, the EC basically extended the GSP and food aid to the ALA group. Then in the 1970s, following the first enlargement of the Union, a limited number of cooperation agreements were concluded to make financial aid and technical assistance available to the group. During the 1980s, cooperation agreements were concluded with ALA countries in areas where they did not already exist, or were reinforced where they did. The 1990s have been characterized by the exploration of opportunities for greater interaction with regard to intensifying trade, promoting investment, and promoting fundamental European values, such as multiparty democracy or private sector development.

Interactions between the ALA countries and the Union began in earnest with the formation of the EEC in 1958, when India and Pakistan promptly established diplomatic relations with it. Following a tour of Latin America by a delegation from the European Parliament in 1964, the Commission and a host of Latin American countries instituted a joint committee for dialogue in Brussels. Nevertheless, it was not until 1972 that the EU concluded its first bilateral, nonpreferential trade pact with an ALA country—Argentina—which was quickly followed by the first bilateral ALA commercial cooperation agreement—with India—in 1973. Later, the EU concluded a handful of similar bilateral agreements—with Brazil and Uruguay in 1974, Sri Lanka in 1975, Bangladesh and Pakistan in 1976, China in 1978, and others. Additionally, in appreciation for and encouragement of regional integration schemes around the world, the EU signed pacts with the ASEAN group[9] in 1980 and with the Andean pact[10] in 1983.

It is important to bear in mind that virtually all of these EU-ALA bilateral and multilateral agreements have been renegotiated and renewed.

Moreover, they have been nonpreferential, equipped with some financial and technical assistance, and fitted with limited mechanisms for political dialogue. Finally, some ALA countries have also been able to benefit from the Union's STABEX program, which otherwise is the preserve of the ACP group.[11]

Despite the limited trade concessions contained in the EU-ALA agreements, according to Table 7.1, Asia's exports to the EU have increased markedly, from about $10 million (1976) to more than $140 million (1995). Asia's share of total EU imports from the LDCs increased from 11 percent (1976) to 37 percent (1995), and its share of EU exports to the South increased from 11 percent (1976) to 31 percent (1995) in nominal terms. Latin America's share of EU imports from the South, in contrast, remained unchanged at 11 percent, and its share of EU exports to the LDCs during the 1976–1995 period ranged from 10 percent to 13 percent.

In sum, it is evident that the Union has deliberately concluded differential agreements with the three clusters of LDCs since the onset of the EEC in 1958. The ACP group has a nonreciprocal, duty- and quota-free access to the EU market. The MENA group, instead, has limited duty- and quota-free access to the EU, and the ALA group has reciprocal trading arrangements with the Union. All three clusters of countries benefit in varying degrees from the EU's financial and technical assistance programs, of which the most generous historically has been the ACP group's EDF program. In the same vein, although all three groups benefit from various oversight institutions set up to implement the agreements, none is as elaborate as Lomé's. Further, the Lomé convention is the only one of the EU-South agreements that is contractual and thus requires the consent of the EU and the ACP group before changes can be adopted.

Rationale for the EU's Presence in the South

This section identifies the common strands in the EU's development strategies in the South and reveals *whys* and *hows* of the EU's visibility in the South.

Trade Cooperation

Trade is the central component of the EU's relationship with the South. Based on their own individual and collective experience, the EU and other Northern countries believe that trade is a reliable vehicle for stimulating economic growth and development. Export revenues, the argument goes, are the main source of finance for importing heavy machinery, equipment for infrastructure, and other vital development inputs. The additional rationale is that opportunity for increased exports by the LDCs will facilitate the diversification and development of the export sector and the domestic economy. Thus, since the inception of the EU, trade has been touted as a key ingredient in the recipe for the economic emancipation of the LDCs. Not surprisingly, therefore, virtually all EU-South relationships have included some provisions for trade, typically in the manner of encouraging unfettered exports by the LDCs to the EU. According to Table 7.1, EU imports from the LDCs increased from around $90 billion in 1976 to $388 billion in 1995 (in nominal terms), representing more than 300 percent growth during the period. Put into perspective, overall exports of the LDCs to the Union in 1995 accounted for roughly 24 percent of their total exports, and 20 percent of the EU's total imports. The EU market has proven to be a resilient, reliable, and sizable market for the South. Still, the benefits of the trade instrument of EU cooperation with the South have accrued differentially. As noted in the preceding section, the different groups—and the countries that constitute them—have availed themselves of the trade concessions/opportunities to differing degrees.

Economic Assistance

If trade occupies the first layer of the EU's instruments of relations with the South, economic assistance programs occupy the second. In the early 1960s the EC began encouraging member states to increase their contributions to the Community's economic assistance programs. The rationale for this has been to use the funds to remedy short-term imbalances and infrastructural problems in the LDCs. To that end, the EU has been a leading provider of economic assistance to the LDCs since it was founded, not least because virtually all of its relationships with the South, with the notable exception of the GCC, have been accompanied by some financial assistance. Otherwise referred to as development cooperation, the allocated funds are typically utilized to promote, for example, regional development, rural development, basic amenities, and infrastructural development. These amenities, it is widely believed, are necessary preconditions and complements of the development-via-trade initiative.

Whereas total EU multilateral and bilateral economic assistance to the LDCs hovers around 0.43 percent of total EU gross national output (GNP), still short of the 0.7 percent of GNP prescribed by the United Nations, the performance of the EU and its member states compares well with that of other countries. Furthermore, ODA constitutes a small fraction of the total economic assistance program, and standard market loans constitute another small fraction. Export credit facilities comprise the bulk of the program. It must further be borne in mind that most of the economic cooperation of the EU is disbursed bilaterally by member states, albeit the EU Commission encourages the coordination of economic assistance programs among member states.

Technical and Industrial Cooperation

Another common ingredient in the EU's development strategy for the South is the promotion of technological and industrial cooperation. This development instrument has been inspired by the belief that sharing Northern know-how with the South will augment the benefits of the development initiative through increased production efficiency. It is widely believed that EU technology can bring a much needed factor of production to the LDCs, presumably at very minimal cost. This goal would be achieved through joint venture initiatives and other creative mechanisms. Additional mechanisms for industrial and technical cooperation include, but are not limited to, nurturing private sector development and promoting investment flow to the South. Similarly, EU technical know-how could be brought to bear to help the LDCs market their products in competitive Northern markets through market appraisal studies, participation in international trade fairs, and so forth.

Commodity Insurance Schemes

The two schemes covered by the EU in its agreements with the LDCs are the STABEX and the SYSMIN. Both were inaugurated in the 1970s, specifically for the ACP group. However, as noted above, poorer economies outside of the Lomé convention have also been accorded the privilege. The rationale for this is to help ease the burden of shortages in export revenues that has resulted from unfavorable and inevitable developments in the global arena, and to help maintain the export capacity of the LDCs in question.

Generalized System of Preferences

Another aspect of development strategies, and a feature of all EU agreements with the South, is the Generalized System of Preferences (GSP). Launched within the GATT in 1971 and renewed in 1995, the GSP was designed to foster the economic development and industrialization of the South. It was also designed to provide yet additional concessions to the LDCs in order to encourage exports of certain products to the EU. One of the purposes of reducing import levies on semimanufactured products entering the EU was to use trade to stimulate industrialization and industrial development in the South. The EU, however, is solely responsible for the scope of the scheme. Although the privileges enjoyed by some countries and products are being eroded, the scheme has featured prominently in the EU's presence in the South. Beginning in 1986, however, the Commission introduced a policy of differentiation in its implementation of the GSP in order to ensure that the program is not dominated by a small number of LDCs.[12]

Debt Relief

Another instrument of development that has become a standard provision in agreements between the EU and the South is debt forgiveness. As far back as 1981–1982, many LDCs—especially in the ACP group, Latin America, and some parts of Asia—have fallen victim to chronic and soaring debt. The governments of the affected countries have moaned about the unnecessary distraction the debt crises have posed with respect to their quest for economic, social, and political emancipation. Students of development have likewise noted that mounting indebtedness is severely inhibiting development. For example, it is widely documented that several African countries expend between 20 percent and 34 percent of their export revenues to finance their debt. While this issue has been raised repeatedly in the Group of Seven (G-7) summits, very little has been done about it on this level. The EU and some member states, on the other hand, have undertaken some positive measures in this regard. Specifically, the EU forgave the multilateral debt owed it by the poorest members of the ACP group. France also wrote off the debt owed it by Francophone African countries, and the UK partially forgave debts owed it by some LDCs.[13]

Institutions for Dialogue

Another mainstay of the EU's presence in the LDCs has been the establishment of opportunities for institutional dialogue. This has assumed a variety of configurations. They include, but are not limited to, forums for cabinet-level deliberations, parliamentary-level conferences, and ambassadorial-level exchanges. Not only does the European Commission maintain delegation offices in most of the LDCs with which the EU has concluded cooperation and development agreements, but the Southern countries, in turn, maintain diplomatic representations in Brussels. These institutions exist to imbue Western values of participatory democracy and to administer the imperatives of the agreements.

Overall, it is apparent from the discussion thus far that the EU has emphasized certain key policy instruments in defining its relations with the South. Since 1958 the development of the South and the bridging of the North-South gap have constituted the foundation of the Union's relationships with the LDCs. The differential nature of existing EU-South agreements suggests a strategy of "thinking globally" while acting "regionally." In other words, although it seems the EU has regarded development as a universal Southern challenge since its inception, existing agreements with the LDCs appear to be regionally fitted.

Factors Influencing EU-LDC Relations

It is evident from the foregoing that the relationship between the EU and the LDCs has grown by leaps and bounds since its genesis in the 1950s.

Not only has the EU expanded its policies toward the South in terms of the sheer number of countries with which it has agreements, but it has also assumed larger roles with regard to its international obligations. Changing EU relations with the LDCs, as with other parts of the world, can be attributed to two interrelated factors, namely internal and external.

Endogenous Forces

Two broadly defined, yet interrelated, internal forces have inspired the changing nature of the EU's policies toward the South: institutional and bureaucratic expansion and the widening and deepening of European integration.

Institutional/bureaucratic expansion. Since the genesis of the EU in the 1950s, and since the establishment of an EU policy on the South in the 1958 EEC Treaty, the Union's Eurocracy has noticeably expanded. On the one hand, the size of the Commission has doubled between 1972 (12,000) and 1996 (24,000). On the other hand, not only has the number of Directorates General (DGs) increased over the years, but they have also elaborated their competencies. In the process, directorates and subdivisions within the DGs have proliferated. What is more, as a result in part of the EU's own internal dynamics (such as the Commission reorganization of 1993), many DGs are now headed by multiple commissioners. Specifically, DG I, which traditionally has enjoyed sole responsibility for coordinating the EU's external relations, has lately been assigned to more than one commissioner. During the second Jacques Delors Commission (1989–1993), for example, the eleven directorates of DG I were divided between two commissioners, Frans Andriessen and Abel Matutes. In the present Jacques Santer Commission, three commissioners have been assigned to oversee the affairs of DG I—Hans van den Broek, Manuel Marin, and Sir Leon Brittan.

Similarly, in the third Delors Commission (1993–1995), only one commissioner, Manuel Marin, had the portfolio for relations with the LDCs, but in the present Santer Commission, that responsibility has been divided between two commissioners, Manuel Marin (Latin America, Middle East, and Asia) and João de Deus Pinheiro (other non-European developing countries). This development was the product of an acrimonious and distrustful relationship between the ACP group and Commissioner Marin during the third Delors Commission, as well as of bureaucratic infighting and turf protection within the Commission. Furthermore, bureaucracies, by nature, are known not only for their conservative values but also for their tendency to justify their existence by expanding their competencies. A growing Commission has thus to rationalize its existence, and one way to do that is to re-engineer and expand its competencies. In this context then, the proliferation of EU relationships with the South is an inevitable consequence of divided portfolios and the growing number of directorates in charge of external relations in general and relations with the LDCs in particular.

The widening and deepening of European integration. The dynamic nature of the EU itself also bears on its growing and changing relationship with the South. To the degree that the EU has not stood still but has grown since its advent in the 1950s, it is only natural to expect its policies also to have evolved. The widening and deepening of European integration inevitably means growing EU policy areas, including its policy toward the LDCs. Indeed, each enlargement of the EU has seen a redefinition and elaboration of the EU's relationship with the South. Between 1958 and 1975, when France dominated the EU, the external economic policy of the EU toward the South was primarily directed toward former French colonies. At the time of the first enlargement in 1973, when the UK acceded to the EU, a more comprehensive policy was developed, accommodating the interests and concerns of British Commonwealth LDCs, first in the Lomé convention in 1975 and later in the form of bilateral agreements with India, Pakistan, and others. In the same vein, following the full membership of Spain and Portugal in 1986, the EU's external policy toward Latin American countries gained more recognition and currency within the Commission. The enlargement of 1995, which included countries that historically had no colonial ties with the South, coupled with the debate about the eventual accession of Central and East European (CEEC) countries, necessitated a redefinition of the EU's relationship with the South in general. The 1989–1990 revolution in Eastern Europe, along with the evolution of reforms that were already underway in the region, has suddenly catapulted the CEEC to the apex of the EU's external economic relations, displacing traditional friends, particularly the ACP group.[14]

Finally, the deepening of European integration is a major internal factor affecting the EU's changing relationship with the South. As the EU assumes greater commitment toward completing the internal market and achieving the goals set out in the TEU, it is inevitable that some traditional relationships, such as its policy toward the South, will be affected and revisited. In the bid to adopt a single currency by the beginning of the next millennium, traditional relationships have fallen by the wayside or have become expendable. For example, the CFA Franc, which the French government established and defended as far back as the 1960s, was allowed by the French to be devalued in 1994. This sent two messages to the Southern countries in general and to the Francophone countries in particular. First, the devaluation meant that the priorities of France (and by extension of other member states) might always be subject to the demands of a deepening European integration. Second, the 1994 event also meant that if France, a traditional ally, could be forced to abandon an age-old commitment such as defending the CFA Franc, instruments of EU-LDC accords—

even entire agreements such as the Lomé convention—could be expendable. In short, relationships between the EU and its Southern partners have undergone, and will continue to undergo, changes as long as there are major developments taking place within the Union.

Exogenous Forces

Several external forces have also motivated and molded the EU's relationship with the LDCs, and continue to do so. These forces have at one time or another inspired a reinvigoration and reformulation of EU-LDC relations. Naturally, some of these forces also border on the internal dimension.

Postwar division of Europe and the world. The partition of Europe after the Second World War, and the Cold War that swiftly ensued, played a large role in the EU's increasingly close relationship with the LDCs in general and with African countries in particular. Although Europe remained at the heart of the Cold War between the U.S.-led Western alliance and the Soviet-led Eastern camp, the battleground was in the South. In the final analysis, what was at stake in the Cold War for both camps was access to and control of vital resources. In that context, therefore, the loyalty of African countries (and the South) was of vital concern to the EU countries. When France, in particular, insisted on including its overseas territories in the Common Market in 1958, its prodigious investment in those territories, especially those in Africa, was at stake. The same argument could be advanced for other members of the EU during much of the Cold War period, especially in light of the Soviet Union's unpretentious overtures to the young and impressionable nations of Africa. That is, in order to contain Soviet expansionist tendencies—which, where successful (as in Ethiopia and Angola), promptly placed in extreme jeopardy existing investments and potential opportunities for Western investors—it became imperative that the EU maintain a visible and meaningful presence in Africa.

To do so, the Union steadily cultivated an unrivaled, comprehensive relationship with the former colonies of its member states, exemplified by the Yaoundé and Lomé conventions. Nearly a century earlier, at the 1884–1885 Berlin Congress, the motivation for the partition of Africa among European powers was to gain access to, and control of, the resources of the African continent for Europe's industrial development. Between Berlin in 1884–1885 and Rome in 1958, the motivation for maintaining visible contacts with Africa changed very little for the Europeans. Whereas, initially in the post–Cold War context the expressed interest in Africa seemed to have been a French concern, it soon emerged in the early 1960s, and again a decade later, that the continent was important for other member states of the Union as well. In acknowledgment of growing global interdependence, and in recognition of the growing importance of Africa's raw materials, a unified policy toward the continent was thus developed.

Southern challenges the to North. In 1964 when the General Assembly of the United Nations created the United Nations Conference on Trade and Development (UNCTAD), the LDCs mobilized for the first time to challenge the Northern countries' control of international resources. At the conference, LDCs demanded export assistance in meeting their economic challenges. Later in 1968, at the New Delhi UNCTAD meeting, the LDCs demanded both a generalized system of preferences for semimanufactured products from the South and the elimination of reverse preferences in trade between Northern and Southern countries. Following the 1972 third UNC-TAD conference in Santiago (and subsequent meetings), earlier demands were reiterated. In addition, the Group of 77 in particular demanded a New International Economic Order, whereby the production, distribution, and consumption of global resources were to be radically altered.

Member states of the EU attempted a unified response to these demands. Not only was the European Commission given a large role in representing the Union in international forums, such as at the UNCTAD meetings, but the EU responded by elaborating its trade arrangements in the 1960s, inaugurating its GSP in 1971, and thus unveiling a steadily expansive but coherent development strategy for the South. In particular, at a European summit in October 1972, it was decided that a comprehensive and coherent policy for the South be formulated.

The energy crises of the 1970s presented the next challenge to Northern hegemony by the LDCs. In general terms, these crises elicited a range of responses from Northern countries, which exposed, at least in the case of the EU, the growing importance of maintaining meaningful relationships with the MENA group and the urgency of a cohesive EU global strategy toward the South. In any event, consequent to the first oil crisis of 1973–1974 and the disparate responses by member states, the European Commission developed a far-reaching global strategy, which included definition of the EU's policy toward the South. It was about this time, coupled with other developments within the EU such as the first enlargement, that many of the EU-South accords took form and took off. In addition, the energy crises of the 1970s forced the EU and its members to address some fundamental structural problems, particularly in relation to consumption of energy.

Alternative strategies for development. By the mid-1980s, many LDCs, especially African countries, were experiencing chronic economic problems. In response, the international financial institutions of Washington, D.C., and other international creditors demanded profound structural adjustment by the affected societies. These financial entities made adjustment a precondition for debt rescheduling and for other concessions as well. The ubiquitous Structural Adjustment Initiatives (SAIs) were subsequently blamed by the implementing LDCs for unleashing major havoc on their economies. The response by the EU was manifold and immediate. The EU intensified its promotion of regional cooperation schemes in many parts of the South, such as in Central America. It also supported the notion of giving SAI "a human face" in many implementing countries by providing measures (safety nets) to mitigate the impact of adjustment. In addition to the regional integration scheme and the "human face" adjustment alternatives, the EU began in the late 1980s to link democracy and human rights in the South to development in these societies.[15]

The fall of the Berlin Wall and the changing European landscape. When the Berlin Wall, which had divided Europe since the onset of the Cold War, came crashing down in 1989–1990, its dismantling jolted the relationship between the EU and the LDCs. The lifting of the iron curtain and the Eastern European revolution have affected the EU-South relationship in two major ways. On the one hand, the collapse of the totalitarian regimes of the Soviet bloc has meant an immediate redefinition of the EU's priorities. The CEEC countries, with which Western Europe shares a great deal of history and geography and from which it was radically and abruptly separated after the Second World War, must now be welcomed back into the "European" fold. This also means, for the EU, that the CEEC countries, which have seriously embarked on transforming their economies into market-oriented structures, must be given the utmost assistance. Almost instantaneously, therefore, the CEEC not only has emerged as a formidable competitor with the LDCs for finite EU resources, but has also been promptly catapulted to the top of the scale of preference in the EU's external economic relations.[16]

On the other hand, the readiness and enthusiasm of virtually all of the CEEC to embrace the basic tenets of liberal democracy, including accepting the outcomes of free and fair elections, has reinvigorated the EU's demand for a democratic South. In fact, the democratic wave that swept across CEEC countries in the wake of the 1989–1990 revolution has strengthened the EU's readiness to assert Western cultural and political priorities in general in its relationships with many LDCs. After all, from its perspective, the key Western value of liberalism has been vindicated. In this same vein, as preconditions for better concessions, the EU is reviving and promoting values such as the prevention of human rights abuses, the preservation of the environment, the proscription of child labor, and the promotion of participatory democracy. The experience of the CEEC countries, particularly those in the vanguard of democratization and economic liberalization schemes (e.g., Hungary, Slovenia, Estonia, Czech Republic, and Poland), lends credence to the argument that political reforms and economic reforms are not mutually exclusive. If anything, they complement each other, and both must be vigorously pursued. Thus, the EU is encouraging the LDCs to pursue those twin goals, and indeed the countries that have abided by this wish of the EU appear to have been accorded more favorable attention. A final factor, as was argued earlier, that has inspired the EU to pursue these goals is the TEU, which called on the EU to promote its values on a global scale via the CFSP framework.

Conclusion

Several conclusions can be drawn from this chapter's discussion about the EU's relations with the South. First, this analysis has demonstrated the incrementalist character of EU policy development toward the South. New initiatives occurred as a result of enlargement, as a consequence of the expansion of the European Commission, and in reaction to a changing international political economy. As new members acceded to the EU, they brought with them historical relationships with former colonies and other trading partners. These relationships were then embraced under Union provisions, having the effect of expanding its development role. In addition, as the Commission grew in size, so did its competencies, including its relations with the South. Developments external to the Union have also induced augmentation of the EU-South relationships. Typical of the EU's neofunctional tradition of expansive and spillover tendencies in policy-making, the creation of instruments that have characterized EU-LDC relations since the 1950s has steadily increased. It began primarily with trade and economic assistance in the 1950s and 1960s. A new generation of development tools was introduced in the 1970s when the GSP, technical cooperation, and commodity insurance schemes were added. Then, by the 1980s and 1990s, policies regarding economic and political reforms as well as human rights were introduced.

Second, it is evident that the role of the EU as a global actor has grown over the years. The impulse of national bureaucrats to vigorously defend their turfs initially meant a limited policy by the EU in the South (and the world). However, a constellation of factors—among them a tenacious and unrelenting European Commission and developments in the global economy—heightened the importance of devising mechanisms that would enable the EU to speak with one voice and act in unison. In addition, it increasingly became evident within the Union that some external economic relations, particularly with the South, required pan-European strategies. Put differently, if member states were to truly make a difference in alleviating the development burdens of the LDCs, it was imperative that a European strategy be devised that would harness all their resources. Thus, at the UNCTAD meetings of the 1960s, the European Commission received a negotiating mandate from the European Council to represent the six EC member states. In those international forums, the Commission interacted with national officials in presenting a unified Community position. Furthermore, each time the Union has negotiated trade arrangements with any country or group of countries from the South, the Commission has been given a negotiating mandate by the European Council, albeit with certain constraints.[17]

Other demonstrations of the EU as a global actor in the South commenced in its formative years. Interestingly enough, the countries that quickly recognized the EC as a global entity in 1958 and promptly requested diplomatic exchanges with it were from the South. Notably, Israel (1958), India (1962), and Pakistan (1962) sought and obtained early diplomatic exchanges with the EC. Today, more than 130 countries from all over the world have diplomatic accreditation with the EU in Brussels. By the same token, the EU maintains delegation offices in more than a hundred countries around the world.

Furthermore, the Commercial Policy provision of the EEC Treaty has enabled the EU to behave as a global actor. To the extent that the member states had to work toward a Common Commercial Policy (Articles 110-116, EEC Treaty), a role for the EC as a global actor became a foregone conclusion. It would be impossible, for instance, to achieve a Common Commercial Policy, especially where the treaty called for coordination of member states' commercial relations with third countries, if the European Commission could not negotiate with those countries on behalf of member states. Finally, with respect to providing succor for victims of natural calamities (e.g., earthquake and flood victims) and manmade catastrophes (e.g., refugees of war and civil war), the EU has been an unrivaled global leader. It has also been a leader in funding countless projects intended to alleviate poverty and promote development in the LDCs and ultimately to help bridge the yawning North-South gap.

While this chapter has not attempted to evaluate the efficacy of EU efforts, it has demonstrated that the EU-LDC relationship is a longstanding, institutionalized feature of EU foreign policy whose future appears to be assured. Its history demonstrates that any assessment of the EU in world affairs must take into account the crucial role played by the EU in expanding and formalizing its trade relationship and development assistance efforts toward the South. The EU-LDC relationship is a fundamental feature of the international political economy in general and of North-South relations in particular.

Notes

1. For elaborate discussions of this group, see, among others, Babarinde 1994; Stevens 1990; and Ravenhill 1985.

2. Treaty Establishing the European Economic Community 1957.

3. Ibid.

4. Exempted from this provision are those ACP products that are directly or otherwise covered by the EU's Common Agricultural Policy (CAP). Additionally, the conventions contain special provisions for some primary products, such as bananas and sugar.

5. The gradual increase in the EDF programs since 1975 reflects, among other factors, the enlargement of the ACP group from forty-six in 1975 to seventy-one at present.

6. For further discussions on the EU's interactions with countries of the Middle East and North Africa, see, among others, Lieber 1976 and Stevens 1990.

7. In 1958, Israel had even applied to establish diplomatic relations with the EC.

8. For more information on the group, see, for example, *Official Journal of the European Communities*, L144, 1980, 1–8; Council Regulation (EEC) No. 1440/80, 30 May 1990; Han 1992 and Kaufman Purcell and Simon 1995.

9. They include Indonesia, the Philippines, Thailand, Singapore, Malaysia, Brunei, Viet Nam, Laos, and Kampuchea.

10. The group includes Bolivia, Colombia, Ecuador, and Peru.

11. Notable among them are Bangladesh, Nepal, Laos, Maldives (since 1986), and Burma (since 1988).

12. *Trade Relations Between the European Union and Developing Countries* 1995.

13. *The Courier,* March–April 1992, xv.

14. See Babarinde 1995 for details.

15. See, for example, *The Courier,* July–August 1991.

16. This is reflected both in the flow of Direct Foreign Investment and in the channeling of Official Development Assistance, which have steadily increased for the ECE countries. See, for example, Miller and Sumlinski 1994, quoted in "Global Investment Flows Bypass Poorer Developing Nations," *Financial Times,* 8 July 1994, 6.

17. While negotiating mandates are being formulated, national bureaucrats have ample opportunities to ensure that their national interests are neither overlooked nor compromised.

8

The Transatlantic Relationship: A Case of Deepening and Broadening

Alberta Sbragia

As the European Union enhances its global role, no relationship is more significant to it than the transatlantic. The United States provides a constant referent, exerts an important external pressure, and is a key potential partner in world affairs. Given the complexity and centrality for the United States of U.S. relations with several of the EU's member states, and given the U.S. preoccupation with redefinitions of European security, the gradual emergence of the Union as an interlocutor for the United States is significant. Outside of the trade arena, the Union has faced fierce competition for U.S. attention. The fact that it is being granted—sometimes reluctantly—an increased share of that attention is pivotal in understanding the enhanced role of the EU in international affairs.

Transatlantic relations are typically thought of in terms of security, trade, and diplomacy. Over time, these traditional elements of the transatlantic mosaic have become surrounded by new elements. Two are of concern in this chapter. The first has to do with significant changes in the political economy of the transatlantic community. The second has to do with the politics of how the United States deals with Europe. While the political economy of transatlantic relations certainly includes the traditional component of trade, it also is underpinned by the extraordinary investment relationship between these two regions of the world. In fact, while trade relations show a high degree of consistency over time, the investment relationship has changed significantly. It has become far more symmetrical. The United States has become much more of a "normal" country, has become "Europeanized" if you will. Its economy has become, for the first time this century, the host of significant foreign direct investment from abroad, Europe in particular.

In the new European-U.S. political economy, U.S. business in Europe and European business in the United States emerge as more important interlocutors than previously in the transatlantic relationship. The business presence is such that European-U.S. relations are no longer confined to trade, armies, and diplomacy. In fact, it leads us away from thinking of a "bilateral" relationship in the traditional international relations sense and toward a type of relationship that is increasingly manifested "behind the border" as well as at the negotiating table. Transatlantic relations now are composed of both a "private sphere" and a "public sphere."

Transatlantic business belongs to the transatlantic community whether or not it participates in "relations" understood as interactions in the public sphere. For example, even if the Transatlantic Business Dialogue (TABD)—a private initiative aimed at achieving common goals including product standards—should fail to become institutionalized, transatlantic business will nonetheless remain an interlocutor, albeit a "private" one.[1] European and U.S. businesspeople have taken their place at the transatlantic table alongside diplomats, trade negotiators, and generals, not only as exporters/importers but as producers, employers, and taxpayers. Their importance, in fact, lies precisely in the fact that, in contrast to the "public" interlocutors, they are producers and employers. The "private" European-U.S. relationship is now so important that it needs to be analyzed along with the "public" transatlantic relationship.

The second new element in transatlantic relations has to do with the relative role of national capitals and the Union in the perception of U.S. policymakers. The upgrading of the European Union in U.S. eyes has changed the political dynamic of European-U.S. relations. Within the Union, the Commission has gained the lion's share of the U.S. acknowledgment. While national capitals are still very important, it is clear that under the Bush and Clinton administrations the Union has become more of a focal point for U.S. concern, pressure, and cooperation. London, Bonn, and Paris each have debilitating weaknesses from the U.S. point of view, making none as useful an interlocutor as the Commission is perceived to be.

The upgrading of the EU/Commission is tied to the perceived need on the U.S. side to fashion a stronger link with Europe at the global level. As global issues (such as transnational organized crime) become more visible with the end of the Cold War, the EU is seen as a more fitting, and indeed a more needed, counterpart over the long term.

Of these two new elements in the mosaic, that of business is the most clearly defined. For its part, the new role of the EU—and of the Commission in particular—is still in the process of being formed, and its future will depend, at least to some extent, on decisions made about integration in future negotiations among the Europeans themselves. Yet if the Commission manages to continue to be included as an actor in the EU's external relations outside of the trade arena, it is probable that the United States will try to nurture and strengthen the Commission's role.

The Traditional U.S. Presence

Although NATO is often viewed as the "centerpiece of the transatlantic relationship," it is useful to remember that at the time of its founding the

United States viewed economics rather than security as the primary mechanism by which to help war-torn Europe. Furthermore, the United States saw even its role as an economic helpmate as relatively short-lived. In Michael Howard's words, the United States was "anxious to withdraw from the European theater as quickly as it decently could."[2] As to security, becoming a key actor in European security was not an immediate postwar goal of the United States; only within the context of global communism[3] was this role defined as in the U.S. national interest. When North Korea invaded South Korea on 25 June 1950, the world in American eyes was redefined.

Forty years after the North Korean invasion, a great deal had changed. The end of the Cold War, the fall of the Berlin Wall, and subsequent events, culminating in the disappearance of the Soviet Union and the re-emergence of Russia, brought about a reassessment of the military relationship between Europe and the United States. Yet NATO not only survived and expanded its activities but attracted the French back into its fold.[4]

It may be worthwhile to speculate on what would have changed if the United States and/or the Europeans had decided that it was time for all U.S. troops to return home. What would the transatlantic community look like if security had been taken out of the equation? Given the visibility of the U.S. military and diplomatic role in NATO among policymakers and foreign policy specialists, it may be useful to imagine a Europe without NATO—if only to throw into relief dimensions of the transatlantic relationship that tend to be overshadowed by the salience of generals and discussions of the "architecture of security." This imaginative exercise illuminates what has changed in the forty years since the decision was made to reverse U.S. policy and send troops to Europe.

Removing U.S. troops would obviously have changed the political/ diplomatic dimension of the transatlantic relationship. Handling the uncertainty in Eastern Europe would have been much more difficult, for example; the instability of that region may well have spilled over into the trade dimension, especially in the short term. Yet given that traditionally NATO has been viewed as central to the transatlantic relationship, it is striking that at least one important economic relationship would have been left relatively unchanged if U.S. troops had been repatriated.[5] It is to that relationship that we now turn.

The Changing Political Economy
of Transatlantic Relations

In contrast to trade, which has chronically provoked visible clashes between the United States and Europe, the broadening of the transatlantic business community has been carried on comparatively quietly. U.S. firms in Europe and European firms in the United States have been in some sense "silent" members of the transatlantic community. Yet these multinational firms form an important pillar in European-U.S. relations. Flows of foreign direct investment "represent long-term commitments by companies to build viable businesses in one another's markets."[6] Such commitments are very different from those embodied in trade relations.

Although at one point (as we shall discuss below) U.S. investment in Europe was controversial, that controversy has been superceded by the debate over Japanese investment in Europe. On the U.S. side, increased European investment has also been overshadowed by Japanese foreign direct investment in the U.S. car industry. Japanese foreign direct investment in both Europe and the United States seems to have pushed transatlantic investment into the shadows of both scholarly inquiry and political debate.[7]

U.S. Foreign Direct Investment in Europe

Although U.S. businesses established European subsidiaries in the early part of the century, it was not until after the Treaty of Rome that U.S. investment in Europe surged.[8] U.S. business then began to invest and produce in Europe to such a degree that over a decade ago Michael Smith concluded that it was "difficult to draw the line between what was properly 'European' and what 'American' in the balance-sheet of economic policy."[9]

And at least some Europeans did feel dominated. The "infusion" or "invasion" of U.S. capital during the 1960s was so pronounced that Jean-Jacques Servan-Schreiber (who founded *L'Express*) wrote *Le Defi Americain* to wide acclaim and denunciation.[10] It is interesting to reread *Le Defi Americain* thirty years later—after the creation of the European internal market and the construction of a more symmetrical U.S.-European investment relationship:

> One by one, American firms are setting up headquarters to coordinate their activities throughout Western Europe. This is true federalism—the only kind that exists in Europe on an industrial level . . . Most striking of all is the strategic character of American industrial penetration. One by one, U.S. corporations capture those sectors of the economy most technologically advanced, most adaptable to change, and with the highest growth rates. This flexibility of the Americans . . . is their major weapon. While Common Market officials are still looking for a law which will permit the creation of European-wide businesses, American firms, with their own headquarters, already form the framework of a real "Europeanization" . . . Their investments do not so much involve a transfer of capital, as an actual seizure of power within the European economy.[11]

Although many Europeans agreed with Servan-Schreiber, from the U.S. perspective, U.S. investment in Europe was very much overshadowed by security concerns, the European role in the Cold War, and the negotiations in the Kennedy Round. Moreover, U.S. foreign direct investment (FDI) did not involve a great deal of interaction between European governments and the U.S. government (U.S. investment in France was an exception).[12]

In addition, although the creation of the EEC spurred U.S. investment, the Community as an institution did not profit in the transatlantic relationship from its role in creating such an attractive economic environment. Ambassador Schaetzel, writing of that period, argues that U.S. attitudes toward the Community "were conditioned" by the negotiating dynamics of the Kennedy Round. "The friction of these negotiations became the core of the new American view of the Community as a hard bargainer, an adversary."[13] In this view Europe was perceived only secondarily as the host of billions of dollars of U.S. capital, and an important source of profits for U.S. companies; primarily, it was seen as an adversary at the negotiating table.

Foreign direct investment in Europe continued throughout the 1970s and leveled off in the first half of the 1980s. If we consider the entire period between 1972 and 1985, and exclude the UK, we find that U.S. investment in the EC grew 200.6 percent.[14] It exploded after the acceptance by the EC of the 1992 program.[15] Whereas it totaled $72 billion in 1984, U.S. investment had risen to $173 billion by 1990.[16] In 1994, the National Association of Manufacturers in the United States pointed out that "Europe is the dominant market for U.S. investment abroad, and will remain so indefinitely."[17]

Interestingly, given the sensitivities of the French government toward the United States, France during the 1980s emerged as an increasingly important recipient of U.S. foreign direct investment in the manufacturing sector.[18] In 1993, for example, the planned capital expenditures of U.S. affiliates in France in manufacturing were equal to their counterparts' planned capital expenditures in Mexico.[19]

Much of the increased U.S. investment in the latter part of the 1980s was undertaken by U.S. multinationals already in Europe rather than by firms seeking initial entry. After all, as Edward Graham points out, "most US multinational firms of any consequence already had a European presence long before anyone thought of 1992 as being anything other than the eighth year after 1984."[20] Given that "over one thousand US firms . . . control affiliates in Europe," and that manufacturing has been the dominant activity of such affiliates, it is not surprising that most of those firms seeking entry were in nonmanufacturing sectors.[21]

U.S. business, however, did not only invest in Europe. Increasingly, in the 1990s, U.S. business "teamed up" with European firms. In fact, Jacquemin and Wright found that non-European partners are often preferred to European ones when companies forge cooperative agreements.[22] European firms are often no longer competing against U.S. firms—European-U.S. coalitions of firms are increasingly competing against other European-U.S. coalitions of firms. In fact, such coalitions sometimes now include a Japanese member.[23] This phenomenon is so important, according to Dick Nanto, that in order to increase their competitiveness, nations should try to ensure that "their industries are successfully integrated into such triadic consortia and networks."[24]

Nonetheless, it is still true that U.S. and European firms seem to find it easier to collaborate with one another than in triadic consortia.[25] Triadic consortia may be more difficult because U.S. firms in Europe seem to differ in important ways from Japanese firms in Europe. U.S. firms are responsible for much more employment, and they seem to be more "Europeanized" and therefore better integrated into the European context. A recent OECD study concluded that when it came to employment, "Japanese firms have created or saved 120,000 jobs in Europe, including 33,000 in the United Kingdom, 24,000 in Spain, 20,000 in France and 16,000 in Germany. This is to be compared with the 2,600,000 jobs created or saved by United States firms in Europe." Furthermore, the study showed that U.S. multinationals' European firms differed from those of Japanese multinationals in that they were more integrated into the European economy than were Japanese.[26]

Again, however, that component of the transatlantic relationship conducted in the public sphere seems to be disconnected from developments in the private sphere. FDI is, in DeAnne Julius' words, "the neglected twin of trade."[27] In the U.S. bureaucracy and in Congress, concern with trade heavily outweighs attention paid to outward FDI. Furthermore, since trade issues are negotiated with Brussels rather than with national capitals, the European Union is viewed as a trade negotiator rather than as an institution that has allowed U.S. companies not only to increase their profits (but also, in some cases, to avoid losses).

Smith and Woolcock in 1993 concluded that "US views of the EC are affected by years of accumulated experience in trade negotiations."[28] Given the seemingly ever increasing number of actors involved in formulating U.S. trade policy (State Department, Commerce, Agriculture, Treasury, U.S. Trade Representative, Congress, and to some extent state governments), the view of the Union formed during trade negotiations is widely dispersed through the U.S. policymaking community.[29] Thus, the private transatlantic relationship—institutionalized in FDI—has been overshadowed by the public relationship institutionalized in trade negotiations. The two in fact seem often to be disconnected in the minds of policymakers.[30]

European Investment in the United States: Achieving a Balance

The 1980s represented a turning point for the United States. Until that period, so-called U.S. exceptionalism was evident in its political economy as well as its political institutions and cultural values. Whereas other OECD countries had watched foreign direct investment become an important feature of their economies, the U.S. economy had remained comparatively insular. Two surges of FDI—which occurred in 1978–1981 and 1986–1989—changed that. During the 1980s, foreign investment in the United States increased so significantly that "the share of US manufacturing assets controlled by foreign investors roughly doubled, well exceeding ten percent."[31] Graham and Krugman conclude:

> It is arguable that the United States is simply becoming more normal—that is becoming, like other countries, a host as well as a home for multinational firms . . . the role of foreign firms in the United States, while still less than that in Europe, has converged to a considerable degree toward the European situation.[32]

European direct investment in the United States began to be noticeable in the period after 1972. The period 1972–1982 saw so much investment that "the ratio of the US direct investment stake in the EC-9 to the EC investment stake in the US fell from 2.80 to 0.97."[33] Investment by European firms in the United States continued at a rapid pace. In fact, more new investment came in between 1985 and 1988 than had existed in the middle of 1982.[34] By the end of 1989, roughly two-thirds of all foreign direct investment flowing into the United States was European. (Canada in 1989 accounted for less than 4 percent of inward flows of FDI.)[35] By the end of 1995, the United States' Mission to the European Union reported that "almost 60 percent of European firms' investment, or $237 billion, comes to the United States."[36]

Given the emphasis that political debate has placed on Japanese FDI, it is important to highlight the fact that in 1989 roughly one-quarter of FDI coming into the United States was Japanese; the rest was overwhelmingly European (British, Dutch, German, and Swiss). By 1992, Japan did overtake the UK as the most important investor that year, although Britain still held first place in the total stock of foreign direct investment.[37] Nonetheless, Japanese investment is far surpassed by European investment taken as a whole. By 1990, the European countries with significant investment in the United States, in addition to the United Kingdom, were the Netherlands, Germany, France, and Switzerland.[38]

The investment relationship between the United States and Europe has remained the most important in the world, with nearly half of total U.S. direct investment targeted in Western Europe and half of all foreign direct investment in the United States originating from Europe. For example, roughly the same number of German workers are employed by U.S.-owned firms as U.S. workers employed by German-owned firms in the United States. A Congressional Research Service report to the U.S. Congress in December 1994 summarized the bedrock importance of the transatlantic business community:

About 41 percent of all U.S. foreign direct investment abroad (FDI) ($200.5 billion of a total of $486.5) is in the EU, and half of all U.S. direct investment abroad is in Europe (including EU and non-EU countries). Planned capital expenditures in Europe by majority-owned foreign affiliates of U.S. companies in 1993 amounted to $33.4 billion, or more than planned capital expenditures in the rest of the world combined, notwithstanding the European recession. In 1992, 51 percent ($924 billion out of $1,810 billion) of total foreign direct investment in the United States (FDIUS) is European in origin. U.S. affiliates of European firms employed 2.9 million workers and paid $112 billion in employee compensation . . . In Europe, foreign affiliates of U.S companies had 2.97 million employees in 1991 and paid $114.1 billion in employee compensation.[39]

The friction that U.S. investment had created in Europe—and that was so eloquently expressed by Servan-Schreiber—has lessened as European firms have invested in the United States. Although foreign direct investment in the service sector (airlines and telecommunications for example) is still restricted in both the United States and Europe, Woolcock finds that "there are no significant barriers to investment in manufacturing in the EC."[40] Servan-Schreiber's analysis could now be applied to the United States nearly as much as it could be applied to Europe. As McCulloch points out, by 1990

> The economic landscape was . . . far different from that envisioned by Servan-Schreiber two decades earlier. For one thing, the United States had itself become a major host region for inward direct investment, with European companies accounting for about two-thirds of the total . . . Thus, rather than the one-way process foreseen by Servan-Schreiber and other early analysts, FDI had come to resemble trade in goods and services, with substantial flows in both directions.[41]

Implications of Symmetry

In general, the investment relationship is an absolutely critical one in tying the United States to Europe. In Featherstone and Ginsberg's words, "Investment interdependence between the US and EC more tightly enmeshes their economies than does bilateral trade. There is no larger investment partnership in the world between two separate economic entities."[42] The increased symmetry between the two bodes well, for example, for a future multilateral accord on investment addressing issues such as the extraterritorial application of laws to multinationals. The United States now has to consider the consequences of its policies on FDI for its own inward investment. In Graham and Krugman's words,

> The United States, for the first time in this century, possesses a large and visible foreign-controlled sector within its domestic economy; therefore the United States must consider the implications of its own policies with

respect to outward FDI upon inward FDI, and vice versa, whereas until quite recently US policy toward FDI was almost solely determined by the outward component.[43]

Even though foreign direct investment is at least as important as trade in European-U.S. relations, it has been the trade relationship that has dominated discussion. U.S. views of the EU are shaped by negotiations between governments—interactions in the public sphere—rather than by the economic "private" reality represented by investment statistics. Transatlantic foreign direct investment has come to be so taken for granted—or perhaps overshadowed by Japanese investment—that it is not perceived as the kind of glue that can absorb the shocks of trade disputes. Typically, the security relationship rather than the investment relationship is assigned that role by both practitioners and analysts.

Nonetheless, businesspeople have clearly taken their place alongside diplomats and generals in the construction and shaping of the transatlantic relationship. As a recent study for the Office for the Secretary of Defense in the United States pointed out: "Trade and investment in both directions have . . . created a growing cadre of industrialists, managers and professional people who move comfortably between the European and American worlds, amplifying the small group of statesmen, soldiers, and diplomats who, until mid-century, had been the principal interlocutors of the transatlantic relationship."[44] This new role, however, has not yet reshaped transatlantic perceptions, especially on the U.S. side of the Atlantic.

One reason why the investment relationship is often downplayed on the U.S. side is that trade and FDI respectively are characterized by different political dynamics. When the investment relationship was asymmetrical, U.S. FDI in Europe simply meant investments that theoretically could have been made in the United States but were not. FDI could be seen as symbolizing foregone U.S. jobs, whereas increased trade symbolized more jobs in local constituencies. John Peterson points out that although the Bush administration supported FDI in Europe, Congress was more worried about exports to Europe for "export-dependent manufacturers and farmers . . . localized in Congressional constituencies."[45] As the U.S.-EU relationship has become more symmetrical, politico-economic concerns are predictably more apparent on the European side. One of the implications for European governments of European FDI in the United States has to do with the "exit" option that the United States provides for European firms unhappy with European regulatory frameworks. The case of biotechnology may be illustrative. The figures given above on the takeovers of U.S. biotechnology firms by Europeans may well reflect the fact that many European businesspeople see current European regulations on biotechnology research as anticompetitive. Moving research to the United States allows European firms to benefit from the more permissive regulatory framework in place in the United States. Bayer, for example, has moved all its biotechnology research to Berkeley. As the CEO of U.S.-Bayer recently put it, "now that it is here [in the United States], it will stay here. It will not be moved back."[46]

Finally, multinationals with European operations can have an effect on U.S. and/or European trade policy, and European firms with U.S. affiliates may try to affect European and/or U.S. policy. Surprisingly little, however, seems to have been written on this relationship. It is possible that multinationals with affiliates in Europe act to "soften any official US response to European policies." For example, it is has been suggested that multinationals with German subsidiaries are able to act as advocates for German policies, whereas they are unwilling to act similarly vis-à-vis Japan, given the relatively low level of U.S. foreign direct investment in Japan.[47]

At the EU level, U.S. corporations have formed an important association to represent their interests in the EU's policymaking process. The EU Committee of the American Chamber of Commerce in Brussels, the members of which are U.S. multinational firms, is widely acknowledged to be one of the most powerful—and most discreet—of the lobbyists in Brussels.[48] It is not surprising that U.S. multinationals would seek access and influence. As Gary Hufbauer pointed out at the beginning of the decade, "for the great majority of large American firms, the business climate inside Europe, and their place in the European economic scheme, have become far more important than their exports to Europe."[49] European firms in the United States do not seem to have formed an institution of equivalent access and clout, but that could conceivably change.

The expansion of European direct investment into the United States has made the transatlantic business community a new pillar of the transatlantic community, and has added a very significant "private sphere twin" to the traditional "public" transatlantic relationship. The 1990s have also seen a change, however, in the "public sphere" in which the transatlantic relationship has typically been conducted. It is to that change that we now turn.

The Upgrading of the European Union's Role

Historically, the United States has had its most important bilateral political relationships with European national governments rather than with the Community. The United States found it difficult to deal with an evolving Europe in which both national and Community institutions exercised power. Most importantly, the United States treated security as the primary issue in European-U.S. relations, an arena in which national capitals rather than Brussels were the key decisionmakers. In brief, London, Paris, and Bonn were always more politically important to Washington than was Brussels.[50]

The European Union has gradually become a more important institutional actor in the international arena generally, and this increase of influence has been reflected—and reinforced—by the way in which European-U.S. relations have evolved. Whereas it was possible in the 1970s and 1980s to compartmentalize the role of the EU in transatlantic relations as that of a trade negotiator, it is no longer possible to do that in the 1990s.

A variety of reasons account for why the EU has increased its status. At the global level, the Union has raised its profile, especially in the environmental arena. There, the member states have allowed the Commission to negotiate for the Union and have fought for the right of the Union to sign international global treaties and thereby to become a contracting party. The Vienna convention and the Montreal protocol were key events in the process of upgrading the Union's international role—especially as the member states supported the Commission in the face of strong U.S. resistance to the Union's new role. Thus, the Commission is no longer an international actor simply in the trade arena.[51]

Turning more specifically to the transatlantic relationship, the 1992 single-market program and the collapse of the Berlin Wall made the Bush administration take a closer look at the EC as an ally and key facilitator of the changes that were occurring in Europe. Finally, the acceptance by the United States of a "European Defense Identity" has raised the profile of the EU/WEU in the security field. The Bush administration's upgrading of the Community's status came after a long period of neglect by U.S. administrations. As Pascaline Winand has shown, both Eisenhower and Kennedy were firm supporters of European integration. The period after Kennedy's death until the advent of the Bush administration was, however, one of benign neglect at best and near disdain at worst.[52]

The relative neglect of the Community outside of trade negotiating arenas began to change as a result of the 1992 program and was accelerated by the geopolitical changes that transformed Europe after the fall of the Berlin Wall.[53] The Transatlantic Declaration of November 1990 was the first major outcome of the Bush administration's reassessment of the Community's possible role in the management of change on the European continent. It "committed both sides to more intensive and institutionalized political consultations outside the North Atlantic Treaty Organization (NATO), which traditionally had acted as the primary channel for exchanges of views between the US and EC."[54] It marked the first time that an institutionalized channel parallel to that of NATO had been developed. In retrospect, although proponents of closer collaboration criticized it as not going far enough, the declaration was an important building block in the construction of an EU-U.S. relationship outside multilateral institutions.

The Transatlantic Declaration had been preceded, in 1989, by the Bush administration's acceptance of the EC (i.e., the Commission) as the lead actor in channeling aid to Eastern Europe. The administration also accredited the permanent representative of the Community to the White House; by contrast, he or she had previously been accredited to the State Department, along with the heads of other international organizations.[55] The Bush administration clearly viewed the Community as a more important international actor than had previous administrations.

It was the Clinton administration, however, that gave the EU a much greater role in European-U.S. relations. Although consultations had gradually become more institutionalized throughout the Bush administration, they were still lacking substantive underpinning and, above all, focus. Summits, for example, were not well prepared and seemed to have no cumulative impact. Consultations at various levels were not linked together; as a result, out of the tangle of consultative meetings that had gradually been institutionalized during the Bush administration and the first years of the Clinton administration, no overarching framework emerged.

On 2 June 1995 Secretary of State Warren Christopher, in an important address in Madrid, "called for a major transatlantic effort to define a framework for broad U.S.-EU cooperation extending beyond trade."[56] That framework came to be known as the New Transatlantic Agenda. Although the Union and the United States had different reasons for desiring a new diplomatic initiative aimed specifically at strengthening the EU-U.S. relationship, they also had common ground. In Anthony Gardner's words, both the United States and the EU were convinced "that the most pressing problems . . . are of a transnational character and cannot be addressed satisfactorily by either acting alone."[57]

The New Transatlantic Agenda

The New Transatlantic Agenda was signed in Madrid at the U.S.-EU Summit on 3 December 1995. In addition, a more detailed "Joint U.S.-EU Action Plan" came out of the meetings. A press release from the White House defined the new initiative as "an ambitious agenda for U.S.-EU cooperation on a wide range of issues." Whereas the Transatlantic Declaration had called for consultation, the agenda and the action plan called for joint action. Cooperation between the United States and the Union was to be deepened.[58]

Among the goals delineated, the action plan called for the two to cooperate (1) in promoting peace and stability in a variety of areas including the former Yugoslavia, the Central and Eastern European countries, Russia, Ukraine, and the other new independent states, as well as Turkey and Cyprus; (2) in responding to global challenges such as organized crime, terrorism, drug trafficking, immigration and asylum, legal and judicial matters, preservation of the environment, population issues, nuclear safety, and communicable diseases; (3) in supporting the World Trade Organization and creating a New Transatlantic Marketplace; and (4) in building bridges across the Atlantic, with encouragement for the Transatlantic Business Dialogue.[59]

Interestingly, the agreement included areas that, on the European side, are not covered by the Treaty of Rome. The case of transnational organized crime is particularly intriguing in this regard. Cooperation in confronting transnational organized crime is a high priority for the United States, but the European interlocutor in that case is far from defined. The Commission under Santer did indeed for the first time include a commissioner for justice and law enforcement (Anita Gradin from Sweden), but the general field of justice and home affairs is not subject to the decisionmaking procedures used for those policy arenas in which the Commission exercises a monopoly of initiative. Instead, the Council of Ministers adopts binding directives, and the European Court of Justice has jurisdiction. The "third pillar," as this arena is known, is intergovernmental, in terms of policy formation and decisionmaking procedure, reserving these prerogatives for the member states.

As Albrecht Funk points out, rather than the Union institutions acting as decisionmakers, "national officials develop 'common policies' . . . The Council then recommends that member states adopt these 'common policies' in keeping with their respective constitutional law. As far as the Third Pillar is concerned, the powers of the Commission are restricted."[60] The third pillar has worked so badly, however, that it has continued to be the subject of proposals for treaty reform.

The Clinton administration seems to have been fully aware that it would be very difficult to actually improve transatlantic coordination in combatting organized crime. Disorganization at the EU level was such that most analysts despaired of improving intra-European coordination! Yet the administration thought that transatlantic attention might in fact "contribute to improved intra-European coordination."[61] In the meantime, the United States (Federal Bureau of Investigation in particular) would keep using its bilateral relations with national governments.

Although some of the goals would be extraordinarily difficult to implement, the New Transatlantic Agenda was meant generally to extend the ties that already existed between the EU and the United States. The importance of this new initiative in binding Europe and the United States together was stressed in nearly all the press releases issued by the U.S. government. In President Clinton's opening remarks at a press conference following the U.S.-EU Summit, for example, he stated, "Our destiny in America is still linked to Europe. This action agenda makes it clear that we will remain as firmly engaged with Europe in the post–Cold War era as we have for the last fifty years."[62] Given the importance of multilateral arrangements for the conduct of U.S.-EU relations, it is noteworthy that the agenda calls for coordination of positions in multilateral institutions.[63] Such a commitment is made particularly forcefully in the case of global environmental issues.[64]

Whatever the concrete results may be, it is clear that the wide range of issues covered by the action plan is pulling many new actors in the U.S. executive into U.S.-EU relations. It is quite possible that the single most important contribution of the action plan will be to act as an educational tool for those within the U.S. executive branch who have failed to keep abreast of the remarkable degree of integration that Europe has witnessed since the Single European Act was ratified in 1987.

The EU and National Governments

It is clear that the New Transatlantic Agenda gives the Union a higher profile with Washington than it has previously had. Whereas the Bush administration recognized the new importance of the Community, significant segments within that administration remained wary. The Clinton administration acknowledged the Community/Union in a much more wholehearted and comprehensive fashion. Clearly, the Union had moved to a stage in which it was more equal to the member states than it had ever been before, though still lacking the weight of a large sovereign power. In the case of global environmental issues, for example, the United States recognized that the Union was now a global actor, one very active and important in key multilateral institutions concerned with environmental issues. The Union negotiated, rather than the individual member states.

While acknowledging the role the Union had acquired in the international arena in the previous decade, the Clinton administration also went further. It recognized as events unfolded in the 1990s that each of its three main national allies—the United Kingdom, France, and Germany—had key weaknesses from the U.S. perspective, which were not going to vanish and which made the EU a more promising ally for the future.[65]

The EU in fact allows the United States to find a new partner—one more attractive in many ways than individual partnerships with the British, French, or Germans. The weaknesses of the respective bilateral relationships with France, the UK, and Germany became particularly apparent with the end of the Cold War. Rather than turning to other capitals in Europe, the United States turned to Brussels as the capital of the European Union. It is clear, however, that the United States will continue to use bilateral relations—even with nonpreferred partners—when it suits its purposes. The "open skies" agreements, for example, with Austria, Belgium, Denmark, Finland, Germany, Luxembourg, and Sweden have allowed U.S. airlines to improve their position in the European market. The unwillingness of the European member states to allow the Union to negotiate for them has provided an opportunity for the United States, and, given the upper hand, the United States has used the bilateral negotiations strategically and skillfully.[66]

Bilateral relations are still paramount in the area of foreign and security policy.[67] Yet even there, Frellesen and Ginsberg argue, "foreign policy cooperation between the EU and the United States is a 'growth area' in transatlantic relations."[68] In fact, most member state governments are developing the habit of using "Europe" as a benchmark. Unilateralist reflexes certainly exist, but the evolving European context is slowly redirecting them. Anthony Gardner, analyzing the role of member state national governments from a U.S. perspective, concludes that "many EU Member States are gradually becoming less unilateralist and more Europeanist . . . [where] actions taken by individual countries contrary to a European consensus or policy are no longer taken for granted; they must be justified."[69]

Implications

The evolution of transatlantic relations illuminates larger trends in international affairs while simultaneously deepening the European-U.S. relationship. The growth of European FDI in the United States has made the U.S. economy more comparable to other economies. Most significantly, perhaps, it has led to the development of a "private" sphere in transatlantic relations. The growing importance of "private" actors in European-U.S. relations—business firms who employ and produce rather than simply trade—is likely over time to change the dynamics and scope of those relations. Business is interested in policy areas—such as regulatory frameworks that have not been the subject of traditional diplomacy either in security or trade negotiations. It is likely that the emergence of a private sphere in transatlantic relations will eventually expand the range of issues important to that relationship.

The transatlantic relationship has also witnessed the emergence of a new actor in the "public" sphere. The 1992 single-market program and the fall of the Berlin Wall enhanced the weight and importance of the EU, a fact acknowledged by the Bush administration. The new Transatlantic Agenda, agreed to by the Clinton administration, continued the process of recognizing the Union's increased weight in many issue areas. The implementation of the New Transatlantic Agenda through the action plan is likely over time to broaden the U.S.-EU relationship. New actors in the U.S. bureaucracy will view the Union as a key negotiator and as an actor with power in important areas.

Still, in areas of crucial importance to the United States (such as combatting transnational organized crime), the Union is not a unified actor. The United States will, therefore, continue to rely primarily on bilateral relations with national capitals. It will also continue, however, to pressure the EU for a more unified policy and cohesive institutional frameworks. While national capitals have certainly not been supplanted by the Union in the eyes of U.S. diplomats and strategists, even in areas not falling under the rubric of traditional security, Brussels is emerging as an important actor in transatlantic relations.

As the United States moves from a Cold War to a more diffuse international agenda, the Commission, at least for the moment, seems to offer the best potential for serving as a counterpart to the United States in the international arena. Yet it is important to remember that the Commission's latitude in external relations outside the trade area is always strongly influenced by the willingness of the member states to allow it to act.

In spite of institutional uncertainties in the European Union, we may be witnessing the general emergence of at least some symmetry in transatlantic relations. The "private sphere" in the transatlantic relationship has achieved a significant degree of equilibrium as European business has invested in the U.S. economy. Similarly, the "public" relationship seems to be inching toward one that at least potentially could be more balanced than it has been in the past. The European Union in its current form is of course far from a "match" for the United States, but it at least has the potential to evolve in that direction.

Notes

This chapter is a revised version of a paper presented to the conference on Policy Making and Decision Making in Transatlantic Relations. Université Libre de Bruxelles, 3–4 May 1996.
1. Harrison 1995. For a more recent assessment, see Cowles 1996a.
2. Howard 1995, 708.
3. Ibid., 709.
4. Menon 1995, 19–34; *Financial Times*, 26 April 1996, 3.
5. Kahler 1995, 1.
6. Julius 1991, 6.
7. Ibid., 6, 8.
8. Costigliola 1984, 149–157. After 1957, the value of U.S. foreign direct investment in Europe surpassed that of European direct investment in the United States. Hu 1973, 7; see also Dunning 1991, 157–162.
9. Smith 1984, 52.
10. Servan-Schreiber 1968.
11. Ibid., 5–6.
12. Graham and Krugman 1995, 97.
13. Schaetzel 1975, 43.
14. Dunning 1991, 164.
15. Harrison 1995, 3, n. 5.
16. Jackson 1992, 273.
17. Cooney 1994, 8.
18. Ibid., 15.
19. Ibid., 19.
20. Graham 1991, 180.
21. Ibid., 183. However, U.S. banks did not seek entry. In fact, some of the banks already in Europe began to withdraw. Even though the United States and the European Union agreed that "national treatment" would be an acceptable way of dealing with each other's banking investments, U.S. banks, for a variety of reasons, did not see post-1992 Europe as an attractive business location. Ibid., 193–196.

22. Jacquemin and Wright 1994, 223.

23. Nanto 1992, 363.

24. Ibid., 364.

25. See, for example, Peterson 1993, 136.

26. Alter 1994, 33, 35–36.

27. Julius 1991.

28. Smith and Woolcock 1993, 55.

29. Ibid., 58.

30. Harrison 1995, 3–4.

31. Vernon 1992, 3.

32. Graham and Krugman 1995, 31–32.

33. Dunning 1991, 167.

34. Ibid., 170.

35. McCulloch 1991, 175.

36. The New Transatlantic Marketplace, 3 December 1995. *USA Text,* Fact Sheet, Public Affairs Office, United States Mission to the European Union, 1.

37. Okubo 1995, 2.

38. Ibid., 4.

39. Harrison 1994, 8.

40. Woolcock 1992, 53.

41. McCulloch 1991, 171.

42. Featherstone and Ginsberg 1993, 153.

43. Graham and Krugman 1995, 170.

44. Van Heuven 1994, p.2.

45. Peterson 1993, 90.

46. Duquesne Club 1996 (discussion), Pittsburgh, PA, 20 March. A similar dynamic may be emerging in the development of new chemicals. See "EU Rules 'Hinder' Chemicals Groups," *Financial Times,* 26 April 1996, 16.

47. Graham 1991, 201.

48. For analysis of the EU Committee, see Cowles 1996b, 1996c.

49. Hufbauer 1990, 24.

50. Featherstone and Ginsberg 1993, 81.

51. See Sbragia (forthcoming) and Sbragia 1996.

52. Winand 1993.

53. Featherstone and Ginsberg 1993, 7.

54. Peterson 1993, 18.

55. Gardner 1997, 4–5. I have drawn very heavily from Gardner's work in my discussion of the Clinton administration. Anthony Gardner until recently served as director for European Affairs in the European Directorate of the National Security Council. He was the official responsible in the NSC staff for coordinating the input of U.S. government agencies and the U.S. Mission to the European Union as the New Transatlantic Agenda was being developed.

56. Gardner 1997, 64.

57. Ibid., 68.

58. President's Trip to Madrid, 2 December 1995, Public Affairs Office, United States Mission to the European Union. *USA Text,* 1–2.

59. Burros 1996.

60. Funk 1996, 5. Funk points out that in the field of internal security "cooperation was well established long before the idea of a Single European Market emerged. The police experts involved in this cooperation played a crucial role in the debate on the future controls at the borders and in the EU." Funk 1996, 8.

61. Gardner 1997, 74.

62. President Clinton's Opening Remarks at a Press Conference Following the U.S.-EU Summit, 3 December 1995. Public Affairs Office, United States Mission to the European Union. *USA Text*, 2.

63. For a discussion of the importance of multilateral institutions for EU-U.S. relations, see, for example Featherstone and Ginsberg 1993, 125–130.

64. *The New Transatlantic Agenda: Statement of Purpose*, 3 December 1995, 4.

65. Gardner 1997, 17–18.

66. Ibid., 8; Staniland 1995, 19–40.

67. Gardner 1997, 25.

68. Frellesen and Ginsberg 1994, 1.

69. Gardner 1997, 31.

9

The EMU and International Monetary Relations: What to Expect for International Actors?

Madeleine O. Hosli

One of the most potentially significant developments in the evolution of the EU's international role is Economic and Monetary Union (EMU). The creation of a common currency and a common monetary policy will clearly affect patterns of global currency investment and the character of exchange rate management. Interestingly, international perception about the significance of the European Economic and Monetary Union project and the chances for its success lags behind reality. Many international actors have assumed that the project will never come into fruition. The exchange rate turbulence involving several European currencies in 1992 and 1993 contributed to the view of EMU as a nonstarter. Public skepticism toward EMU in several EU states—tending to rise with deepening economic recession— and disbelief about the utility of fixed European exchange rates in the United Kingdom have also contributed to the perception of dire prospects for EMU. Despite all of this, however, economic and political realities increasingly suggest that the project is a realistic one. Hence, it is imperative for international actors to start preparing for EMU in order to react appropriately to this new era in international monetary affairs.[1]

EU states are aiming to comply with the convergence criteria encompassed in the Treaty on European Union (TEU), in order to have the option of joining the project when it commences. The race to comply with the criteria, moreover, is not limited to Western Europe. Central and Eastern European countries are aiming to fulfill the criteria in an effort to increase both their prospects for early EU membership and their prospects, once admitted, of joining the EMU. Finally, business and financial sectors in several EU member states are increasingly preparing for, and counting on, the realization of the EMU.

The growing role of the EU in the international economy appears to both justify and necessitate an enhanced leverage for EU members in international monetary affairs. In order to assess the likely role of the new currency (the euro) that will be created as a result of EMU, this chapter is structured as follows. The first section provides background information on the European Monetary System and its two component parts, the Exchange Rate Mechanism (ERM) and the European Currency Unit (ECU). Additionally, it provides information on the roles of EU member states in the context of this regional exchange rate regime and the effects of the regime on both the level and relative dispersion of inflation rates among the EMS members.

The second section describes the "convergence criteria" as laid down in the TEU—which will crucially determine the selection of members qualifying for EMU membership—and provides data on the EU members' actual performance with respect to these monetary and fiscal "benchmarks." Moreover, the section outlines the EMU's institutional structures, which are likely to crucially influence the EMU's policy outcomes.

Section three shifts the focus to the possible effects of a common European monetary policy and the potential role of the euro as a unit of account in global affairs. In the framework of the EMS, the ECU partially functions as an (official) *numéraire,* and some national European currencies play a rather strong role, for instance, with respect to the denomination of international trade. The euro is likely to enhance these functions. Additionally, the section reveals the total shares of EU members in global trade and the significance of national currencies in this framework.

The fourth section focuses on the euro's potential role as an international means of payment. Some EU currencies currently have a significant function as intervention tools in international exchange markets. For instance, the deutsche mark has been used extensively for foreign exchange intervention, not only in the framework of the EMS, but also by the U.S. Treasury to influence the dollar's external exchange rate.

The final section builds upon these considerations and looks at the euro's potential role as a store of value. With respect to official use, reserve holdings of major central banks provide an indication of the relative importance of national currencies, and as will be shown, some EMS currencies already play important roles as global stores of value. Similarly, in terms of private investment, the ECU and some major European currencies are rather significant. Depending on the shape and actual composition of the EMU, the euro may take over these roles from the present individual national European currencies.

From the "Snake" to the European Monetary System: Reducing Exchange Rate Volatility in the Union

When the Bretton Woods fixed exchange rate system collapsed in the early 1970s, the Western European states, strongly trade interdependent, had to find ways to reduce exchange rate fluctuations among their national currencies. In 1970, the Werner Plan—named after the prime minister of Luxembourg at that time—called for the establishment of a European Economic and Monetary Union (EMU) within a decade. The plan foresaw three stages to reach this goal. Overall, these stages were rather similar to the present steps foreseen to move toward EMU as contained in the respective provisions of the TEU. The original project turned out to be premature.

In a more moderate approach, in March 1972 the EC member states created the "snake in the tunnel." This system established bilateral exchange rate fluctuation margins for all participating EC member states of ± 2.25 percent, whereas this "snake" was allowed to commonly fluctuate ± 6 percent from the value of the U.S. dollar. However, in 1973, the first oil price crisis caused major strains for the "snake." The subsequent economic recession forced several EC members either to drastically adapt their monetary policies or to leave the system. At the end of the 1970s, the "snake" was little more than an "extended deutsche mark zone," with only Germany, Denmark, and the Benelux countries left as participants.

During this time, calls for stronger monetary convergence in the EC were once again articulated. The president of the European Commission, Roy Jenkins, strongly advocated enhanced currency stability for the Community. Moreover, German Chancellor Helmut Schmidt and President Giscard d'Estaing of France called for the establishment of a new regime to moderate exchange rate volatility among the currencies of the Community member states. The Hague summit in 1978 officially sanctioned the plan and the European Monetary System (EMS) was introduced in March 1979.

The EMS was designed to resemble the "snake in the tunnel," but most importantly, it would involve only the currencies of the EC member states, without the U.S. dollar as the formal focal point or "anchor." The system contained two major elements: the Exchange Rate Mechanism (ERM) and the European Currency Unit (ECU). The ERM established a grid of bilateral parities, in which currencies were allowed to fluctuate within a margin of ± 2.25 percent around their bilateral "central rates." The national central banks were obliged to intervene when currencies reached their fluctuation margins. Moreover, short-term and long-term borrowing facilities in the framework of the European Monetary Cooperation Fund (EMCF) were established to enable national central banks to borrow and to intervene in financial markets.

The Community's national currencies, in this system, were designed to create a new common unit of account, the European Currency Unit.[2] Bilateral rates between the ECU and the national currencies—the EMS "central rates"—were to be agreed upon in the framework of the Council of Ministers of Economics and Finance (ECOFIN). The "weights" of the national currencies in the ECU "basket" could be revised every five years. Such a general revision of central rates was conducted in both 1984 and 1989.

In between these "five-year revisions," however, market pressures on participating currencies caused a series of realignments within the EMS. The respective new bilateral central rates were agreed upon in the Council. In the first years of the EMS's existence, quite a few realignments occurred, involving several EMS currencies. Pressures to appreciate were strong mainly for the deutsche mark and for the Dutch guilder, joined since 1983 by the Belgian and Luxembourg franc. By contrast, the French franc and the Italian lira, as well as the Irish punt, were devalued several times during the course of the 1980s. Every time the ECU was reweighted, capital gains and losses occurred. Investors holding ECU bonds, for instance, normally lost when the weight of a strong currency was decreased.[3] If not corrected in the framework of these five-year revisions and the several "realignments" in between, the shares of the strongest currencies— and hence their respective contributions to the ECU basket—would have been enhanced steadily.[4] In the late 1980s and early 1990s, however, few realignments of the central rates took place, leading observers to assess that the EMS had significantly contributed to exchange rate stability within the Community.

The currency turmoil in the fall of 1992 and in the summer and fall of 1993 partially changed this image. Caused not least by the introduction of EMU's Stage I on July 1, 1990—implying the full abolition of capital controls—and reinforced by the German Bundesbank's policy of high interest rates to fight inflationary pressures after German reunification, financial speculation put several EMS currencies under stress and forced the pound sterling and the lira to abandon the system.

Today, the ECU still constitutes a basket of the currencies of almost all EU members (with the exception of recent members Austria, Sweden, and Finland). However, since the ratification of the Maastricht Treaty in 1993, the "weights" of the national currencies in the ECU basket are frozen.[5] Table 9.1 provides an overview of the weights and central rates and percentage shares of currencies in the basket as they apply since the November 1996 realignment. The deutsche mark, the French franc, the Dutch guilder, and the pound sterling—the latter not taking part in the ERM—hold the largest shares in the ECU basket.

In the late 1980s, the relative stability of the EMS most likely contributed to the phase of "Euro-optimism," reinforced by positive accounts of the economic potential of the single European market.[6] EMS stability at this time was paralleled by a period of economic upturn. Hence, in the late 1980s, monetary integration in the EU appeared to be feasible within a reasonable time frame. The optimistic mood was reinforced by analyses conducted by the European Commission on the additional gains to be obtained by establishing the monetary union, most decisively the 1989 "Delors Report"[7] (crucially influenced by the Committee of Central Bankers) and the study by the European Commission on "One Market, One Money."[8]

Table 9.1   The Currency Composition of the ECU Basket (Summer 1996)

Currency	Relative Weight in the ECU Basket	Percentage Share of the Component Currencies[a]
Deutsche mark	0.6242	32.41
French franc	1.332	20.62
Dutch guilder	0.2198	10.13
Belgian franc	3.301	8.31
Luxembourg franc	0.13	0.33
Italian lira	151.8	7.96
Danish krone	0.1976	2.69
Irish punt	0.008552	1.07
Pound sterling	0.08784	11.08
Greek drachma	1.44	0.49
Spanish peseta	6.885	4.20
Portuguese escudo	1.393	0.71
Total	1 ECU	100

Source: Eurostat.
a. On the basis of the central rates in force since 25 November 1996.

The EMS members have indeed experienced relatively beneficial effects with respect to convergence and improved monetary performance. Most prominently, not only have inflation rates decreased for most members, but the divergence in their relative price level performance has narrowed. Table 9.2 shows these trends from the establishment of the EMS in March 1979 until 1995.

Whereas in 1980 the (unweighted) average inflation was 13.94 percent for the twelve EC members, this group's average inflation decreased to 6.52 percent by 1990. A further significant reduction in inflation rates has been experienced in recent years, probably because of strict formulation of the convergence criteria in the TEU. Average inflation rates among EU members in 1995 were merely 3.36 percent, with a similar record low in their standard deviation of 2.25. Note that this trend applied both for countries participating in the ERM and other EMS members, such as the United Kingdom, as well.

However, the EMS may only partially have induced this shift toward improved inflation performance. Generally, during this period, EU members developed a stronger belief in the merits of price stability, especially by abandoning the traditional view of a trade-off between price stability and employment (as expressed by the Phillips Curve). Instead, member state governments started to view price stability as generating beneficial effects on long-term economic growth and employment.[9] Moreover, the relative decrease in inflation was not restricted to Europe, but significant changes in inflation performance also occurred for other world actors (especially the United States and Japan), as Table 9.3 demonstrates.

The reduction and stabilization of inflation rates in the member states is significant for the establishment of the EMU. A major goal of the new

Table 9.2   A Time-Series of Inflation Rates,[a] EMS 1979–1995

	1979	1980	1981	1982	1983	1984	1985	1986	1987	1988	1989	1990	1991	1992	1993	1994	1995
Belgium	4.5	6.6	7.6	8.2	7.7	6.3	4.9	1.3	1.6	1.2	3.1	3.4	3.2	2.4	2.8	2.4	1.5
Denmark	9.6	12.3	11.7	10.1	6.9	6.3	4.7	3.6	4.0	4.6	4.8	2.7	2.4	2.1	1.3	2.0	2.1
France	10.8	13.6	13.4	11.8	9.6	7.4	5.8	2.7	3.1	2.7	3.6	3.4	3.2	2.4	2.1	1.7	1.8
Germany	4.1	5.5	6.3	5.3	3.3	2.4	2.2	-0.1	0.2	1.3	2.8	2.7	3.6	4.0	3.6	2.7	1.8
Greece	19.0	24.9	24.5	21.0	20.2	18.4	19.3	23.0	16.4	13.5	13.7	20.4	19.5	15.9	14.5	10.9	9.3
Ireland	13.3	18.2	20.4	17.1	10.5	8.6	5.5	3.8	3.1	2.1	4.1	3.3	3.1	3.1	1.4	2.3	2.6
Italy	14.8	21.2	17.8	16.6	14.6	10.8	9.2	5.8	4.7	5.1	6.3	6.5	6.3	5.2	4.5	4.0	5.2
Luxembourg	4.5	6.3	8.1	9.4	8.7	5.6	4.1	0.3	-0.1	1.4	3.4	3.7	3.1	3.2	3.6	2.2	1.9
Netherlands	4.2	8.5	6.7	5.9	2.7	3.3	2.3	0.1	-0.7	0.7	1.1	2.5	3.9	3.2	2.6	2.8	1.9
Portugal	23.9	16.6	20.0	22.4	25.5	28.8	19.6	11.8	9.4	9.7	12.6	13.4	10.9	9.0	6.4	4.7	4.1
Spain	15.6	15.6	14.5	14.4	12.2	11.3	8.8	8.8	5.2	4.8	6.8	6.7	6.0	5.9	4.6	5.2	4.7
United Kingdom	13.4	18.0	11.9	8.6	4.6	5.0	6.1	3.4	4.1	4.9	7.8	9.5	5.9	3.7	1.6	2.5	3.4
EC 12 (unweighted average)	11.48	13.94	13.58	12.57	10.54	9.52	7.71	5.38	4.25	4.33	5.87	6.52	5.93	5.01	5.28	3.55	3.36
Standard deviatn. (σ_{n-1})	6.43	6.28	6.02	5.69	6.82	7.43	5.88	6.61	4.72	3.84	3.94	5.49	4.88	3.94	4.88	2.58	2.25

Sources: Qvigstad, *Economic and Monetary Union,* 1992 (for figures 1979 to 1990); 1991–1995, *Eurostat;* author's calculations.
a. Percentage change of the Consumer Price Index (CPI).

European Central Bank (ECB) is to guarantee price stability. Furthermore, relative inflation rates are one of the five "convergence criteria" that will assess EU members' ability to join the EMU.

Institutional Structures, Membership, and Powers of the EMU

The TEU—and the protocols on EMU attached to the treaty—describe the variables that will be crucial for the decision on whether EMU will start with a majority of the EU members, as in Article 109(J), and which members will qualify to enter EMU from its inception. The criterion with respect to price level stability is that in the twelve months prior to evaluation, a member's inflation rate may not have exceeded by more than 1.5 percentage points that of the three best performers. Judged at the beginning of 1992, for instance, this relative figure would have been 4.4 percent (compare Table 9.2).[10] Judged in 1988, however, it was 1.3 percent. In the beginning of 1995, according to Table 9.2, this benchmark would have been 3.5 percent.

Similarly, interest rates on government bonds during the twelve months prior to examination may not have exceeded the (unweighted) average of the three best inflation performers' long-term interest rates by two percentage points. Since the three best inflation performers in 1991 were Denmark, Luxembourg, and Ireland, and the (unweighted) average of their long-term interest rates was 9.1 percent,[11] the relative benchmark on interest rates for 1992 would have been 11.1 percent.

The criterion with respect to exchange rate stability is somewhat difficult to interpret in practice: a country's exchange rate must have remained, in the two years prior to the examination date, within the "normal fluctuation bands" of the ERM.[12] However, when these criteria were defined, the normal fluctuation margins within the EMS were still ±2.25 percent; they were widened to ±15 percent after the 1993 currency turmoil. Hence, the interpretation of this criterion and of what constitutes a "normal fluctuation margin" may be subject to political judgment.

Two important criteria refer to the EU members' fiscal performance. The first stipulates that the ratio of general government deficit to GDP may not exceed 3 percent. The second prescribes that government debt to GDP has to be equal to or less than 60 percent (or at least clearly moving toward this target). The two fiscal criteria may be of special importance; although the EMS has led to harmonization with respect to inflation and reduced exchange rate volatility, it has not induced fiscal convergence that can significantly affect monetary performance.

To judge the capacity of different EU members to join EMU according to these criteria, Table 9.4 provides an overview of the performance of present EU members with respect to inflation, interest rates, government

Table 9.3   Inflation and Inflation Variability[a] in Selected Major Industrialized Countries, 1970–1980 as compared to 1980–1990

Country	1970–1979		1980–1990	
	Inflation Rate	Inflation Variability	Inflation Rate	Inflation Variability
Germany	4.9	1.5	2.9	2.0
France	8.9	2.6	7.0	4.2
Italy	12.5	5.6	10.9	5.8
United Kingdom	13.3	5.6	7.6	4.2
USA	7.2	2.8	5.5	3.3
Japan	9.1	5.9	2.6	2.1
Switzerland	5.0	3.2	3.5	1.8

Sources: Tavlas 1993, 568; IMF, *International Financial Statistics*
a. Variability is measured by the standard deviation (on the basis of quarterly data for the indicated time period).

deficit, and government debt. (It abstracts from the requirement with respect to exchange rate stability.) As Table 9.4 illustrates, the inflation rate in 1995 for the average of all EU members was 3.1 percent. The inflation rate of the new members—Austria, Finland, and Sweden—was below this average. Additionally, the relative distribution of inflation among the fifteen members was relatively low (with a standard deviation of 2.12).

Nonetheless, some members face difficulties in meeting this criterion. For instance, Greece—despite an impressive decrease in its inflation rate as compared to earlier periods in its EMS membership (Table 9.2)—still experiences a relatively high annual change in consumer prices. In contrast, Italy, Portugal, and Spain, although showing inflation rates above the EU average, managed significantly to moderate their price level increases in an effort to belong to the EMU's core group. EMS members with weaker currencies also tended to have higher long-term interest rates. Principal among these strates were Greece, Italy, Portugal, and Spain; it should be noted, however, that long-term rates were also relatively high for EU members such as Denmark, Ireland, Sweden, and the United Kingdom.

In the years in which the convergence criteria were formulated, the prospects for enhanced fiscal discipline appeared to be rather positive for Community member states: Germany, for instance, had a budgetary deficit of –2.7 percent in 1990 and a ratio of government debt to GDP of 44.5 percent. Other member states obtained similarly good fiscal balances.[14] Hence, fiscal indicators were another measure according to which moving toward monetary union appeared to be feasible. The situation changed, however, with the advent of the economic recession in the early 1990s. Government deficits for 1994 were highest in Greece and in Sweden. The largest figures on government debt—resulting from a series of deficits during the 1980s—can be seen for Belgium, Greece, and Italy.

Table 9.4   Relative Performance of the EU Member States with Respect to Four Convergence Criteria (1995)

Country	Inflation rates	Long-term interest rates (percent)	General Government Deficit (in percentage of GDP)	General Government Debt (in percentage of GDP)
Austria	2.3	6.5	5.9	69.0
Belgium	1.5	7.4	4.1	133.7
Denmark	2.1	8.3	1.6	71.9
Finland	1.0	7.9	5.4	59.2
France	9.3	7.7	4.8	52.8
Germany	1.8	6.8	3.5	58.1
Greece	1.7	17.3	9.1	111.8
Ireland	2.5	8.3	2.3	84.8
Italy	5.4	11.8	7.1	124.9
Luxembourg	1.9	7.6	−0.4	6.1
Netherlands	1.9	7.2	4.0	80.0
Portugal	4.1	11.4	4.9	71.7
Spain	4.7	11.0	6.6	65.8
Sweden	2.9	10.2	7.9	79.4
United Kingdom	3.4	8.2	5.7	53.9
(Non-weighted) average	3.10	9.17	4.83	74.87
Standard Deviation (σ n–1)	2.12	2.81	2.47	31.39

Source: Based upon Tables 1 and 2 in David Cameron, "Economic and Monetary Union: Transitional Issues and Third Stage Dilemmas," presented at the European Community Studies Association Conference, Seattle, Washington, May 29–June 1, 1997.

The recession that started in the early 1990s forced several EU members to increase government spending, for instance, for unemployment benefits. Simultaneously, tax incomes dropped. Hence, budget deficits increased rather than decreased, also aggravating the ratio of debt to GDP. In Germany, reunification placed the budget under additional strain. In order to cover new financial needs and to fight inflation, German interest rates were kept elevated. This forced other EMS members—despite an urgent need to stimulate domestic demand by reducing interest rates—to keep their domestic rates high in order to defend their bilateral parities. This dynamic, along with full abolition of capital controls in 1990, enhanced speculative capital movements and reinforced, if not largely induced, the 1992–1993 exchange rate turbulence.

Latest figures for Germany indicate that the country partially fails to comply with the fiscal convergence criteria: its 1995 budget exceeded the 3 percent deficit-to-GDP threshold. Similarly, it has exceeded this target in 1997. Moreover, most EU members fail to comply with at least one of the criteria (with Luxembourg constituting a remarkable exception to this rule).

In the wake of members' difficulties with fulfilling the criteria, considerable debate about postponing EMU has ensued. Since the European economies, however, are gradually moving out of recession, it seems likely that the overall timetable can be adhered to. Moreover, since the criteria allow latitude in interpretion, it seems unlikely that they will be weakened formally. Modification of the criteria might prove to be detrimental to the EMU's role in the global economy: should the convergence criteria be adapted to facilitate early acceptance of members with weak economic and monetary fundamentals, EMU's role in the world economy would most likely be weakened.

The judgment on which members are considered to comply with the criteria and whether a majority of EU members fulfills them will be made by the European Council in May 1998. The basis for the decision will be a report by the European Commission and a recommendation by the ECOFIN Council (on the basis of a qualified majority vote). The "recommendation" by the ECOFIN Council will certainly be rather decisive in practice. Under the present institutional arrangement, a blocking minority of twenty-six votes could suffice to prevent members from participating in EMU.[14] Hence, the core group of members qualifying for membership needs to be large enough to prevent a minority of members from blocking the others from going ahead.

The future position of the United Kingdom remains an open question. Given the importance of London as an international financial center and of the pound sterling in international commerce—for instance, in invoicing primary commodity trade—it's difficult to imagine that the UK will abstain forever. At this moment, the possibility cannot be excluded that eventually the UK as a whole, aided by increasing pressures from its financial sector, might perceive a "higher return" from EMU membership than from staying aside.[15]

The present monetary system in the Union, the EMS, is designed as a "symmetric" system. The central rates are determined by agreement between the member states, and the obligation to intervene to defend bilateral exchange rate parities holds for all participating members. Nonetheless, the system—as in the "snake" previously—is clearly dominated in practice by one player: the German Bundesbank. The Bundesbank sets its monetary policy rather autonomously, whereas the other members are essentially forced to react to it. One of the reasons why the Bundesbank is able to exert this power is its full independence from political pressures and its credibility with respect to price level stability—supported by the German public's profound aversion to high inflation as a result of the traumatic experience of the Weimar period.

Members that presently have little leverage in the EMS strongly favor creation of a monetary union on the basis of symmetric influence among participating members, in the framework of a new "EuroFed"—which would replace the de facto hegemony of Germany in the EMS. For instance, a more symmetric institutional foundation has been crucial to

France, including the French central bank and the Ministry of Finance.[16] The provisions foreseen on decisionmaking as well as the overall institutional structure of EMU reflect this desire for more symmetry. The EMU is constituted as a system in which all participating members hold equal influence irrespective of factors such as population size or economic weight. The European System of Central Banks (ESCB), composed of the European Central Bank (ECB) and the national central banks (Article 106.1 TEU), will be governed by the ECB's governing council. According to Article 109a, this council comprises both the governors of the national central banks and members of the ECB's executive board. Executive board members have a term in office of eight years, which is nonrenewable to shield them from political pressure. In moving toward EMU, national central banks must also be fully independent. This requirement has been set in place to further protect EMU from political influence.

The determination of the Union's monetary policy will be the responsibility of the ECB's governing council. All national central bank governors will hold equal voting power within this institution on the basis of the principle "one member state, one vote." The implementation of the EMU's monetary and exchange rate policies by the national central banks will be supervised by the ECB's executive board.

Historical experience may somewhat qualify the importance of such formal symmetry. Both the Bretton Woods system and the EMS were designed as symmetric institutional structures, but both evolved into highly asymmetric regimes in practice,[17] the U.S. dollar being the effective anchor in the framework of the Bretton Woods fixed exchange rate regime and the deutsche mark in the framework of the EMS. Since the EMU is more institutionalized than either Bretton Woods or the EMS, however, this formal symmetry may indeed be more realistic in the framework of the ESCB—bearing more resemblance to the U.S. Federal Reserve than to the EMS.

In contrast to the EMU, structurally, the EMS was based on the principle of "voluntary membership," in that members could leave the ERM when their currency came under severe pressure (although such action could cause economic and monetary repercussions). Exchange rate adjustments were generally possible; the EMS constituted a system of fixed but adjustable rates. In some sense, the EMS constituted its own kind of multispeed approach to European integration, since only some Community members, although a majority, participated in the ERM. However, all Community currencies formally participated in the EMS and especially in the ECU currency basket.

How independent and how committed to low inflation will the EMU be? The TEU defines the main policy objective of the ECB to be price level stability (adopted into the treaty largely on the basis of German insistence) and subordinates other goals to this principal orientation: "The primary objective of the ESCB shall be to maintain price stability. Without prejudice to the objective of price stability, the ESCB shall support the general economic policies in the Community with a view to contributing to the achievement of the objectives of the Community as laid down in Article 2."[18]

How well the ECB will be able to adhere to the priority of price level stability is a matter of debate. Two main challenges to this goal are internal inflationary pressures and a certain conflict with exchange rate stability. Internally, inflationary pressure could, for example, stem from a free-rider problem with respect to budget deficits.[19] This problem has been mitigated somewhat by the December 1996 agreement on the "pact for stability and growth," stipulating that members incurring high fiscal deficits have to pay fines (determined by the ECOFIN Council), but are exempt from this procedure if their economy experiences negative economic growth of more than 2 percent.[20]

Nonetheless, a potential conflict exists between price stability and exchange rate stability. In terms of policy functions, the management of reserves and the implementation of the EMU's day-to-day exchange rate policy will be the responsibility of the ECB. In contrast, other decisions—especially regarding the conclusion of formal exchange rate arrangements—will be brought into the (political) purview of the Council of the EU.

As formulated in the TEU, the influence of the ECOFIN Council is likely to be most pronounced with respect to the EMU's exchange rate policy (but constrained, to a considerable extent, by the ECB's primary goal of price stability). Garrett points out that the relevant provisions in the TEU—mainly Articles 105, 109.1 and 109.2—partially contradict each other as to which institution will determine the EMU's exchange rate policy.[21] This ambiguity in all likelihood reflects dissent on this issue among Union members in the framework of the EMU negotiations.

Formal international exchange rate agreements, such as linking the value of the euro to other currencies, will have to be agreed upon unanimously in the Council of the EU.[22] Hence, every participating EMU member, in principle, obtains a veto with respect to such decisions, irrespective of its economic or fiscal performance.[23] This veto power will be extended to all newly admitted EU states that qualify for EMU membership. The requirement of unanimity in the framework of extended EMU membership, however, is likely to significantly reduce the prospects for international formal exchange rate arrangements that involve the EMU. But, in the more recent history of international monetary relations, such formal agreements are a rare event anyway.

However, "general orientations for exchange-rate policy" in relation to "one or more non-Community currencies" (Article 109.2) can be formulated on the basis of a qualified majority in the Council of the EU (among the EMU member states and with the usual consulting power of the European

Commission and of the EP). Hence, informal agreements may be some-what easier to conclude, in the sense of the 1985 Plaza agreement among the major industrialized countries or the 1987 Louvre accord, than more formal regimes—for example, those to be concluded with EU members outside EMU.[24]

How may this institutional structure affect the EMU's orientation with respect to monetary and exchange rate policy? A stable euro, supported by a generally high level of political stability in the EU, is likely to enhance the potential for international use of the EMU's common currency. The primacy of price stability, on the other hand, may limit the EMU's possibilities and willingness to actively influence the exchange rate vis-à-vis third currencies. This can be illustrated with an example in the framework of the EMS.

The tight monetary policy of the Bundesbank after German unification served primarily to counter inflationary pressures (as caused by the terms of the internal German monetary union). The Bundesbank's priority of price stability led it to maintain high interest rates against the wishes of its EMS partners, who were forced to follow suit despite recession in their own country. Hence, an internal primacy of price stability—although gen-erating beneficial effects for long-term growth and enhancing prospects for international use of the currency—may prevent the monetary actors from engaging in international efforts aimed at maintaining international ex-change rate stability.

For the German government, the level of the exchange rate of the deutsche mark was also crucial in this episode because of the high impor-tance of exports for the German economy. The German government viewed a stable exchange rate, with little pressure to appreciate, as bene-ficial for the economy, putting it at odds with its own central bank. Simi-larly, the relatively profound trade openness of the European economies in the aggregate may cause tension between the EMU's governments on the one hand (aiming at a stable and rather low level of the euro) and the ob-jectives of the ECB, on the other. Generally, countries with a longer tradi-tion of political influence on central banks may be inclined to carry ex-change rate policy partially into the ECB (whereas the statutory rules for the ESCB clearly counter such endeavors).

Fixing currencies irrevocably in the framework of the EMU will de-prive economic agents of the macroeconomic tool of adjusting external ex-change rates—for instance, in order to enhance the international competi-tiveness of their export industries. In such a context, the French practice during earlier stages of the EMS to aim at high growth rates and reduced unemployment, accepting relatively high levels of inflation—but correct-ing by consecutive devaluations of the French franc—will no longer be feasible in the framework of the EMU.

The liberalization of European capital markets in the framework of the EU's single market is crucial to a potential international use of the euro.

As foreseen in the Delors Committee Report, the full integration of financial and banking markets is significant.[25] However, trade relations may
also influence the euro's potential role. In the framework of the Bretton
Woods system, for instance, it is likely that the United States cared somewhat less about the stability of the dollar vis-à-vis other currencies because
of its low dependence on international trade. Measuring intra-Union trade
as "domestic trade" will similarly reduce the relative international "trade
dependence" of the EU.

How will the creation of the common currency influence international
monetary relations? To analyze the potential role of the euro in more detail, three main functions of an international currency can be distinguished:
(1) unit of account; (2) means of payment; and (3) store of value. An
overview of these tasks for both private and official agents is provided in
Table 9.5.

The Euro as an International *Numéraire*

The ECU as a basket currency was established as a European "unit of account," with the intention that it develop into the EU's official reserve currency. Yet, it neither managed to evolve into a significant *numéraire* nor
into a common European reserve asset. The official use of the ECU was
limited mainly to measuring the size of revolving credits through the European Monetary Cooperation Fund (EMCF). As a (private) store of value,
however, its role was somewhat more significant, especially with respect

Table 9.5   The Roles of an International Currency

Function	Sector	
	Private	Public
Unit of account	Currency used for invoicing foreign trade and denominating international financial instruments	Currency used in expressing exchange rate relationships
Means of payment	Currency used to settle international trade and to discharge international financial obligations	Intervention currency in foreign exchange markets and currency used for balance-of-payments financing
Store of value	Currency in which deposits, loans, and bonds are denominated	Reserve asset held by monetary authorities

Source: Tavlas 1993, 567.

to ECU-denominated asset markets such as ECU commercial paper, notes and bonds.

The increasing importance of the EU in international trade is likely to require an adaptation of the presently modest role of the "European currency" as a unit of account in international commercial and financial affairs. Since the inception of the Community, the share of intracommunity trade as compared to Union members' total share in global trade has gradually increased. Early studies concluded, however, that with the establishment of a customs union, trade creation in the EC—the shift from a high-cost domestic production source to a lower-cost partner source—exceeded trade diversion.[26] Developments with respect to the relative shares of intra versus extra-Community trade for 1960, 1975, and 1990 are demonstrated in Table 9.6.

Whereas extra-Community trade in 1960 clearly exceeded intra-Community trade, the shares were about equal in 1975. By 1990, however, this relationship was clearly reversed. Table 9.6 shows this trend for the aggregate of the twelve EC members as of 1986. An additional factor increasing the relative share of intra-Union trade is enlargement: the successive admission of new members increased the relative proportion of intra-Community trade as compared to extra-Community trade for the EC members. *Ceteris paribus*, this development enhanced the need to reduce exchange rate variability within the Community and necessitated a move toward a system such as the EMS. Similarly, a need increasingly arose for a common *numéraire,* a unit of account. The ECU partially took over this function in the framework of the EMS, but it was strongly rivaled by member states' domestic currencies, especially the deutsche mark.

Most EU members have relatively "open" economies (measured as the ratio of imports plus exports to total GDP). Hence, as compared to other major world actors such as the United States or Japan, the European economies will be more affected by international exchange rates. The relatively high degree of "trade openness" of EU members may induce the EMU countries to aim at external exchange rate stability. It may similarly

Table 9.6   Intra-EU Versus Extra-EU Trade (EC 12, values in million ECU and in percentage of total)

	1960	1975	1990
Intra-EU	17,712	130,262	663,797
	(37.92)	(49.49)	(58.92)
Extra-EU	28,999	132,932	462,720
	(62.08)	(50.51)	(41.08)
Total	46,711	263,194	1,126,517
	(100.0)	(100.0)	(100.0)

Source: Eurostat; author's calculations.

enhance incentives to increase the role of the euro as a unit of account and a means of payment in trade relations. However, the larger the share of intra-Union trade will be as compared to extra-Union trade, the lower will be the incentives to aim at external exchange rate stability. Nevertheless, a factor encouraging international use of a currency is the relative share of its own domestic region in global trade. For the EU, this share is already considerable, and can be expected to grow in the future.[27]

A currency that functions as an international unit of account may also have an unofficial use in invoicing practices. For instance, at present the U.S. dollar is widely used for international trade invoicing. In exchanges with actors in developing countries, generally, either the currency of the industrialized partner country is used or the U.S. dollar. Moreover, the U.S. dollar is widely used as vehicle currency (that is, for the denomination and settlement of trade between countries without involving the United States). Additionally, primary commodities are traditionally invoiced in either dollars or the pound sterling.

Hence, U.S. traders enjoy a considerable advantage by being able to invoice mostly in their domestic currency, and hence to forgo exchange rate risk. Similarly, in the framework of the EMS, an increasing share of intra-Union trade has been invoiced in German marks, the share evidently being largest for trade that involves Germany. Generally, the share of imports invoiced in a country's domestic currency exceeds the respective share in exports. This is largely due to the fact that imports contain an automatic "hedge" against exchange rate risk, since domestic prices of imports are adaptable, but such a hedge does not exist for exports. As a general rule, the more stable a national currency and the lower its inflation rate, the more attractive is its use for international trade invoicing. Additionally, the larger the total volume of trade invoiced and settled in a specific currency, the lower the effects of single actions on its overall value. (In addition, effects of economies of scale in the use of the currency are likely to materialize.)

With respect to currency-invoicing patterns, recent developments involving the German mark may indicate possible future trends for the euro. During the 1980s, little change occurred in German export invoicing with respect to the relative shares of the deutsche mark, the dollar, pound sterling, or other currencies (with the exception of a slight increase in the role of the yen). By contrast, with respect to German imports, the dollar's share decreased from 32.3 percent in 1980 to 22.0 percent in 1987, whereas the share of the deutsche mark increased from 43.0 to 52.7 percent during the same years, paralleled by a moderate increase in the share of the yen and a decrease in the share of the pound sterling.[28]

In this period, the deutsche mark was backed by relatively lower inflation rates compared with its EMS partners (Table 9.1). It is likely that its relative price stability as compared to other currencies was crucial for its increasing share in currency invoicing. In order to accept German imports denominated in German marks, traders needed to "trust" its stability (as similarly holds with respect to private international investment). In the early stages of EMU, it is to be expected that more EMU imports will be denominated in euro than will be exports. Table 9.7 provides an international comparison of invoicing currencies, using data from a period of stability within the EMS, prior to German reunification and the 1992–1993 currency turmoil.

As Table 9.7 illustrates, in 1988 as compared to 1980—that is, just after the establishment of the EMS—invoicing in German marks remained relatively stable for German exports. By contrast, the share of deutsche mark invoicing for German imports rose considerably, from 43 to 52.6 percent between 1980 and 1981. This phenomenon can also be seen for the French franc, which experienced a moderate decline in its share of exports invoiced in the domestic currency, but a relatively sharp increase in its share of imports, from 33.1 to 48.9 percent. The same trend holds for Italy. In contrast, the share of UK exports invoiced in pounds sterling declined considerably during the 1980s, from 76 percent of its exports in 1980 to 57 percent in 1988. However, the share of imports denominated in pounds sterling remained relatively stable. The United States experienced little effect in the period analyzed, in terms of either exports or imports denominated in U.S. dollars. Expanded use of the yen in both export and import invoicing, on the other hand, has been of increasing significance to Japan, primarily reflecting the yen's increasing share of Asian trade invoicing.

In the framework of the EMS, trade invoicing rested on the reputations of the domestic currencies in terms of stability and inflation. However, the EMS may have contributed to the use of these currencies—for instance the French franc—by allowing them to "borrow credibility" from the German Bundesbank and by providing a framework for a relatively high degree of exchange rate stability, thus reducing traders' exchange rate risk. With the establishment of the euro, the "domestic" size of the economy backing the currency will be considerable. Hence, the share of invoicing in euro may be at least as large as the sum of the shares of domestic currencies as indicated above. The large share of EU trade in global commerce supports the use of the euro in future trade invoicing. Since the relative shares of trade from most EU neighbors—including Central and Eastern Europe, the members of the European Free Trade Association (EFTA), and northern Africa—are highest with the EU, the incentive to use the euro for trade denomination is further enhanced.

It is likely that an actual "euro zone" will be created.[29] Members not belonging to the EMU (either EU members or third countries) may have strong incentives to peg the value of their domestic currencies to the euro. For example, in the framework of EMS—at least until the 1992–1993 currency turmoil—the Nordic countries pegged their domestic currencies to

Table 9.7   Currency Denomination of Trade Invoicing, 1980 and 1988

	France	Germany	Italy	Japan	United Kingdom	United States
1980						
Exports						
Domestic Currency	62.5	82.3	36.0	29.4	76.0	97.0
Other	37.5	17.7	74.0	70.6	24.0	3.0
Imports						
Domestic Currency	33.1	43.0	18.0	2.4	38.0	85.0
Other	66.9	57.0	82.0	97.6	62.0	15.0
1988						
Exports						
Domestic Currency	58.5	81.5	38.0	34.3	57.0	96.0
Other	41.5	18.5	62.0	65.7	43.0	4.0
Imports						
Domestic Currency	48.9	52.6	27.0	13.3	40.0	85.0
Other	51.1	47.4	73.0	86.7	60.0	15.0

Source: Modified from Tavlas and Ozeki, *Internationalization of Currencies,* 1992, 32.
Compare Peters 1996.

the ECU. Similarly, Switzerland has de facto pegged its currency to the deutsche mark. In the short to medium term, a peg to the euro may be all the more attractive for large regions in Central and Eastern Europe because of their officially declared goal of EU membership. Pegging to the euro may also be attractive for a large part of the former Soviet Union and even for the Middle East. The non-EMU EU members will be induced, because of their strong trade links within the Union, to denominate an increasing share of their trade in euros, particularly since denomination in German marks or, for example, in French francs, will no longer be possible. Hence, in regions strongly involved in trade with the EU, the U.S. dollar may partially be replaced by the euro for trade invoicing and payments.

In contrast, it appears rather unlikely that the euro will be used in either the Asian region—where the yen is increasingly taking on the role of a regional *numéraire*—or regions geographically close to the United States, such as Latin America. Similarly, although the United States is the EU's largest trade partner, U.S. traders are not likely to denominate their exports in euros. On the other hand, an increasing share of invoicing in euros may be expected for U.S. imports, especially regarding exports from EMU member states.

Weaker international currencies generally peg to either a single strong currency or to a basket. In recent decades a trend has emerged for several developing countries to shift from pegging from one currency to a currency basket, in order to reduce exchange rate risk. The attractiveness of pegging to the euro will increase for these regions in proportion as their relative trade share with the EU, as well as price stability within the EMU, increases.

Settlement of Financial Obligations and Intervention in Foreign Exchange Markets

A second major role that the euro may play is as a means of payment. In this function it can, for instance, be used to settle international trade debts and to discharge international financial obligations. Considerations brought to bear on the euro as a unit of account are largely valid for its potential in discharging private international financial obligations as well. In its official use, the euro can serve as an instrument for balance-of-payments financing and as an intervention device in foreign exchange markets. This section principally looks at developments of European currencies for intervention purposes in foreign exchange markets.

Whereas the Bretton Woods system was largely dominated by the dollar as a means of payment, and the earlier "gold standard" period (spanning from about 1870 to 1914) by the pound sterling, the present international monetary system has increasingly obtained the character of a multicurrency system. This trend can be seen, for instance, with respect to interventions in the framework of the EMS and in the activity of the U.S. Federal Reserve in international foreign exchange markets. Table 9.8 provides an overview of the currency distribution (given as percentages) used for intervention in the EMS during the 1980s.

Table 9.8 demonstrates that intervention in the EMS occurred increasingly in EMS currencies, with a strongly increasing share of deutsche marks, at the expense of the U.S. dollar. However, for the U.S. Federal Reserve and the U.S. Treasury, the deutsche mark lost ground in this period with respect to the yen as an intervention currency. This trend is illustrated in Table 9.9.

Table 9.8 Currency Distribution of EMS Intervention (as a percentage of total)

	1979–1982	1983–1985	1986–1989
U.S. dollars	71.5	53.7	26.3
EMS currencies	27.2	43.5	71.7
(deutsche marks)	(23.7)	(39.4)	(59.0)
Others	1.3	2.8	2.0

Source: Modified from Tavlas 1993, 573.

Whereas the role of the deutsche mark as an official means of payment and intervention currency for the EMS has strongly increased, it has been used less by the United States to affect the value of the dollar. Moreover, the currency turmoil in the EMS of 1992–1993 has further enhanced the attractiveness of the deutsche mark (and the Dutch guilder) for intervention purposes in the framework of the EMS at the expense of other ERM currencies. If the euro is strong and based on a large EMU "domestic region," it may become increasingly attractive to the United States for intervention purposes and may be used more than is the deutsche mark at present.

What other indicators exist with respect to the use of currencies as a means of payment? The turnover of currencies on foreign exchange markets provides an indication of the use of national currencies to settle international financial obligations. Table 9.10 illustrates the turnover of currencies in relation to the U.S. dollar as well as the respective development of the deutsche mark, the French franc, and the pound sterling, during the existence of the "stable" EMS.

As Table 9.10 illustrates, the share of the deutsche mark in total turnover was relatively stable for the period examined. In contrast, the

Table 9.9 U.S. Federal Reserve and Treasury Intervention

Currency	1979–1982	1983–1985	1986–1989
Deutsche marks	89.7	67.9	57.5
Yen	10.3	32.1	42.5

Source: Modified from Tavlas 1993, 573 (based on data from the Federal Reserve Bank of New York and the Deutsche Bundesbank).

Table 9.10 Currency Composition of Turnover on the New York Foreign Exchange Market (percentage of total, 1980 and 1989)

Currency (against U.S. dollar)	1980	1989
Deutsche mark	31.8	32.9
French franc	6.9	3.2
Pound sterling	22.7	14.6
Swiss franc	10.1	11.8
Japanese yen	10.2	25.2
Canadian dollar	12.2	4.0
Others	6.1	8.3
Total	100.0	100.0

Source: Modified from Tavlas 1993, 575.

French franc and the pound sterling declined considerably in their share of turnover in exchange with the U.S. dollar. Similarly, the volume of the Canadian dollar as exchanged against the U.S. dollar decreased significantly. Turnover, however, was larger with respect to the Japanese yen (partially explaining the increased use of the yen by the U.S. Treasury to intervene in foreign exchange markets). Again, provided the euro will be strong and stable, it is likely to be utilized in foreign exchange markets and more generally as a means of payment.

The Role of the Euro as a Store of Value in Global Monetary Relations

The international use of a currency is also determined by its function as a store of value. On the one hand, individuals can use a currency for (private) purposes of borrowing and investment. Official actors, by contrast, predominantly hold (foreign) currencies as reserve assets. In terms of its private use, the ECU has been rather attractive for investors: because of the nature of the ECU as a basket currency, ECU international bonds constitute a diversified portfolio with "automatically" reduced exchange rate risk. This character of the ECU has led to a considerable increase in the issue of international ECU-denominated bonds. Between 1986 and 1991, the increase in total volume was from US$6.3 billion to US$32.6 billion. In 1991, in fact, ECU international bond issues were a close second to U.S. dollar issues.[30]

The significance of ECU bonds was greatly affected, however, by the 1992–1993 EMS currency turmoil. As measured in billion ECU, whereas by 1991 the total of ECU bond issues had risen to 27.2, it subsequently dropped to 19.2 (1992), 6.9 (1993), 5.5 (1994), and 5.6 (1995).[31] Hence, instability within the EMS significantly affected the trust of international investors in the ECU. A similar effect can be assumed in regard to the potential role of the euro in international (private) investment, providing a considerable incentive for the EMU to maintain monetary and price level stability.

With respect to developing countries, recent data for the Asian region indicate an increasing share for the yen in the denomination of governments' external debts. The euro may likewise be used in the future to denominate the official debt of developing countries in geographical regions closer to Europe or where trade and foreign aid ties with Europe have historically been strong.

Moreover, if the euro takes over from the deutsche mark as the EU's "hard currency," interest rates on ECU bonds may fall to the German level, causing capital gains for their holders.[32] This will increase the attractiveness of international borrowing in euros. If the euro is used more widely as a reserve currency, it may not be as easy as it has been for the United States to sell treasury bonds, which are now held internationally by central banks as reserve assets.

Table 9.11 illustrates the share of national currencies in total identified official holdings of foreign exchange in an international overview. As the table illustrates, the total share of currencies in official foreign exchange holdings between 1983 and 1992 reflected a relative decline in the importance of the dollar (from 71.1 percent to 64.4 percent). Nonetheless, the share of the U.S. dollar in total holdings is still clearly dominant internationally. The data show a considerable increase in the share of the deutsche mark during this period, with a tendency to decrease, however, following German reunification. The yen also gained overall in importance, from a share of 4.9 percent of total holdings in 1983 to 8.1 percent in 1992. The shares of the pound sterling and the smaller European currencies, in contrast, remained relatively stable in the course of the 1980s, with individual shares under 4 percent for each currency. The sum of the shares of major European currencies, Table 9.11 illustrates, tended to increase rather than decrease through the mid to late 1980s.

The establishment of the euro will abolish holdings by international central banks in national European currencies (with the likely exception of the pound sterling). Similarly, for the EU members participating in the EMU, official foreign reserves will be pooled and managed by the ESCB (in accordance with Article 105.2 TEU).

Generally, official holdings show a slightly higher share for the U.S. dollar in industrialized countries (as well as for the pound sterling and certain "unspecified" currencies) as compared to the nonindustrialized world. The decline in the relative importance of the dollar, however, appears to be more pronounced within industrialized countries; its share remains rather constant in developing countries. This trend suggests that the euro may rival the U.S. dollar principally in the official reserves held by actors in the industrialized world. When additional members of this group join EMU, moreover, the decline of the dollar relative to other currencies will be reinforced in the developed countries.

Additionally, the above figures on the composition of official reserves indicate that a global multicurrency system is already in existence. The end of a clearly hegemonic structure—in terms of the use of certain currencies as official reserve assets—appears not to have significantly reduced international monetary stability. The gradual decrease in the use of the U.S. dollar, however, with respect to central banks' official reserves, may cause more dollars to flow back to the United States in the medium term, possibly paralleling increasing domestic inflationary pressure.[33] In contrast, under the hegemonic global monetary system, the United States was largely shielded from inflationary effects by increases in its money supply.

Table 9.11 Share of National Currencies in Total Identified Official Holdings of Foreign Exchange (end of year, percentage, all countries)

	1983	1984	1985	1986	1987	1988	1989	1990	1991	1992
U.S. dollar	71.1	69.9	64.8	67.0	67.8	64.6	60.2	57.5	58.4	64.4
Deutsche mark	11.7	12.6	15.1	14.6	14.4	15.6	19.0	18.6	16.5	13.0
Pound sterling	2.5	2.9	3.0	2.5	2.4	2.7	2.7	3.4	3.6	3.2
Japanese yen	4.9	5.8	8.0	7.8	7.5	7.7	7.7	8.8	9.4	8.1
Swiss franc	2.3	2.0	2.3	2.0	1.9	1.9	1.5	1.4	1.4	1.3
French franc	0.8	0.8	0.9	0.8	0.8	1.0	1.4	2.3	2.8	2.5
Dutch guilder	0.8	0.7	1.0	1.1	1.2	1.1	1.1	1.1	1.1	0.7
Unspecified	6.0	5.4	4.9	4.1	3.9	5.4	6.5	6.9	6.9	6.8
Total	100.1	100.1	100.0	99.9	99.9	100.0	100.1	100.0	100.1	100.0
Sum of deutsche mark, pound sterling, French franc, and Dutch guilder	15.8	17.0	20.0	19.0	18.8	20.4	24.2	25.4	24.0	19.4

Source: International Monetary Fund, Annual Report; author's calculations.

When the euro is more extensively used internationally, exchange rate risk will be eliminated for all intra-EMU trade (and most likely for the largest part of intra-EU trade, since trade will by and large be denominated in euros for the EU's non-EMU members as well). Furthermore, as use of the euro by non-EU countries increases, privileges for traders based in the EMU will likewise increase. Should the EMU be able to issue a kind of treasury bond, a further advantage will accrue to it in terms of an inexpensive way to obtain international financing.

The larger the volume of trade invoiced in euros, the larger the pressure from non-EMU traders and investors to either peg their national currency to the euro or enter EMU. If the euro suffers instability, however—as a result of high inflation, for example—a larger role might be assumed by European currencies such as the pound sterling or the Swiss franc. On the other hand, if the euro proves to be stable and strong, the currencies of these countries will probably decline in importance in both international payments and investment. Given the institutional factors within the EMU that favor price stability, the latter outcome seems most likely.

Conclusions

A full-blown failure of the EMU currently appears to be a rather unrealistic scenario, since the monetary and fiscal performance of EU states according to the convergence criteria indicates that quite a few EU members may qualify for EMU membership. Nonetheless, in the medium term, the EMU and the EU will probably not be congruent. For instance, the United Kingdom and Denmark may choose to stay out of the arrangement, and other member states may not qualify for the EMU "core group" because of failure to comply with specific convergence criteria (especially those in the fiscal domain).

Asymmetry of influence within the EU is one factor motivating some actors to move toward the EMU. A common currency for EU members appears to be desirable and even necessary, furthermore, because of the EU members' relatively large share in global trade relations, as contrasted with their more modest role in international financial affairs. The strong position of EU members in global commercial relations indicates that once the euro is established, its potential for use in international trade invoicing and global payments is rather significant.

Institutionally, the primary objective of the ECB and the ESCB is price stability. Low inflation is thus likely to be realized in the EMU framework, constituting another factor that could enhance the attractiveness of the euro for international use. The disadvantage of this factor is that it might possibly be detrimental to the EMU's flexibility with respect to external exchange rate policies. The TEU is somewhat ambiguous with respect to who carries responsibility for the EMU's exchange rate policy. Formal exchange rate agreements to be concluded by the EMU will require unanimity of EMU members in the ECOFIN Council. This hurdle will be difficult, especially in view of a future enlargement of both the EMU and the EU. Therefore, in addition to the ECB's priority of price level stability, institutional decisionmaking requirements may also contribute to an increasing reluctance—or inability—of the EMU to conclude formal international exchange rate agreements. The unanimity requirement could provide an additional reason for the EMU to focus on price level stability rather than international exchange rate coordination. In the present state of international monetary affairs, however, such formal agreements constitute relatively unlikely events anyway.

Currently, the EU is not a significant actor in global monetary relations. However, the role of some individual members in international monetary and financial affairs is strong for purposes of investment, trade invoicing, and intervention in foreign exchange markets. In particular, the German Bundesbank plays a major role in international monetary affairs, largely because of the high credibility of its low-inflation policies, strengthened by the full political independence of the Bundesbank from political pressures. The use of other ERM currencies in international markets is partially strengthened by their "borrowed credibility" from the Bundesbank. The euro, based on an EMU in which institutional structures guarantee a policy of price level stability, can significantly enhance the potential of the common European currency to be used in international finance.

Inflation presently tends to be lower than in earlier decades for several international actors (including, for instance, the United States and Japan). Low inflation rates, therefore, are not likely in and of themselves significantly to popularize a currency's international use. Additional factors that enhance this capacity are large and open financial markets, a strong role in international trade, and domestic political stability. On the whole, these factors appear to be realized in the framework of the present EU and hence to strengthen the euro's potential in global monetary affairs.

Notes

This chapter has profited from valuable comments by Carolyn Rhodes and several participants of the workshop on "The European Union as an International Actor" in Jackson Hole, Wyoming, April 1996. Helpful comments were also given by Hans Labohm.

1. Compare Henning 1996.

2. Note that the ECU, then termed the European Unit of Account (EUA)—also a basket of the EC members' currencies—was already used in the 1970s in the framework of the European Development Fund, the European Investment Bank, and as a unit of account for calculating the Community's budget.

3. Compare Hallwood and MacDonald 1994, 315.

4. An easy way to see this is to calculate the percentage shares in the ECU basket on the basis of the ratio of the central rate to the amount in the basket: the central rate of the German mark to the ECU, for instance, is 1.91 as at present. To calculate the percentage share in the ECU basket, divide the fixed share of the deutsche mark in the basket (0.6242) by the central rate (1.91) to obtain the percentage share in the ECU basket (32.68 percent) (0.5242/1.91 = 0.3268). When the German mark appreciates vis-à-vis the ECU, the central rate between the mark and the ECU decreases (that is, more ECUs are obtained for a mark). Hence, the denominator decreases, leading to an increase in the percentage share of the mark in the currency basket.

5. Article 109(G) of the Maastricht Treaty reads: "The currency composition of the ECU basket shall not be changed."

6. The empirical analysis of beneficial impacts mainly goes back to the quantitative assessments of the "Cecchini Report," Cecchini 1988.

7. Committee for the Study of Economic and Monetary Union, 1989.

8. Commission of the European Communities, 1989.

9. Compare Sandholtz 1993.

10. The figure is calculated by taking the inflation performance of the three "best performers" in 1991—Denmark, France, and Ireland—summing their rates (2.7 + 3.0 + 3.0), dividing by 3, and adding 1.5 percent to this (nonweighted) average.

11. Compare Qvigstad 1992.

12. Compare Article 109(J): "The observance of the normal fluctuation margins provided for by the exchange-rate mechanism of the European Monetary System, for at least two years, without devaluing against the currency of any other Member State."

13. For exact figures on these variables, see Qvigstad 1992.

14. Recall that presently, the voting weights of the EU members are distributed as follows: Germany (10), France (10), Italy (10), United Kingdom (10), Spain (8), Belgium (5), Greece (5), Netherlands (5), Portugal (5), Austria (4), Sweden (4), Denmark (3), Finland (3), Ireland (3), and Luxembourg (2). The qualified majority is 62 out of the vote total (87). Institutional revision and EU enlargement may cause adaptation of the voting weights.

15. In the short term, a separate market for the pound sterling might persist, although it is likely to be gradually substituted by the euro in international finance if the euro is a strong currency.

16. Compare Dyson and Featherstone 1996.

17. McKinnon 1993.

18. Treaty on European Union 1992.

19. Compare Garrett 1994.

20. Moreover, another serious inflationary potential will be eliminated, since national central banks will no longer be allowed to finance deficits (according to the "no bail-out clause" as another precondition for EMU membership). Hence, monetary financing of budget deficits will be prohibited.

21. Garrett 1994.

22. In more detail, the procedure also involves other institutions. The first part of Article 109.1 reads as follows: "By way of derogation from Article 228, the Council may, acting unanimously on a recommendation from the ECB or from the Commission, and after consulting the ECB in an endeavour to reach a consensus consistent with the objective of price stability, after consulting the European Parliament, in accordance with the procedure in paragraph 3 for determining the

arrangements, conclude formal agreements on an exchange-rate system for the ECU in relation to non-Community currencies." (The "ECU" is now replaced by the name "euro.")

23. Compare Henning 1994; Kahler 1995.

24. Formal exchange rate agreements between the currencies of EU members inside and outside EMU gain in importance the larger the number and economic weight of EU states that formally remain outside the EMU.

25. Compare also Frenkel and Goldstein 1993.

26. Measured as the shift from a low-cost external source to a higher-cost partner source, resulting from the creation of the customs union, i.e., the abolition of tariffs on intra-Community trade and their substitution by a common external tariff. For such studies, compare Balassa 1967 and Viner 1950.

27. See Cameron Chapter 2 of this volume.

28. See Tavlas 1993.

29. Compare Kenen 1992.

30. Hallwood and MacDonald 1994, 315–316.

31. Figures based on *Eurostat*.

32. Hallwood and MacDonald 1994, 316.

33. Peters 1996.

10

Divided but United: European Trade Policy Integration and EU-U.S. Agricultural Negotiations in the Uruguay Round

Sophie Meunier

In international trade negotiations the European Union* speaks with one voice. Yet, this obligation to present a common front internationally is in constant tension with the need to take into account internal divergences among member states. This chapter analyzes the bargaining constraints and opportunities for the EU created by the requirement to negotiate as a single entity. It argues that the internal decisionmaking structure of the EU affects the process and outcome of its negotiations with third countries. The voting rules at the EU level and the amount of autonomy exercised by EU negotiators are central to determining (1) whether the final international agreement reflects the position of the median or of the most extreme member state; and (2) how the institutional structure of the EU influences its effectiveness as an international actor.

These factors are developed in the case study of the EU-U.S. negotiations on agricultural trade liberalization in the Uruguay Round of the General Agreement on Tariffs and Trade (GATT). This particular case provides a good illustration of the impact of the EU institutional structure on its external bargaining capabilities, because the EU's international negotiating efforts took place during a series of formal and informal institutional changes in the Union that affected the ways in which decisions were made.

The following discussion is divided into three parts. The first section traces the evolution of shared competencies on trade issues between the member states and the Commission and explores the impact of the EU

---

*While the activities discussed in this chapter reflect "first pillar" responsibilities under the Treaty on European Union, and therefore technically refer to European Community responsibilities, the decision was made to utilize the term "European Union" except for references to historical circumstances that predate the Maastricht Treaty's ratification.

institutional structure on its external bargaining capabilities. The second section reviews the "Blair House agreement" in 1992—which was reached after years of unsuccessful negotiations between the EU and the United States—as well as its subsequent renegotiation and the effect that this renegotiation had on the final arrangement. The conclusion examines the institutional changes in EU trade policymaking brought about by the experience of the Uruguay Round and suggests how these changes might affect EU bargaining capabilities in the future.

Divided but United: Impact of EC Institutional Structure on International Negotiations

Negotiating mandates for international trade negotiations are elaborated successively by the Commission and the Council. During the Uruguay Round, EU bargaining proposals were first developed by the external affairs (DG I) and agriculture (DG VI) directorates of the Commission. They were then examined by the "113 Committee,"[1] composed of senior civil servants from the member states, including representatives from the ministries of agriculture and trade. Once approved by the 113 Committee on a consensual basis, proposals were transmitted to the Committee of Permanent Representatives (COREPER) and subsequently to the General Affairs Council. Formally, the Council decides on the negotiating mandate under qualified majority, according to Article 113. In practice, however, the aggregation of the divergent interests of the member states into one single bargaining position still follows unanimity. Decisions are not adopted if a country, especially one of the three major countries, firmly opposes it. The actual conduct of the negotiations is carried out by members of the Commission. In principle, as long as they remain within the directives set by the Council, Commission negotiators are free to bargain and conclude agreements with third countries as they wish. In the end, the Council approves or rejects the trade agreement.

Member states tie their trade policy fate to their EU partners and transfer bargaining power to the supranational Commission in the hope of deriving some external negotiating benefits from combined action. Yet the institutional structure of the EU, which often necessitates consensus to aggregate the divergent interests of the member states into a coherent whole, is traditionally assumed to handicap the EU in international negotiations.[2] The internal EU divisions and the political process through which they are mediated are visible to the EU's negotiating opponents, which can sometimes use them to their advantage. This section explores the impact of the EU institutional structure on its external bargaining capabilities and presents the various negotiating outcomes that can result from the Union's character as "divided but united."

EU Institutional Structure: Bargaining Handicap or Advantage?

"Let's unite. And the world will listen to us" was an ad campaign used to mobilize the pro-European camp in France during the 1992 referendum on the Maastricht Treaty on European Union. This slogan referred as much to foreign policy as it did to trade policy, recalling the traditional assumption that integration would enable the European Community to talk on an equal footing with the United States. The rationale is that unity brings strength, and therefore that European integration and Europe's external bargaining capabilities are positively correlated. In other words, the stronger the EU is internally, the stronger the EU gets externally.[3]

Proponents of the view that internal unity brings external strength suggest that the cumbersome EU institutional structure facilitates the achievement of gains by a negotiating opponent. Their solutions for fixing these institutional handicaps involve further devolution of authority to the supranational Commission. Hugo Paemen, who was chief EU negotiator during the Uruguay Round, identified three "fundamental institutional flaws" of the EU in his own account of the negotiations.[4] First, EU decisionmaking procedures tend to produce a bargaining position that is the lowest common denominator of all member states' positions. This prevents the Union from making innovative proposals and therefore from having a lot to offer to its negotiating opponent in order to extract concessions of a similar nature.

Second, the institutional design of the EU deprives Union negotiators of one crucial bargaining element: uncertainty. The Union cannot hide its bottom line, first, because each member state reveals its position during Council meetings and, second, because member states must agree on a negotiating mandate setting the limits within which Commission negotiators are allowed to proceed. According to Paemen, exposure of its "hand" is a major handicap that seriously impairs the European Union's negotiating capability.[5]

Finally, the Union is ill-equipped to act swiftly in the final hours of a negotiation, when agreements are always hammered out. The limited size of the EU negotiating staff, combined with the necessity to shuttle proposals back and forth between the Commission negotiators and the member states, makes it extremely difficult for the Union to negotiate effectively with a deadline pending.

Despite these drawbacks, however, there are bargaining advantages that do accrue from the need to achieve member state consensus. Under the right conditions, the EU can use its "institutional flaws" strategically in order to gain concessions from its negotiating opponent. As Thomas Schelling suggested in *The Strategy of Conflict*, having one's hands tied internally can be useful for extracting concessions externally and the power to bind oneself, for instance through divisions highly visible to the opposite party, can confer strength in negotiations.

> The well-known principle that one should pick good negotiators to represent him and then give them complete flexibility and authority—a principle commonly voiced by negotiators themselves—is by no means as self-evident as its proponents suggest; *the power of a negotiator often rests on a manifest inability to make concessions and to meet demands.* Similarly, while prudence suggests leaving open a way of escape when one threatens an adversary with mutually painful reprisal, any visible means of escape may make the threat less credible.[6]

Thus, as Schelling's analysis suggests, the EU can make strategic use of internal divisions over the negotiating mandate and of the ratification requirement of the external agreement in international negotiations. The case study that follows demonstrates that when the Union is put in a "defensive" position, in which the negotiating opponent demands change in EU policy, the voting rules at the EU level and the amount of autonomy exercised by EU negotiators determine whether or not the EU gains external bargaining effectiveness from its internal divisions, and whether or not the final international agreement reflects the position of the median or deviant member states.

Voting rules. If each country possesses the power of veto, the terms of the final agreement are dictated by the most reluctant country. The practice of unanimity means that the negotiating position adopted is the lowest common denominator. In this case, it takes only one deviant country to block progress in the negotiations, and consensus can only occur around that country's position. The threat of having one outlying country eventually overturn an international agreement makes the other member states prefer to settle on this country's position, rather than being left with no agreement at all. Once the Union has adopted this position as its own, the institutional impossibility to alter it—also known to the negotiating opponent—*makes the EU a very tough bargainer since it cannot deviate from its offer.* Therefore, the negotiating opponent has to make concessions acceptable to the most recalcitrant state. In that sense, unanimity reinforces the bargaining strength of the EU. In contrast, if majority rule is implemented, the terms of the final agreement satisfy the median rather than the deviant countries. The EU cannot use its institutional features (or "handicaps") as bargaining leverage. Under majority rule internal divisions are more conducive to gains for the negotiating opponent, as it can use a "divide and rule" strategy or reward some member states for their positions.

Commission autonomy. The Commission's negotiating autonomy can be limited by the requirement constantly to report to the member states and to await further negotiating instructions. In this case, negotiators have very little room for maneuver, which enhances the proposal's credibility as a "take it or leave it" offer, prompting the negotiating opponent to make concessions for fear of being left with no agreement at all. In practice, however, in a number of cases the Commission can seize more negotiating autonomy. Indeed, the authority of the Commission emerges in the context of a day-to-day struggle, where Commission representatives attempt the delicate balance of exercising as much autonomy as possible without provoking a backlash from the member states worried about their own sovereignty. In these instances EU negotiators work within the limits set by the negotiating mandate agreed to by the Council of Ministers but are left free to conduct the bargaining as they wish until the final agreement is submitted to the member states for approval. Negotiations proceed faster and are more likely to lead to a final agreement, but—since it is less plausible that a member state will veto the whole agreement rather than several individual elements of the agreement—the partial removal of the internal constraint deprives EU negotiators of some key leverage over their opponents.

In practice, Commission autonomy and voting rules are most often positively correlated. Commission negotiators have more autonomy when integration is deep and decisions are made according to the majority rule. When unanimity is used, the member state holding the extreme position tends to keep a tight leash on the Commission to ensure that the negotiating mandate is respected.

EU Negotiating Capabilities in Practice

In practice, the EU has successfully reached many international trade agreements on nonconflictual issues when its bargaining position easily converged with that of its negotiating opponent or when trade-offs between sectors were possible, such as the successive reductions of industrial tariffs since the 1960s and the agreement on services during the Uruguay Round. There have been a few conflictual cases in which the EU went on the offensive and tried to pry open the U.S. or Japanese markets, for example, through the reciprocity demands of the original Second Banking Directive in 1988 or the third-country provisions of the Utilities Directive on public procurement in 1990.[7] Except for these few often unsuccessful market-opening efforts, however, the vast majority of conflictual trade negotiations in which the EU has participated involved preserving the status quo while deciding on a unanimous basis. Agriculture has provided the bulk of EU-U.S. trade disputes, although issues such as broadcasting and civil aircraft have also been much publicized.

The EU-U.S. agricultural negotiations in the Uruguay Round provide a particularly good illustration of the external consequences of the EU's institutional structure in a "defensive" situation. These negotiations were representative of EU behavior in most conflictual trade negotiations, with the defensive attitude combined with the "extremism" of one stubborn member state. As in the EU-U.S. agricultural negotiations in the Kennedy and Tokyo Rounds of GATT, the position of a reluctant EU crystallized around French demands for preserving the status quo in agriculture. At the same time, the Uruguay Round agricultural negotiations provide some unusual contrasts—for example, between the apex of Commission autonomy versus the subsequent reining in of Commission negotiators, or between the institutional confusion following the Single European Act versus the subsequent reinstatement of veto power.

Of course many factors influenced the EU-U.S. agricultural negotiations in the Uruguay Round, including domestic politics and interest group pressure, trade-offs between sectors, and side payments. The following case study shows, however, that the EU's institutional structure also influenced the Uruguay Round negotiations, because it determined in part the bargaining position of the EU. The evolution of the autonomy exercised by EU negotiators and the practice of unanimity voting contributed first to the conclusion of the EU-U.S. agricultural agreement and later to its exceptional renegotiation.

EU-U.S. Agricultural Negotiations in the Uruguay Round

The initial impetus for the Uruguay Round came from the United States, which wanted to bring trade in services within the multilateral system, strengthen GATT rules and disciplines, and once and for all tackle agricultural liberalization. Agricultural trade disputes between the United States and the EC had intensified in the early 1980s, with each side retaliating by imposing costly protectionist measures.

The EC initially rejected the concept of a new round including agricultural talks because of its potentially highly divisive nature within the Community. The ten, and then twelve, EU countries had extremely divergent interests with respect to agriculture. Great Britain and the Netherlands, both net financial contributors to the Common Agricultural Policy (CAP), hoped that the multilateral negotiations would provide an "external push" enabling the EC to slow the increasing costs of the CAP. Other member states, above all France, but also to some extent Belgium, Ireland, Italy, and Germany, wanted to keep a high degree of agricultural protection in Europe. As Europe's first and the world's second agricultural exporter, France was particularly adamant about maintaining the current system of export subsidies and protected market access for agricultural products, especially given the importance of the rural vote in French domestic politics.[8] The breakthrough enabling the EC finally to accept the launching of a new round of multilateral trade negotiations occurred when France, a major services provider, agreed in March 1985 to discuss agriculture in exchange for the inclusion in GATT talks of its most important concerns, such as liberalization of investment and services, the issue of exchange rate fluctuations, and the "rebalancing" of former privileges.[9]

Negotiating Stalemates

The United States was first to officially put its negotiating proposal before the GATT group dealing with agriculture in July 1987. It called for complete elimination of all domestic subsidies in agriculture by the year 2000—a negotiating position called the "zero option" by analogy to ongoing arms control negotiations.[10] It also demanded a phase-out over ten years of quantities exported with the aid of export subsidies and a phase-out of all import barriers over ten years.[11] The EC was taken aback by the extreme nature of the U.S. negotiating proposal and did not submit its own proposal until late October, reiterating its initial plea for short-term measures, non-negotiability of the CAP, and reduction of all forms of support. A divided Community was ready to make some concessions on the issue of domestic support, but was unable to offer anything on either market access or export subsidies.

The wide gap separating the U.S. and EC positions and the inability of the EC to offer concessions going beyond its lowest common denominator led to a series of negotiating stalemates, which almost terminated the Uruguay Round altogether. It seemed that EC negotiators "evidently assumed that, as in past GATT rounds, agriculture would be taken off the table before the end of the negotiations."[12] The Commission, however, was resolved to cut agricultural support, which was costing up to 60 percent of the total EC budget. The Agriculture Council rejected the Commission's agriculture proposal in September 1990 for going too far. Most member states vigorously defended their farmers' interests in Brussels, especially Germany, which was in the midst of reunification. In November, the Council adopted a much watered-down text, which proposed a 30 percent cut in domestic support over five years, to be calculated from 1986, as well as a correcting mechanism to take into account currency fluctuations and improved conditions for export competition.

The EC representatives' lack of negotiating autonomy prevented a successful conclusion of the Brussels ministerial meeting of December 1990, originally intended to close the Uruguay Round. After an initial crisis triggered by a U.S. ultimatum, Renato Ruggiero, the Italian trade minister and president of the Council, asked the Commission to continue the negotiation while exercising "a degree of flexibility in keeping with the spirit of its mandate."[13] The United States and other countries agreed to a compromise by Mats Hellstrøm, Swedish agriculture minister, which proposed import restrictions, a reduction of 30 percent in export subsidies, and domestic supports from 1990 levels to be implemented over five years. In the end the Hellstrøm proposal proved to be beyond the Commission's negotiating mandate. The Brussels meeting consequently collapsed, and participants criticized the crucial lack of flexibility of EC negotiators.

Negotiations made no progress until December 1991, when Arthur Dunkel, the director general of GATT, drafted a proposal providing specific terms for reductions in export subsidies, domestic support, and import restrictions. Most countries accepted the Dunkel Draft as a basis for the final agreement on agriculture, but the EC Council rejected the text.[14] Dunkel also introduced the principle whereby no amendment to his draft would be taken into consideration unless the proposing country had held informal negotiations beforehand with the other parties and obtained their support. For the European Community, this meant that a bilateral pre-agreement on agriculture had to be concluded with the United States.

Capping the CAP

The U.S.-EC agricultural negotiations were put on hold while the EC, facing increasing isolation internationally and rising budgetary pressures, undertook an internal reform of its Common Agricultural Policy. By redefining the negotiating mandate, quieting internal divisions, and granting more flexibility to Commission negotiators, this reform enabled the bilateral negotiations to move forward and eventually result in an agreement.

On 21 May 1992, after a year of intense debate, the EC Council of Ministers adopted a revolutionary reform of the CAP designed by Agricultural Commissioner Ray MacSharry, which limited production, entailed a substantial reduction in support prices (to be compensated by aids), and a reduction in land set aside from production. Unlike the negotiations in GATT, however, the reform did not address the crucial issues of market access and export subsidies. The Commission wanted a reform in order to avoid a budgetary crisis and to diffuse internal criticism of the EC's wasteful and protectionist policies. The Commission also hoped to derive a more flexible negotiating mandate from the reform in order to successfully reach a deal with the United States. Countries reluctant to change the CAP, such as France, eventually agreed to the reform because the combination of budget constraints, Commission agenda setting, and outside pressures made such a reform inevitable.[15] France could also use the strategic advantage of locking in the CAP reform now to avoid making further concessions to the United States later.

European and U.S. officials disagreed over the meaning of the CAP reform. European policymakers argued that this reform represented the upper limit of changes that the EC could make to its agricultural policy. In contrast, the United States argued that the reform was an internal EC matter, addressing only the issue of internal support. It interpreted the reform as the basis for a future U.S.-EC agreement that would also include provisions on market access and export subsidies. Above all, the United States wanted to avoid rigidity in the European position and therefore rejected EC attempts to "lock in" a negotiating position by reaching internal agreements first—that is, having its "hands tied" by a prior internal agreement. When EC negotiators first demanded reciprocal concessions as a result of the CAP reform, Carla Hills, the United States Trade Representative (USTR), suggested instead several ways in which the reform could be expanded to deal directly with the issues in the trade talks.[16]

Internal Divisions, Commission Autonomy, and Conclusion of the Blair House Agreement

A series of intense bilateral negotiations on agriculture started in Brussels in October 1992. However, negotiations failed to produce results as France pressured the Community to make new demands and brandished its veto threat, suggesting that the Commission negotiators were going beyond their mandate as defined by the CAP reform.[17] The United States responded to the failure of the negotiations by linking the oilseeds dispute to the ongoing discussions and by menacing the EC with a full-blown trade war.[18] Carla Hills announced a retaliatory 200 percent punitive tariff on $300 million of European food imports effective December 5 if the EC did not reduce its oilseeds production from 13 to 8 million tons. By targeting not only French, but also German and Italian products for retaliation, the United States tried to capitalize on internal divisions in the EC and hoped to increase member states' pressure on France.

Negotiations resumed in Chicago on November 2 and 3 in this tense bilateral context, although the U.S. administration was particularly eager to conclude a deal that would come before the presidential election. The bilateral talks did not produce any progress but resulted in a major internal crisis in the Community. Before concluding a deal, U.S. negotiators wanted to ensure that the agreement negotiated by Commission representatives would be supported by the Council. In a surprise move, Agriculture Commissioner Ray MacSharry offered proof of the Council's likely support in the person of John Gummer, the British president of the Agriculture Council, who was secretly in Chicago to monitor the talks, thus attempting to assure Agriculture Secretary Edward Madigan that the EC would back the deal.[19] This move created a scandal in EC circles: "The Commission and the presidency were going behind the backs of their Community partners in order to stitch up the deal!"[20] That same evening, Commission President Jacques Delors told MacSharry that the agreement would be voted down in Brussels because it was too costly for the Community and exceeded the Commission's negotiating mandate. Denouncing Delors's interference and infringement on the negotiators' autonomy, MacSharry presented his resignation from the Commission on his way back to Brussels.[21]

This internal EC crisis influenced the course of subsequent EC-U.S. negotiations, even though Delors and MacSharry settled their differences a couple of days later (with MacSharry returning to his post as agriculture

Commissioner). Beyond a conflict of personalities, the crisis revealed that the EC institutional system was not functioning properly. According to a Commission official, "the Commission does not meet anymore, leaving the Commissioner in charge of the negotiation to act as he wishes. In other words, it is a mess. We have been in free wheel for two years."[22] The crisis further revealed the extent of internal divisions in the EC, not only among member states but also among and within the various EC institutions. Observers noted that this fact did not elude U.S. negotiators.[23]

Consequently, the U.S. administration reinforced its pressure on the EC through vigorous threats of retaliatory sanctions, in hopes of exploiting the EC's obvious lack of cohesiveness by forcing those member states favorable to its views simply to disregard the outliers and join together to reach a bilateral agreement. The United States attempted to obtain a favorable agreement by playing the "divide and rule" strategy.

Internal EC divisions appeared even more clearly in the following Council meetings. On November 9, EC foreign ministers denied French demands for European retaliation against U.S. trade sanctions. At the Agriculture Council of November 16, expected to adopt a common position for the GATT negotiations to resume that week, an isolated France tried to convince the other member states that the proposed agreement with the United States went far beyond the CAP reform. MacSharry did not address France's concern about compatibility between the proposed agreement and the reform and proceeded with a new round of bilateral talks.

On 18 and 19 November 1992, MacSharry and External Affairs Commissioner Frans Andriessen met with Madigan and Hills in the Blair House residence in Washington. After a series of proposals and counterproposals, MacSharry enabled a breakthrough in the negotiations by offering a reduction of 21 percent in the volume of subsidized exports. The talks later broke down when the U.S. team needed to consult internally, and the Community delegation went back to Brussels. The agreement was concluded, however, by phone the next day.

The Blair House compromise provided for a 20 percent reduction in internal price support over six years, with the years 1986–1988 as reference, but with an exemption from these cuts for U.S. deficiency payments and EC compensation payments. On the controversial issue of export competition, the compromise provided for a reduction of export subsidies in agriculture by 21 percent in volume (and not 24, as in the Dunkel Draft) and 36 percent in budget over six years, using 1986–1990 as the base period. Finally, European and American negotiators agreed to a "peace clause" that would exempt from trade actions those internal support measures and export subsidies that do not violate the terms of the agreement. A separate deal on oilseeds was also concluded, thus ending several years of EC-U.S. disputes and GATT litigation and canceling the promised U.S. trade sanctions against the EC.

The increased autonomy seized by the EC negotiators, which made the Blair House compromise possible, was apparent from the beginning of the talks. When MacSharry agreed to return to the talks as Agriculture Commissioner, newspapers reported that he was given a "free hand."[24] As Andriessen was entering the actual negotiations, he told reporters that he was flexible in his position, shouting: "The message from Brussels? Go ahead and make a deal!"[25] U.S. negotiators were also very conscious that the EC representatives had a fairly broad mandate and adequate flexibility to negotiate.[26] "Madigan, speaking with reporters as he entered the Blair House, where the talks were being held, said that the EC negotiators reportedly were coming to the talks with 'enhanced flexibility.'"[27]

The autonomy of EC representatives during the Blair House negotiations, which took place in the absence of observers from the member states, gave rise to accusations that the Commission had negotiated the agreement in secret.[28] While the Commission held a meeting on November 20 to present to members the broad characteristics of the agreement, the only specific text that the member states had in hand for a week was a two-page USTR press release. Only a week later did the Commission finally send a ten-page document to the member states, including five pages confirming the compatibility of the agreement with the CAP reform.

The Blair House agreement was interpreted at the time as a relative negotiating success for the EC. The agreement was able to occur in spite of strong opposition from France, the most recalcitrant country, because the Commission representatives exercised a particularly high degree of autonomy during the Blair House negotiations. The combination of weakened unanimity and greater Commission autonomy actually "freed the hands" of EC negotiators, thereby breaking the negotiation paralysis. The agreement reached reflected U.S. bargaining strength but served the interests of the majority of member states.

Veto, Tied Hands, and Renegotiation of the Blair House Agreement

The French government opposed the Blair House agreement as soon as it was signed on the grounds that it was not compatible with the CAP reform. Belgium, Italy, and Spain were also skeptical at first of the agreement.[29] Fueled by the fact that the Maastricht Treaty was ratified in France by a perilously narrow margin in 1992 as well as by violent domestic protests from angry farmers and by crucial national elections in March 1993, the French government embarked on a crusade to denounce the content of the agreement and contest the conditions under which it had been reached. Above all, French policymakers blamed the European-level negotiators who, they claimed, had exceeded their mandate. In private, French officials criticized the personalities of Andriessen and MacSharry, but they

also denounced the EU institutions for drifting away from intergovernmentalism and allowing the fundamental objections of a member state to
be overruled.[30] The French goal thus became to reopen the agricultural negotiations and at the same time curb the erosion of "negotiating by consensus" and the growing autonomy of the EU negotiators.

Successive French governments ardently tried to reassert the veto
right in the EU in order to reject the agreement. The possibility of a French
veto was constantly in the minds of U.S. negotiators, who were closely
following the legal arguments in the EU about the constitutionality of a
veto under the provisions of the 1986 Single European Act.[31]This threat
was reinforced by the March 1993 election of a center-right government in
France after a long campaign, in which the protection of French farmers,
the CAP reform, and the Blair House deal negotiated by "foreign" com-
missions were central issues.[32]

The official stance of the newly elected French government on Blair
House was finally unveiled on May 12 in a memorandum accepting the
oilseeds deal but vowing to fight the other parts of the agreement. France
blamed the conclusion of the Blair House agreement on institutional flaws
in the EU. French European Affairs Minister Alain Lamassoure issued a
memorandum stating that EU decisionmaking was not working properly
and the Commission's methods were unsatisfactory, resulting in "a certain
confusion of responsibilities." Citing the Blair House accord, he complained about the unclear definition of competencies in the Union and
asked governments to ensure that the Commission stick to its negotiating
mandate and that national parliaments be associated with the aims of that
mandate.[33]

The French memorandum also complained about the inadequacy of
the EU's retaliatory trade policy instruments and argued that the EU decisionmaking process, which allows a minority of states to block use of such
instruments, had to be reformed. The memorandum suggested a new commercial defense instrument that would speed up antidumping rules and
pleaded for an improvement of the efficacy of the Union's existing trade
instruments in order to match the "impressive arsenal of American unilat-
eralism."[34] The French goal was to change the institutional rules of the
game in the EU by, on one hand, making it easier for one outlying member
state to rally its reluctant Union partners to its defensive position and, on
the other hand, making it more difficult for one outlying member state to
block a trade offensive or retaliatory action against a third country.

In June, Belgium backed French demands for new trade instruments to
fight unfair trade practices by third countries and for strengthening EU
trade defense mechanisms. Ireland, Portugal, and Spain also supported the
French view, but Germany disagreed. External Affairs Commissioner Leon
Brittan argued that the Union had all the instruments it needed, notably the
"New Commercial Policy Instrument" introduced in 1984 and modeled

after the U.S. Section 301 procedure. What was required, he asserted, was the political will to use them.[35] From then on, limiting Commission autonomy, reinstating the veto right, and providing the EU with offensive trade instruments became intertwined with French demands for renegotiating the Blair House agreement.

The U.S. administration made clear that it had no intention of reopening Blair House and treated the renegotiation issue as an internal EU matter. The Commission and all member states, with the exception of France and Ireland, also opposed the renegotiation of a deal that had been legitimately agreed to by the EC representatives. "Opening up Pandora's Box," in Commissioner Steichen's words, could also prove risky, because many U.S. agricultural groups felt that the United States had granted too many concessions to the EU. Finally, renegotiating Blair House could provoke a crisis in the EU about the legitimacy of the Commission's representation, especially in the current atmosphere of mistrust of the EU created by the Maastricht debate.

France spent the next five months trying to find allies to reopen the Blair House deal. In June, Belgium offered France some welcome support by making the compatibility of the Blair House agreement with the 1992 CAP reform a priority of its upcoming presidency.[36] In July the French government formally requested a special "jumbo" meeting of EU foreign affairs, trade, and agriculture ministers to discuss the reopening of Blair House. Despite opposition from several member states, the Belgian government ultimately decided to organize the "Jumbo Council" in order to re-establish Community coherence, fearing that France would ultimately not hesitate to use its veto power if it felt isolated.[37] Belgium also hoped to improve confidence and communication between the Commission and the member states, in order to avoid a repeat of the crisis that followed the secrecy of the Blair House agreement negotiations.[38]

Germany, which initially expressed firm opposition to any reopening of the Blair House deal, played a crucial role in mediating the renegotiation crisis. In late August, Chancellor Kohl surprised everyone, above all his own government, when he announced that Germany shared some French concerns about the Blair House compromise: "Europe should affirm its personality and identity in the trade negotiations and have the means to defend its essential interests. . . . That means the Blair House agreement in its present form is unacceptable for us (and) that Europe should have trade policy instruments that make it equal to the others."[39] Kohl's concessions to France were interpreted as either a trade-off for the financial crisis of the summer or as an extraordinary gesture of Franco-German solidarity.[40]

In a second memorandum sent to the Commission and the member states on September 1, the French government stated that the summer's monetary instability had rendered the Blair House agreement incompatible with the CAP reform, and it demanded the addition of firm protection against currency fluctuations.[41] More controversially, the French memorandum also called for changes in EU internal procedures to ensure national governments closer control over the Commission during multilateral negotiations and to avoid the scarcely transparent conditions under which previous agreements, such as Blair House, were negotiated.[42]

The French government simultaneously revived its veto threat. At the same time France and Ireland engaged in heavy lobbying of their Union partners before the Jumbo Council. On September 13 the Spanish government, concerned about its own fruit, rice, sugar, and wine production, backed France in a memorandum arguing that several provisions of the Blair House accord had to be revised and calling for transparency in future negotiations. The Spanish paper said that the importance of the issues at hand made it crucial that the Council be kept informed at all times of the progress of negotiations, so as to avoid being presented with a fait accompli.[43] Greece also sent a memorandum objecting to certain provisions of Blair House on September 15.

At the same time, France also tried to bypass the Union and negotiate directly with the United States, in the hope of increasing its direct impact on the final outcome of the Uruguay Round. "We would not call this negotiations, but we believe we should speak directly with the United States either bilaterally or with the EU Commission," said a senior Balladur aide in September.[44] This strategy proved fruitless, however, as the United States had no interest in negotiating with France directly when the EU compromise position was less extreme than the French. Indeed, United States officials made clear to France that the EU Commission is the sole European negotiator; they were determined not to be sucked into a bilateral negotiation with France on revising Blair House.[45]

The Jumbo Council and the reclaiming of unanimity and control over the Commission. The exceptional Jumbo Council of September 20 eventually enabled the EU to present a common front in the multilateral negotiations, at the expense of Commission autonomy and majority decisionmaking. After an intense session, thirty-five ministers of trade, agriculture, and foreign affairs agreed on the need for "clarification," "interpretation," and "amplification" of the Blair House agreement and reaffirmed the fundamental principles of the CAP. This was a compromise solution, which achieved the objective of preventing France's isolation while not overtly jeopardizing the results of the Uruguay Round.

The Commission's negotiating autonomy proved to be the dominant and most controversial issue during the Council. Complaining that a Franco-German proposal risked tying his hands in the negotiations, Brittan urged the ministers not to demand any new negotiating mandate.[46] French Foreign Minister Alain Juppé angrily retorted that Brittan, a "petty official

who had exceeded his brief," had no right to oppose member states' negotiating instructions. This internal drama further strengthened suspicions of
the Commission's excessive power.[47] Although in the end no new mandate
was given to Brittan—only "certain general orientations" for maintaining
the EU's export capabilities and ensuring that international commitments
are compatible with the CAP reform—the Council decided to "monitor
constantly the negotiations" on the basis of Commission reports during
each session of the General Affairs Council.[48] This decision was the first
step toward a return to strict intergovernmentalism in trade negotiating
matters and a reining in of the Commission's negotiating powers.

Another result of the Jumbo Council was the clear reinstatement of
unanimity as the basic decisionmaking principle in trade negotiations. The
Council decided to approve the Uruguay Round results by consensus. This
important decision was confirmed informally during the November General
Affairs Council, which also discussed the issue of Commission autonomy
and decisionmaking in external trade negotiations. In October, at France's
demand, the member states agreed to ask the Commission for a written report on the trade talks every two weeks until the December deadline.[49]

Renegotiation of Blair House. The threat of a major crisis if EU demands
for "clarification" of Blair House were not met contributed to a reversal of
the U.S. position on the renegotiation of the agreement.[50] The U.S. administration ultimately agreed to renegotiate specific elements of the agreement, rather than confront a possible breakdown of the talks before the
crucial ultimatum enforced by the expiration of the U.S. Congressional
Fast Track Authority on 15 December 1993.

The Commission's negotiating autonomy was severely limited during
the final days of the negotiations. Brittan shuttled "virtually directly from
the negotiating room to the EU Council meeting to report—and presumably seek approval—from EU foreign and trade ministers."[51] Negotiations
had to be concluded ahead of the deadline, so EU foreign ministers could
review the final text of a GATT agreement before authorizing Brittan to
sign it on their behalf. "One French official boasted that ministers were
keeping Sir Leon on such a tight leash that officials were "practically following him into his bedroom."[52]

The EC-U.S. agricultural agreement, finally concluded on December
6, changed several important elements of the original Blair House accord.
The "peace clause" was extended from six to nine years, and the bulk of
the cuts in subsidized farm exports were postponed to the later years of the
implementation period. Market access for imports was fixed according to
the category of product (animal feed, meat, dairy products, etc.), instead of
the more restrictive product-by-product curbs. Direct assistance to farmers
provided under the 1992 CAP reform was not challenged. Finally, and
most importantly, 1991–1992 was taken as the reference period instead of

1986–1988. The EC could thus export eight million tons of grain over and above the quantity that the original Blair House agreement would have allowed.

In exchange for accepting the agricultural agreement, France demanded tougher EU handling of unfair trading procedures and changes in the EU voting system on antidumping.[53] Germany dropped its longstanding opposition to a measure giving the Commission greater power to impose antidumping duties on unfairly priced imports. The French government had thus succeeded in making it easier for a defensive member state to capture the negotiating position of the EU, and in enhancing the EU's offensive capabilities by making it harder for reluctant member states to reject an offensive trade action.

The EU gained more than mere "clarification" in the final agreement on agriculture, and the United States was forced to retreat during the last weeks of the negotiations. As a result of the constraints created by the EU obligation to negotiate as a whole while retaining the principle of unanimity and tight control over the Commission, the most recalcitrant country exerted a preponderant influence on the final outcome. When the Uruguay Round was concluded on 15 December 1993, the veto right had been reinstated, the Commission's autonomy was curtailed, and Juppé was able to "voice admiration for the way Brittan had obtained a better deal on subsidized farm exports than the 1992 Blair House accord."[54]

Conclusion: From Single to Multiple Voices Again

Voting rules at the EU level and the amount of autonomy exercised by EU negotiators help to explain the shape of the final international agreement. In particular, when decisions are made unanimously and the Commission has limited negotiating autonomy, the fact that no agreement is possible if it endangers the Union's consensus forces the negotiating opponent into making concessions acceptable to the most reluctant country.

The EU's external bargaining capabilities are directly related to its institutional structure. This case study demonstrates that after six years of deadlock in the EC-U.S. negotiations, a breakthrough became possible thanks to an internal agreement to entrust the Commission with a bargaining mandate. The resulting Blair House agreement was renegotiated because the Commission's authority was contested. By reinstating the veto right and tightening member states' control over Commission negotiators, France forced a divided EU to accept its point of view and cornered the United States into relaxing its demands. The capture of EU voting rules and Commission latitude by the most recalcitrant member state resulted in the "lowest common denominator" final agreement and diminished the bargaining strength of the EU's negotiating opponent.

Furthermore, the renegotiation debate triggered questions about the legitimacy of the Commission's representation both inside and outside the Union. The issue of the division of competencies between the Commission and member states was raised again before the signing and ratification of the final act concluding the Uruguay Round in April 1994. Whether the document would be signed by the member states individually or by the Commission on behalf of the EU was the subject of heated political and legal debate. A compromise solution was eventually agreed on: both the Council President and Commissioner Leon Brittan signed the final act on 15 April 1994 in Marrakesh. Representatives of each of the member states also signed, in the name of their respective governments.

A major debate also arose as to EU representation and repartition of responsibilities in the new World Trade Organization.[55] Several member states insisted on being granted their own competencies with respect to the "new issues" such as services and intellectual property. Hoping to maintain Union cohesion, the Commission asked the European Court of Justice for an opinion on the issue of competence. In November 1994 the court ruled that although the Union had sole competence to conclude international agreements on trade of goods, the member states and the Union shared joint competence to deal with trade that did not involve goods.[56] This legal recognition of mixed competencies departs from the founding principle that the Union has a single voice in international trade negotiations and from previous case law on external relations. The court's encouragement of a return to intergovernmentalism in the field of external trade is undoubtedly setting the stage for future disputes over competencies and may affect the future character of the EU as an actor in international trade negotiations.

Notes

I would like to thank Karen Alter, Suzanne Berger, and Carolyn Rhodes, as well as all the May 1996 ECSA workshop participants, for their helpful comments.

1. The "113 Committee" is named after Article 113 of the Treaty of Rome, which sets the rules for trade policy after the transitional period and states that international trade negotiations will be conducted by the Commission assisted by a special committee designated by the Council.

2. Paemen and Bensch 1995.

3. See Meunier (forthcoming 1998).

4. Paemen and Bensch 1995, 95.

5. Ibid., 109–110.

6. See Schelling 1960, 19.

7. For an in-depth analysis of the EC-U.S. conflicts over the Second Banking and the Utilities directives, see Meunier (forthcoming 1998).

8. See Keeler 1996.

9. Paemen and Bensch 1995, 36, 46–48.

10. See Paarlberg 1993.

11. Paemen and Bensch 1995, 106.

12. Schott 1994.

13. Paemen and Bensch 1995, 185–186.

14. Schott 1994, 46.

15. See Keeler 1996.

16. "No Concessions Offered to Europeans in Washington Trade Talks, U.S. Says," *Washington Post*, 28 May 1992.

17. "GATT: Bruxelles négocie, Paris agite son veto," *Libération*, 12 October 1992.

18. The dispute erupted when the United States challenged EC oilseeds subsidies in GATT. Successive GATT panels found against the EC, which refused to comply.

19. "Sutherland, MacSharry Played Key Roles in Complex Agreement," *Irish Times*, 15 December 1993.

20. Paemen and Bensch 1995, 214.

21. "Blood Is Thicker than Rape Oil," *The Economist*, 14 November 1992, 52.

22. "GATT: Le vin blanc européen trinque pour le colza," *Libération*, 6 November 1992. Author's translation.

23. "GATT: une manche aux Etats-Unis," *Libération*, 12 November 1992. Author's translation.

24. "The Anatomy of a Trade Agreement: U.S. Gamble Pays Off in Deal with EC," *New York Times News Service*, 23 November 1992.

25. "U.S., EC Trade Talks Adjourn, to Resume Later," Reuters, 19 November 1992; "Struggle Continues for GATT Formula," *The Independent*, 20 November 1992.

26. Interview with senior USDA official, January 1995.

27. "U.S., EC Begin Talks on Farm Subsidies as Officials Claim Agreement Is Near," *The Bureau of National Affairs*, 19 November 1992.

28. "Obfuscation by the Commission on EC-U.S. GATT Deal," *Agra Europe*, 4 December 1992.

29. "GATT: la France retrouve ses amis latins," *Libération*, 28–29 November 1992.

30. Interviews with French officials, 1994.

31. Interviews with senior USDA official and USTR official, January 1995.

32. Julie Wolf, "Putting CAP on and Making Sure It Fits," *The Guardian*, 27 March 1993.

33. "EC Decision-Making Is Not Working—French Minister," *Reuters*, 22 April 1993.

34. Ibid.

35. "France Wins Some Support for GATT Stance," Reuters, 22 April 1993. See also "French Government Releases Official Position on GATT Talks," *International Trade Reporter*, 19 May 1993.

36. "Belgium to Seek Changes to Blair House Deal," Reuters, 23 June 1993.

37. "The prime objective of the [Belgian] Presidency was therefore to get France out of its corner." Devuyst 1995, 452.

38. Belgium could achieve such an objective because "as a federalist oriented member state, Belgium was in a position to request greater member states scrutiny over the Commission without being suspected of trying to restrict the Commission's treaty powers." Devuyst 1995, 453.

39. "Kohl Leans Toward France in GATT Farm Dispute," Reuters, 26 August 1993; "Bonn Says Not Seeking to Renegotiate Blair House," Reuters, 27 August

1993; "Germany Wavers on Farm Concessions to France," Reuters, 27 August 1993; "Kohl Says Germany Shares Some French GATT Concerns," Reuters, 26 August 1993.

40. "Franco-German Alliance Sought over GATT/ERM Issues," *Agra Europe*, 27 August 1993.

41. "Senior Farm Officials Prepare for Jumbo GATT Council," Reuters, 14 September 1993.

42. "France Calls for Sweeping Changes to Blair House," *Agra Europe*, 3 September 1993.

43. "Spain Backs French Demand for Revised Farm Trade Accord," Reuters, 13 September 1993; "Spain Backs France on Farm Trade," *Financial Times*, 14 September 1993; "France Aiming for GATT Buy-off," *Agra Europe*, 17 September 1993.

44. "France Urges Reopening Dialogue on Blair House Accord," *Bureau of National Affairs*, 9 September 1993.

45. Interview with senior USDA official, January 1995. See also "Brittan Says U.S. Moves on GATT Cultural Position," Reuters, 29 September 1993.

46. "Rift Hits EC as Germany Backs France on Farm Pact," *International Herald Tribune*, 21 September 1993; "Vague EC Plan Defuses French Trade Row," Reuters, 21 September 1993; "EC ministers instruct negotiators to clarify Blair House Accord with U.S.," *International Trade Reporter*, 22 September 1993.

47. "Leap of Solidarity," *European Insight*, 24 September 1993.

48. Devuyst 1995. See also "French Coaxed Back into Farm Trade Fold," *Financial Times*, 22 September 1993.

49. "Balladur Says Trade Jockeying to Go Down to Wire," Reuters, 15 October 1993; "European Council: Franco-German Stratagem Sets Hare Running in Brussels," *European Report*, 30 October 1993.

50. "Airbus, Agriculture Trade-off on GATT Not Impossible," *Agence France Presse*, 2 November 1993.

51. "Hopes Run High for Tariff Cutting Deal," *Financial Times*, 1 December 1993.

52. "France's Trump: U.S. Wanted Pact," *International Herald Tribune*, 16 December 1993.

53. "EC-U.S. Close to Framework Trade Pact, Problems Remain," Reuters, 6 December 1993.

54. "France Could Back Brittan for EC President," Reuters, 14 December 1993.

55. See Devuyst 1995.

56. Court of Justice of the European Communities, *Opinion 1/94*, 15 November 1994, I-123. On the Court's advisory opinion, see Bourgeois 1995.

11

States, Agency, and Rules: The European Union in Global Environmental Politics

Joseph Jupille & James A. Caporaso

Assessing the role of the European Union* in global politics raises numerous empirical challenges. First, the analytical criteria for determining the status of the EU as an actor are unclear. Beyond some weak standard of agency, there is no consensus on what it means to be an actor,[1] yet such standards would seem to be central to discussions of power and influence. Second, the protean nature of the EU is a challenge in and of itself. It is an organization (really a collection of organizations) made up of fifteen member states and numerous institutions that reflect, in varying degrees, territorial and nonterritorial interests. In addition, the EU's involvement in world affairs varies over time and across issues. In this chapter, we propose a number of criteria for considering the EU as an actor, building upon previous efforts treating it as a "presence" in global politics,[2] and then illustrate these criteria with a case study in global environmental politics, the EC's involvement at the June 1992 Earth Summit in Rio de Janeiro. Although this chapter focuses on the Rio summit, offering an empirical illustration of how the EU has behaved as an international environmental actor in one prominent situation, a number of our observations are corroborated by case studies on ozone negotiations between 1982 and 1995 and hazardous waste negotiations between 1987 and 1995.[3]

Prior to our empirical investigation, we must attend to a conceptual question. How do we determine (better, how do we even think about) the role of the EU in external relations? Three broad possibilities present themselves. First, the EU can be seen as a collection of states, a forum for their interaction, with a minimal set of rules guiding those interactions.

---

*While the activities discussed in this chapter reflect "first pillar" responsibilities under the Treaty on European Union, and therefore technically refer to European Community responsibilities, the decision was made to utilize the term "European Union" except for references to historical circumstances that predate the Maastricht Treaty's ratification.

Under this view the EU's status as a "collective actor" is due to the convergence of interests at the unit level, facilitated by internal interaction within an established communication structure.[4] Sometimes units agree and forge common policies, sometimes they don't, but in either case there is no need for introducing a concept above that of the component states and their interactions. The research agenda suggested by this approach is most avidly advanced by realists and intergovernmentalists.[5] The second approach, quite opposite, is to view the EU as a polity, or evolving polity. According to that view, the zig-zagged political transition from nation-state system to polity has been made.[6] Although this approach opens some analytical opportunities (e.g., policy analysis within an extant institutional structure) it also ignores the process of system transformation itself. Third, the EU can be thought of as an evolving entity, composed of numerous issue areas and policy networks, neither a full-blown polity nor a system of sovereign states, which displays varying degrees of "actorhood" across issues and time. This third approach poses the most problems for analysis, and is naturally the one on which we settle in this chapter.

We suggest that it will be more useful to develop criteria for assessing changing relations in the less certain middle ground, where concrete struggles to develop authoritative (or perhaps just effective) politics are taking place, than to undertake a comparative end-point analysis, contrasting a decentralized international system with a streamlined, hierarchically organized EU polity. Doing this requires criteria of "actorness" that are observable, continuously variable, and abstract from any particular institutional form. We suggest four such criteria—recognition, authority, autonomy, and cohesion—that we anticipate to be conceptually helpful when applied to the EU's global political role and to be applicable more generally in assessments of other entities' capacities to act in world politics.

Assessing Actor Capacity

We posit four components of actor capacity in global politics. First is *recognition* understood as acceptance of and interaction with the entity by others. Second is *authority*, which we use in the sense of legal competence to act. Third is *autonomy*, conceived as institutional distinctiveness and independence from other actors. The final component is *cohesion*, or the degree to which an entity is able to formulate and articulate internally consistent policy preferences. The EU's capacity to act, then, is a function of its recognition by others as well as its authority, autonomy, and cohesion. In this section, we provide a brief overview of the EU's standing along each of these dimensions.

Recognition

The first consideration in assessing actor capacity concerns external recognition. This criterion should be seen as a minimum condition that adds little substantive understanding of any given entity, but simply registers it on the analytical radar. Recognition by others allows for presence in global politics, which, not surprisingly is the sine qua non of global actorhood. Robert Jackson has convincingly demonstrated that in many cases full recognition ("negative sovereignty") alone is a sufficient condition for international actorhood.[7]

Recognition can be either de jure or de facto. De jure recognition involves either diplomatic recognition under international law or formal membership in international organizations. Diplomatic recognition is unproblematically and automatically conferred on states, as it is a definitional component of sovereign statehood.[8] Because it is not sovereign, however, the European Union does not benefit from the norm of automatic recognition. Recognition of the EU by third parties is discretionary, and they have traditionally been extremely reluctant to grant it in full. The EU has high-level diplomatic contacts with most countries, but it has not been accorded the same status as sovereign states. Much the same can be said for international organization (IO) membership. The EU can be somewhat opaque to third parties because at any given time it may not be clear whether the Union or its member states are competent to address a given issue or to uphold the responsibilities of membership.[9] Third parties are thus reluctant to fully "recognize" the EU through formal IO membership. Although some argue that such resistance is on the wane,[10] in no way can the EU be said to benefit from the universal and automatic forms of de jure recognition that sovereignty would bring it and that would themselves be sufficient to qualify it as a global actor.

By extension, Jackson's analysis tells us that the EU cannot hope to accede to international society by the "negative sovereignty" route soon. According to Jackson, an entity that is long on the empirical attributes of statehood but short on the juridical aspects is at a critical disadvantage in the current global political climate, which favors the empirically weak but juridically "anointed."[11] However, this is not the only way for an actor to gain recognition. Although sovereignty may be sufficient, it is not a necessary condition for global political actorhood.

De facto recognition of the EU can result from its instrumentality for third states and from the sociality of global politics. Third parties that decide to interact with the EU implicitly confer recognition upon it. However, the simple production of external effects is not sufficient to satisfy the criterion of recognition. That the completion of the single market might have external effects (e.g., trade diversion) is less important than that third parties subject to these effects engage the Union in order to discuss, modify, or simply understand them. For many, this dynamic is what has driven the emergence of the EU in global politics. In Brewin's words,

> The Community's importance as an actor is a consequence as much of its actions as of its legal powers. It has been the creation of a huge internal market which has made it increasingly difficult to treat the Community as an instrumental international organization. This has been the principal reason why, particularly in the decade of the 1970s, third states have negotiated directly with the Community as an autonomous actor.[12]

For our purposes, whenever a third party interacts with the Union, rather than, or in addition to, going to one or more EU member state(s), the criterion of recognition has been satisfied.

Recognition need not be conceived of as a one-shot, all-or-nothing criterion. Rather, as the EU comes to interact with third states bilaterally, regionally, or globally, and as the number and frequency of these contacts increase, a process of socialization occurs according to which EU activity comes to be accepted and expected, and indeed according to which its very identity is formed and the identities of its interlocutors transformed. Wendt in particular has outlined the ways in which actors' identities are mutually constituted, not materially, but socially or relationally. For him, "each identity is an inherently social definition of the actor grounded in the theories which actors collectively hold about themselves and one another."[13] Jackson and Wendt both allow for a transformative and a generative conception of global politics according to which actors can be supported or undermined, *and* made or unmade.[14] It is especially here that analytical space opens up for consideration of the EU as an actor in world politics.

Authority

The second factor that sheds light on the EU's capacity as a global actor is its *authority* to act externally. By authority we mean in particular the EU's legal competence in a given subject matter. Because the EU is a creation of the member states, its authority ultimately derives from these states. Thus, to speak of the EU's authority is to think of authority delegated to EU institutions by nation states. Legal authority or competence to act in such situations is given by a contract under which principals empower agents to act in their interests. Such contracts at once limit the actions of principals and constrain the scope of agents' competence to that which principals will accept.[15]

The 1957 Rome Treaty gave the European Community the greatest external authority in the areas of international commerce and association agreements. The Common Commercial Policy (CCP) provision of the Treaty grants exclusive power to the Community to negotiate trade agreements with third parties. Under Article 113, where a trade agreement is to be reached, the Commission proposes the negotiation, the Council authorizes the Community to negotiate the accord with the "assistance" of a special committee appointed by the Council (the "113 Committee"), the Commission negotiates, and the Council approves the conclusion of the agreement. Along with trade, the Rome Treaty foresees an external role for the Community in the conclusion of "association" agreements between it and third states, one of the principal foci of which has come to be development aid. Article 238 of the Treaty establishes that the Council may conclude such agreements, which can establish "reciprocal rights and obligations, common action, and special procedures," after consulting the European Parliament (EP).

The EC gained the ability to act in international environmental forums by three means.[16] First, the areas of the EC's express competence have evolved to take on an environmental component. Commercial policy now includes trade-related environmental measures (TREMs), and aid increasingly pursues the goal of sustainable development.[17] Second, the European Court of Justice (ECJ) has established a linkage, or "parallelism," between the ECs internal and external powers. In a series of "activist" judgments during the 1970s, the Court established that where the EC has legislated internally, or where external cooperation is necessary to attain the objectives laid out in the Treaty, it has an implied power to conclude agreements with third states.[18] Finally, the amendment of the Rome Treaty by the Single European Act (SEA) gave the EC express authority to conclude environmental agreements with third countries.[19]

Autonomy

The third component of actor capacity is *autonomy*, implying distinctiveness, and to some extent independence, from other actors, particularly state actors. Since this characteristic presents the greatest possibility for misunderstanding, a few words of clarification are in order. By distinctiveness, we mean institutional distinctiveness. An international organization, to be an actor, should have a distinctive institutional apparatus, even if it is grounded in, or intermingles with, domestic political institutions. By independence we mean that these institutions should make a difference, compared to the baseline expectation of a decentralized state system working on the basis of power and interest.

Autonomy presents itself as a criterion as a way of fending off the proposition that, "since things are happening there" (e.g. Brussels) the agents proximally responsible must be important. We reject the view that equates the locus of activity with causal importance. What matters is whether the EU is a "corporate"—rather than a "collective"—entity, which has, or at least can have, causal importance that is more than the sum of its constituent parts.[20]

Autonomy can be said to exist when decisionmaking latitude is wide, when agency slack is considerable, when decisions require going outside standard operating procedures, and when instructions are ambiguous, incomplete, or depend on information that the principals cannot have. Pierson has set out the general conditions under which agents acquire substantial influence.[21] Although we do not try to replicate his argument here, we draw on it in parts of our own analysis. Summarizing what we have said so far, we settle on institutional distinctiveness (or separateness in extremis) and independence (discretionary goal formation, decisionmaking, and implementation) as our two main indicators of autonomy.

Assessing the autonomy of the EU with regard to its member states is notoriously difficult. Part of the difficulty lies in the pervasive intermingling of levels of political authority, a condition Smith calls a "perpetual boundary problem."[22] To cite but one example, arguably the most important Union institution, in terms of the EU's ongoing decisionmaking, is the Council of Ministers, which is itself comprised of ministers in member state governments. Thus, the institutional structure of parts of the EU is barely once removed from the member states. For example, although the Commission enjoys "exclusive" competence to negotiate trade agreements, this "exclusivity" actually entails significant member state influence through the preponderant role of the Council and the 113 Committee. Exclusive competence, defined as a situation in which the Union is competent to act to the "exclusion" of its member states, does not translate directly into Union independence.[23]

Interdependence of the EU and its members is even more pronounced when one considers the case of so-called mixed agreements, which include all of the EU's external environmental agreements. These are defined as agreements to which the EU, some or all of its members, and at least one third actor are parties, but for the execution of which neither the EU nor its members enjoys full competence.[24] Under such agreements, it is not definitively established ahead of time who acts on what issues. Often questions about who acts have to be decided on the spot as new issues arise, causing EU members and institutions to engage in a negotiation-within-a-negotiation in order to decide who can address the point in question. Again, therefore, an assessment of the EU's capacity as an actor cannot be undertaken unless one takes into account the extent to which it is institutionally distinct from the member states and the extent to which it is independent of them and third actors.

Cohesion

Even without policy cohesion, the EU would still make a difference in global politics, judged solely by the standards of its external consequences. This suggests a difference between actor and presence. To be an actor implies a minimal level of cohesion. A random collection of elements could have external effects but would not be judged as being an actor.

A complex international organization such as the EU can act with varying degrees of cohesion. One extreme is exemplified by those organizations that are no more than simple aggregates of member states, producing no more cohesion than a decentralized balance of power system would lead us to expect. The other extreme is represented by the unitary international organization, whose member states display high levels of consensus. International concerts imply some commitment to basic foreign policy goals. Transaction cost regimes imply coordination, the sharing of information, and the revelation of preferences, which in any case there is no strategic reason to misrepresent. Regimes to overcome social dilemmas imply stricter institutional mechanisms, especially mechanisms to foster compliance. If the EU is "more than a regime, less than a federation," we need to think of cohesion indicators appropriate to this level.[25]

Cohesion is a slippery concept. It need not imply substantive agreement, such as on values and goals. Such agreement would imply a harmony of interests that rarely exists even in domestic politics, let alone international politics. To clarify the concept of cohesion, we identify four separate dimensions of the term: value (goal) cohesion, tactical cohesion, procedural cohesion, and output cohesion. Value cohesion simply refers to the similarity or compatibility of basic goals. If goals are somewhat different but can be made to fit with one another through issue linkages and side payments, we speak of tactical cohesion. In such a situation, a similarity of goals in the aggregate obtains, an idea best represented by package deals.

In contrast, procedural cohesion implies some consensus on the rules and procedures used to process issues where conflict exists. For example, qualified majority voting on common external positions may imply procedural cohesion that is stronger than that found under unanimity rules and that is independent of agreement on policy goals. Similarly, Article 5 of the EC Treaty, sometimes called the "loyalty clause," obligates member states to refrain from taking any measures internally or externally that jeopardize the attainment of the EU's objectives. When respected, this clause can be thought of as a requirement of procedural cohesion. Procedural cohesion implies some agreement on the basic rules by which policies are made. An institutional framework, such as the Rome Treaty, does identify some specific policy goals, such as the elimination of tariffs; however, the main institutional work of the Treaty is to establish acceptable rules for dealing with common problems. Overall, in the creation of an institutional framework such as the Rome Treaty, procedural agreement is unlikely to precede substantive agreement. As Karl Deutsch pointed out long ago, states with high levels of transactions and established habits of cooperation are much more likely to agree to common institutions.[26]

The final dimension of cohesion has to do with public policies or "output cohesion." If member states succeed in formulating policies, regardless of the level of substantive and procedural agreement, more cohesion is said to exist. To be sure, output cohesion will be affected by the level of agreement on goals and procedures as well as the degree to which it is possible to link issues tactically. The ability to devise collective positions, apart from the level of agreement, is an indicator of cohesion.

All four forms of cohesion can be threatened by both horizontal conflicts (those *at* a given level of authority) and vertical conflicts (those across levels). Horizontal conflicts manifest themselves in disagreements between member states and in disagreements between EU-level institutions such as the European Parliament and the Commission. Analytically relevant vertical conflicts will occur principally between the EU level and the member states, although national-subnational conflicts are not excluded. Where such conflicts are present, we expect to find the EU less able to act.

Summary

The concepts we have outlined above are, by hypothesis, interrelated. Cohesion, for example, is analytically irrelevant if the entity in question lacks autonomy. Similarly, it makes less sense to talk about the autonomy of EU institutions if these institutions are perfectly instructed by the member states. Outside recognition of the Union can only be an option if its own member states agree to delegate it the authority to represent them externally. Thus these indicators form a coherent ensemble, depending on one another for full meaning.

Before turning to our case study, it will perhaps be useful to trace the broad outlines of the EU's global environmental activity. In brief, the EU's external environmental activity has developed tremendously. The Commission's earliest environmental policy statements put the Community in a clearly subordinate position to its member states, and vowed that the Union would "restrict its [external environmental] activities . . . to complementary work and to using the results obtained by international organizations."[27] In 1973 the Community sought simply to keep tabs on international developments and to cooperate where possible with other international organizations that were active in the field, but by 1987 the EC was vowing to stake out powerful and cohesive positions in a variety of international environmental forums.[28] The Single European Act provided express Community authority for external environmental activity, and this legal grant has received continued and growing political support. By 1992, the Maastricht Treaty elevated international cooperation to one of the fundamental objectives of the EC's environmental policy, and the Community devoted four chapters of the Fifth Environmental Action Program to its external environmental activities, again vowing to step up its global involvement.[29]

On the basis of this evolution, the Union has engaged in almost every conceivable form of global environmental activity. Environment is a part of the EU's bilateral dealings with countries in every region of the world. Regionally, the EU is an active player in environmental forums concerned with all possible media and ranging geographically from the Mediterranean to the North and Baltic Seas and from Iceland to Vladivostok, and it is a party to numerous regional environmental conventions. The EU's interregional links extend to every area of the globe, and at the global level it has participated in and/or concluded almost every major environmental conference or negotiation held since the 1972 UN-sponsored Stockholm Conference on the Human Environment.[30] There can be little doubt that the EU is present in global environmental politics. However, for an analytically sharper picture we turn now to our case study.

United Nations Conference on Environment and Development

The European Union's participation in the United Nations Conference on Environment and Development (UNCED, or the "Earth Summit") is a critical case for understanding its role in global environmental politics, not only because the conference was itself extremely important—it was the largest gathering ever of international heads of state in one place at one time, and dealt with issues of critical importance on the global agenda— but also because the very contentious nature of the issues to be addressed was to prove a significant test of the EU's capacity to act on the global stage.

The UNCED was the product of two legacies. The first was the Stockholm Conference on the Human Environment of 1972, which heralded the birth of international environmental politics as such and, not coincidentally, provided the catalyst for the development of the EC's own environmental policy. The second was the 1987 Brundtland Report, which coined the term "sustainable development" and reframed the terms of the environmental policy discourse from one of antagonism to one of integration between ecology and economy. The objective of the 1992 conference, as given in UN Resolution 44/228, was "to elaborate strategies and measures to halt and reverse the effects of environmental degradation in the context of strengthened national and international efforts to promote sustainable and environmentally sound development in all countries." Various EC protagonists embraced UNCED as an opportunity to demonstrate the vitality, relevance, and potential impact of the EC in global environmental affairs.[31]

Because the UNCED process dealt with many diverse issues (e.g., official development aid [ODA], biodiversity, forest resources, hazardous waste trade, global climate change, etc.), it is difficult to summarize EC authority in the negotiations.[32] Put most simply, competence in the forum was shared between the EC and its member states. According to the European Parliament's Environment Committee, reporting on the role of the EC at UNCED before the fact, the Commission would participate on behalf of the Community in negotiations surrounding the Conventions on Climate Change and Biodiversity, which were foreseen as binding instruments of international law, and it would also negotiate trade-related matters exclusively. In other areas, however, such as the conclusion of the overarching statement of political principles, which came to be known as "Agenda 21," the Commission would take "a subordinate role" to the member states.[33] This ambiguity would color the Community's entire involvement in the Rio process.

The Community played a conflicted role in the Preparatory Committee (PrepCom) meetings leading up to the Rio conference, but one largely in line with its areas of competence. For example, during heated PrepCom III negotiations over the nature and amount of financial assistance that would be provided by developed countries, the EC was compelled temporarily to withhold comment on a G-7 draft negotiating text because its negotiating mandate was not explicit on the issues under discussion.[34] Its lack of authority, or perhaps more accurately its contingent authority (as opposed to the diffuse authority enjoyed by most national representatives) on aid issues at that time compelled it to remain inactive during this phase of the discussions. In contrast, during a discussion of the international economy at PrepCom IV, when the topic turned to questions of international trade—and more specifically, to agricultural protectionism and subsidies—the Community participated actively.[35] In this context, the Commission had the authority and was in fact able to speak on behalf of the member states in defending the EC position. Except for areas of "exclusive competence" such as trade, however, the EC's authority was rarely clear to anyone, including the EC participants themselves.

While it was impossible to delineate *ex ante* the specific contours of the Community's competence, it was at least possible to establish the general principles governing its recognition and participation. After the Council of Ministers agreed in Brussels in March 1992 that the EC should be a full participant at UNCED despite the fact that it had no more than observer status within the UN itself, it seemed that all that was required to "ratify" this status was the acquiescence of the other UNCED participants.[36] A striking turn of events at the New York PrepCom (IV) forced the issue. Portugal, which was then the Council president and the voice of the EC in mixed competence areas, sought to accord European Commission President Delors's wish to "sit at the top table in Rio . . . as the leader of an essentially sovereign entity" during the formal signing and concluding ceremonies. The proposal, however, created a "flaming row" within the

EC and between it and the United States, with the latter accusing Europe of trying to win a thirteenth vote for itself and with very few EC members "prepared to accept the Commission as an actual peer in Rio."[37]

This proposal was rejected in favor of the more moderate solution reached at the end of the New York meetings. Algerian issue coordinator Ahmed Djoghlaf submitted a draft decision under which the EC would have the right to "participate fully" in the proceedings.[38] The EC would be unique among intergovernmental organizations invited to the conference, for, as Rule 63 of the amended rules of procedure for the conference noted, all IGOs except for the EC could participate only as observers, without the right to vote or participate in deliberations.[39] In an extraordinary confirmation of the EC's specificity and special status within UNCED, PrepCom IV chairperson Tommy Koh resumed its status as follows:

> The EEC will represent exclusively the Community's position to the Conference on issues falling within the EEC's exclusive competence. In cases of mixed competence, the EEC and its member States will determine which, as between them will represent the positions of the Community and its member States. The EEC shall inform the UNCED secretariat prior to consideration of an agenda item by the Conference if the EEC will be representing a position of the Community and its member States with respect to specific matters within the scope of that agenda item.[40]

Koh enjoined the EC and its member states not to sidetrack the workings of the conference with their own internecine struggles. He added that the request for such status was put to him by the EC on an ad hoc basis, that this did not constitute a precedent for the future status of the EC within the UN, and that the EC would not have the right to vote even within the UNCED framework. The resulting status of the EC as a "full, but not full" participant in the UNCED proceedings seems to have held firmly throughout the actual two-week Rio meetings, and largely resolved any residual questions surrounding recognition of the EC at the Earth Summit. Brinkhorst, for one, views the precedent set by the EC's "full" recognition at UNCED as a hopeful one that bodes well for its development as a global actor. Corcelle contends more controversially that this state of affairs essentially renders the EC a "sovereign state in the sense of the UN Charter."[41]

While the "presence" of the EC at Rio is indisputable —with Council officials, some twenty Commission representatives including Development Commissioner Matutes, and a five-member EP contingent counted among the EC delegation[42]—their distinctiveness and certainly their independence are much less clear. The EP delegation was peripheral to most actual decisionmaking, and longtime EP Environment Committee chairperson Ken Collins did not go to Rio, choosing not to lend his name to what he called a public relations "sham."[43] The Commission delegation was similarly limited, as Environment Commissioner Carlo Ripa di Meana was also absent from Rio. He had vowed throughout the spring of 1992 to boycott the conference if the Council did not make sufficient progress on several environmental dossiers, including an energy tax to limit carbon dioxide (CO_2) emissions and increased development financing for environmentally friendly projects. When the Council failed to reach agreements on these issues, Ripa di Meana refused to attend the conference.[44] What is more, European Commission President Jacques Delors was unable to deliver his prepared remarks in Rio.[45] Lamented one MEP, "if the Community really wishes to play a political role at world level, we must certainly not be conspicuous by our absence when we are in a position to be involved as full participants in a historic summit conference."[46]

That the EC should have causal importance independent of its member states is an extremely stringent test of its capacity to act. Yet, even the seemingly easier test of its independence relative to third parties reveals circumscribed Community autonomy. A case in point is the effort undertaken by the European Community to assume a leading role before and . during the Rio summit in combatting global warming/climate change. Prior to the Earth Summit, the Commission proposed an energy tax that it hoped would help the EC achieve a "reduction" (on prevailing estimates) of CO_2 emissions in the year 2000 to 1990 levels.[47] The Commission further hoped to convince the other leading industrialized nations (principally the United States and Japan) to commit to similar CO_2 targets. In Zito's words, the carbon tax was a "foreign policy bid to make the EC a leading political actor in global environmental issues."[48] U.S. President Bush, however, refused such a commitment, calling instead for a general framework agreement that would require only that states devise national climate action plans, with or without CO_2 targets. According to EC Environment Commissioner Ripa di Meana, this amounted to "an attack on the very heart of the [Rio] conference."[49]

Even EC member states were reluctant to back the Commission on the energy tax proposal, however.[50] Some were fearful of imposing a competitive disadvantage on their industries vis-à-vis the United States and Japan. Some countries, such as Spain, were totally opposed to a CO_2 tax on the grounds that it would discourage their economic development. Others, such as Germany, favored the tax and sought a unified, independent, and strong stance.[51] Recognizing that a unilateral energy tax was politically unfeasible, the Commission changed its stance in May 1992 by making the EC energy tax conditional on the adoption of similar measures by other industrialized nations, and in so doing it scuttled any chance of a truly independent Community stance on climate change at the Earth Summit. Numerous EC participants encouraged the Commission to drop the conditionality requirement and take a unilateral leadership role on climate change at Rio, but the Commission remained convinced—even after the Earth Summit took a minimalist stance on the issue that a carbon tax should only be imposed as part of a multilateral commitment.[52] In sum, the Community lacked the capacity actively to push a common agenda regarding global climate change.

Community cohesion was recognized early as a prerequisite to effective action within the UNCED. In the words of one MEP, "the weight carried by the Community will depend on its own ability to take decisions and its willingness to act."[53] This contention is borne out not only by the example of climate change, but also by that of development aid. Developing countries had essentially identified the commitment of additional financial resources by the wealthier countries as the sine qua non of their support for the UNCED's environmental components. The EC hoped to achieve output cohesion on this issue during Council meetings before going to Rio, but at the joint meeting of Environment and Development ministers held on 5 May 1992, they were able to reach agreement only on the amount, and not on the timing, of additional aid. At this meeting, France, the Netherlands, Denmark, and Italy all sought to raise the level of aid given by each country to 0.7 percent of GDP by the year 2000. The UK, Germany, and Belgium all sought a vague "as soon as possible" target, and Spain, Ireland, and Greece were reluctant to make any ODA commitment at all—although they ultimately did.[54] Even this minimalist consensus was rescinded at the 26 May Environment Council meeting, with the Council, now led on this question by Germany, Spain, the UK, and Greece, abjuring any commitment to set aside 0.7 percent of GDP for development aid. The Council rejected even a French compromise proposal to allow some members to pick up others' slack by targeting the 0.7 percent figure for the EC as a whole.

The member states tried desperately to achieve some consensus on the issue while at Rio, shifting the target from a scaled figure based on a percentage of GDP to a set figure of ECU 3 billion (which was less than 0.7 percent). Intra-EC agreement on a percentage at Rio had proved impossible, as not all EC member states were willing to join the United States and Japan in agreeing to a text according to which "all UN members who so wish" would honor the 0.7 percent figure. The target of ECU 3 billion, however, was finally agreed upon. Eleven EC members had in fact felt able to commit to 0.7 percent without a specific timetable, but the United Kingdom refused to commit itself even to this.[55] Its lone abstention precluded any corporate activity on the issue by the EC.[56] In the interim, the EC's inability to come to an agreement prevented a resolution of this question within the UNCED framework. Not only could the EC not act in unison, but its inability to do so at that specific time threatened global outcomes.[57]

In sum, where EU's authority is unclear or ambiguous, the EU is at a disadvantage as compared to other actors. However, as Brinkhorst notes, where authority is clear, it correlates with capacity to act. In areas dealing strictly with the environment, where the EU has had a well-developed policy, it has acted relatively effectively; in areas such as aid for sustainable development, where EU policy is relatively underdeveloped, it has been able, as at Rio, to do little.[58]

EU autonomy vis-à-vis its own member states presents a relatively demanding criterion of actor capacity. At the Earth Summit, the EC had great difficulty in distinguishing itself from its member states. In particular, two of its most visible environmental spokespersons were absent; Environment Commissioner Ripa di Meana and EP Environment Committee Chairperson Ken Collins both declined to attend on the grounds that little of any consequence for the environment was going to be done there. What is more, Commission President Jacques Delors suffered at least two setbacks in his efforts to elevate his own and/or the EC's role at UNCED. His request to be granted the diplomatic status of a head of state was roundly rejected at PrepCom IV, and he was compelled to leave Rio without presenting his remarks on the global stage. The energy tax example also demonstrated that EC independence vis-à-vis third countries was limited in Rio, given the interdependencies facing all global actors.

Cohesion proved to be a decisive determinant of the EC's capacity to act at the Earth Summit. Evidence from both the climate change and the development assistance episodes demonstrates that where both value and procedural cohesion were absent, either the EC was driven to embrace watered-down, globally least-common-denominator positions, or its member states were driven to unilateral action outside of the EC context.[59] The aid issue also underscores the importance of procedural cohesion and the relationships between it and EU authority. Because the EC in Rio was not legally empowered to act on the issue of development aid, the attempt to reach agreement among the member states at the conference followed a consensus decision rule. This left the door open for one member (the UK) to block corporate action because EC rules made it difficult to aggregate conflicting preferences.

Conclusion

As the recipient of authority and power delegated to it by its member states, the EU demonstrates a good deal of agency. This is particularly evident in the broad expansion by the European Court of Justice of the EU's external authority dating from its 1970s judgments establishing a "parallelism" between internal and external authority. This expansion has given the EU the "bare minimum" means for external action—the very right to act—and has encouraged its developing presence in global politics. However, the EU has been less effective in fostering those elements of its capacity as an external actor—namely autonomy and cohesion—that are more political than legal or instrumental in nature. The flip side of Schmitter's externalization hypothesis, that a global role might enhance the EU's internal power vis-à-vis its members, appears not to operate very forcefully.[60] The combination of these two observations lends support to Joseph Weiler's "dual character of supranationalism" thesis, according to which growing EU legal authority coexists with a great deal of member state control.[61]

Much remains to be better specified. For example, little is known about the conditions under which member states will either breach or respect Union rules regarding external competence, particularly the rule of loyalty and external unity laid out in Article 5 of the Rome Treaty. Similarly, we need a better understanding of the effects of EU institutional rules on the international efficacy of the Union, and of its members. How do varying levels of EU competence affect its global influence? Under what conditions will the external presence of the EU amplify or attenuate its member states' bargaining strength with third states? Finally, the interrelationships between our conditions of actor capacity need to be more fully and systematically explored.

Notes

1. See Wolfers 1962, 3–24; Young 1972; Frey 1985; Cosgrove and Twitchett 1970, 11–51; Sjöstedt 1977.
2. The term "presence" is drawn from Allen and Smith 1990.
3. See Jupille 1996.
4. Kenis and Schneider 1987, 439–440.
5. See for example Moravcsik 1991; Moravcsik 1993; Taylor 1983.
6. Sbragia 1992b; Hix 1994.
7. Jackson and Rosberg 1982; Jackson 1986.
8. Miller 1986.
9. Groux and Manin 1985, 12; Sack 1995, 1235–1237.
10. Denza 1994, 588–589.
11. Jackson 1987. We recognize that we have stretched Jackson's early notion of empirical statehood, which comprised effective government and a monopoly on the legitimate use of force internally. However, Jackson's later formulation allows for other indicators of empirical statehood such as welfare provision. See Jackson 1990, 21.
12. Brewin 1987, 21.
13. Wendt 1992, 398.
14. Wendt 1994.
15. Moe 1984, 745.
16. For an overview, see Nollkaemper 1987.
17. On TREMs see Demaret 1993.
18. Court of Justice of the European Communities, 1971; 1976; 1977; 1979.
19. Bulletin of the European Communities, 1986, Article 130r(5), 16.
20. Kenis and Schneider 1987, 440–441.
21. Pierson 1996.
22. Smith 1994a, 294.

23. Hession 1995, 155; Weiler 1983, 74.

24. Schermers 1983, 25–26; see also Neuwahl 1991.

25. Wallace 1983.

26. Deutsch 1957.

27. Bulletin of the European Communities, "A Community Programme Concerning the Environment," Supplement 5/72, 1972, 46.

28. *Official Journal of the European Communities* 1973, 47–48; *Official Journal of the European Communities* 1987, 36.

29. Council of the European Union 1992, Article 130r(1)(4). The Fifth Action Program is laid out in CEC 1992a, 81–92.

30. A comprehensive enumeration is given in European Parliament 1995, 59–66.

31. See, for example, Commission of the European Communities 1992b.

32. Robins 1992, 78.

33. European Parliament 1991, 13–14.

34. *Earth Negotiations Bulletin* v. 0, no. 2, 3 September 1991.

35. *Earth Summit Bulletin*, 25 March 1992, and 30 March 1992.

36. Bulletin of the European Communities 3–1992, point 1.2.120, 49; *Europe Environment* no. 382, 3 March 1992; *European Report* no. 1749, 3 March 1992.

37. *New Yorker*, 1 June 1992, 71–72.

38. United Nations 1992a.

39. United Nations 1992b, 17.

40. United Nations 1992c, 14

41. Brinkhorst 1994; Corcelle 1993, 123, translation ours.

42. European Parliament, *Debates of the European Parliament* no. 3–419, 12 June 1992, 298; and no. 3–420, 9 July 1992, 256; Bulletin of the European Communities 6–1992, point 1.3.127, 69. The EP had earlier vowed to be represented in Rio; see *Official Journal of the European Communities* 1992a, 156.

43. European Parliament, *Debates,* no. 3–418, 15 May 1992, 254.

44. *European Report* no. 1750, 7 March 1992, IV/6; *European Report* no. 1770, 20 May 1992, IV/18; "EC Unity Sought for Earth Summit," *Financial Times*, 5 March 1992, 2; "Ripa di Meana Will Not Attend Earth Summit," *Financial Times*, 28 May 1992.

45. European Parliament, *Debates* no. 3–421, 16 September 1992, 179; "The Earth Summit: Winners and Losers," *Financial Times,* 15 June 1992, 15.

46. European Parliament, *Debates* no. 3–420, 9 July 1992, 258; see also "Conflicting Viewpoints— Industrialized Nations," *Financial Times*, 2 June 1992, VI; "EC Drops the Ecological Ball: Energy Tax Snag Keeps It from Rio Talks," *International Herald Tribune*, 28 May 1992.

47. The EU's position on global warming is more fully examined in Skjærseth 1994.

48. Zito 1995, 432.

49. "EC Attack over Bush's Line on Environment," *Financial Times*, 26 March 1992, 7.

50. This relative lack of cohesion is discussed in Brinkhorst 1994, 614.

51. "EC Hitch Ahead of Earth Summit," *Financial Times,* 26 May 1992, 5; *Europe Environment* no. 388, 2 June 1992.

52. European Parliament, *Debates* no. 3–419, 15 June 1992, 294–298; *EP Debates* no. 3–421, 179.

53. European Parliament, *Debates* no. 3–414, 11 February 1992, 55; see also Johnson 1992.

54. "EC Agrees Joint Strategy for Rio Earth Summit," *Financial Times,* 6 May 1992, 4.

55. *European Report* no. 1776, 13 June 1992, V/9; *European Report* no. 1777, 17 June 1992, V/8–9.

56. Several members did make relatively firm commitments. France, Germany, and the Netherlands all agreed to commit some $250 million a year in additional ODA, but these were unilateral initiatives, not to be found in the EU budget. The EU was committed to some ECU 350 million of the ECU 3 billion figure, however; see "Earth at the Mercy of National Interests," *New Scientist,* 20 June 1992, 4. On the budget issue see European Parliament, *Debates* no. 3–423, 28 October 1992, 187, and no. 3–426, 20 January 1993, 233; Council of European Communities, 1994, 33.

57. *Earth Summit Bulletin* v. 2 no. 12, 13 June 1992; Chasek 1994, 60.

58. Brinkhorst 1994, 614.

59. For a more positive assessment of the EU's cohesion in Rio, see the comments by Council President Jones in European Parliament, *Debates* no. 3–420, 8 July 1992, 170; see also Brinkhorst 1994, 614–615.

60. See, generally, Imbrechts 1986; on the Commission's stance, see *Official Journal of the European Communities* 1978.

61. Weiler 1981.

12

Conclusions

Carolyn Rhodes

In reviewing the previous chapters, several observations can be made. First, it is clear that the changing international system has been affected by the deepening and widening character of the European Union, and that the opportunities provided by changes in the international system are challenging the EU to act in realms beyond its historical experience. This has meant that a number of EU initiatives have been taken in the global arena across a wide range of issue areas, raising external expectations about the EU's role in the world community, challenging the historical preferences of member states, and calling into question existing institutional features.

Thus, rising expectations about EU potential in international affairs and associated pressures to take a more proactive role abroad are revealing a number of tensions within the current EU structure. It is apparent that a truly cohesive, strategically guided EU foreign policy is undermined by the division of powers between the more supranationally oriented institutions (the Commission in particular) and the intergovernmental Council. Furthermore, bold initiatives in the international arena, whether made by the Commission or the Council, are often followed by "second thoughts" on the part of member states who then want to qualify their support for certain policy overtures once their implications are more fully considered.

Therefore, a second observation is that the EU's capacity to act is constrained both by its institutional structure and by the disparate interests and historical relationships of its member states. This is most obvious in security affairs, but is evident in trade and the environment as well. Under current decisionmaking procedures, the emergence of a common foreign and security policy that moves beyond nonmilitary support for humanitarian, economic development, and democratic processes will be unlikely. As long as the basic security interests of member states are divergent, a cohesive projection of an EU military force is improbable.

Longstanding international trade concerns regarding competitive imports from third countries will continue to divide member states, despite negotiating mandates from the Council to the Commission. Development assistance and trade overtures toward Central and Eastern Europe and Russia have been impressive, but as the member states have realized their implications in terms of EU market access and budgetary demands, support has diminished. Intergovernmental decisionmaking (even in areas where qualified majority rule supposedly governs decisions) continues to impede the cohesive development and maintenance of external policies whenever member state economic or security interests are seriously affected.

The major exception to this is the disciplined movement (by most member states) toward a common currency at a time when member state economies are sluggish, have high unemployment, and when the convergence criteria are placing strong constraints on national budgetary flexibility. This interesting anomaly seems to be best explained by a high level of consensus among political elites regarding the benefits that will be gained from EMU, as well as from the fiscal discipline and low inflation rates that the convergence criteria require. Once in place, EMU will remove monetary policy from the hands of member state governments to a centralized institution. This centralization of monetary policy will mark a significant new step in the supranational development of the European Union. Its effect on the structure of international monetary arrangements will be profound. However, whether the euro will be easily manipulated to effect changes in exchange rate policy is less clear, because of the fairly rigid discipline of EMU institutional policy. In this particular case the institutional requirements for EMU, requiring total cohesion on the part of participating member states and clear strategic goals for currency stability, may hamper the ability of the EU to project its monetary power in flexible ways.

Third, the legitimacy of the EU role in international affairs generally, as suggested by these case studies, is clearly affected by the evident dynamic between a range of important and influential EU initiatives on one hand and member state reservations about those same initiatives on the other. There is little doubt that the EU is a significant actor in global affairs, and that its authority to broaden that role is being extended in a number of areas. However, its hybrid character (part international organization and part supranational government) sends mixed signals to other actors in the global arena. Increasingly, Brussels and Strasbourg receive attention from foreign lobbyists hoping to influence EU policy; this attention comes not merely from prospective members or lesser-developed trading partners who are clamoring for access to the lucrative EU market, but from the most significant "others" in the global arena. Russia and the United States are both developing new, very meaningful ties with the European Union, alongside their traditional relations with national capitals. Moreover, initiatives taken by the EU in trade, development, and environmental relations have increasingly indicated that the European Union is a locus of new influence.

Still, given the discomfort evidenced in member state capitals over some EU activities abroad, it is clear that the capacity of the Commission and the European Parliament to act remains constrained by the Council. In terms of legitimacy of EU-level actions and responsibility for foreign policy generally, the dichotomous nature of decisionmaking continues to affect the role of the EU in the global community.

Fourth, this dichotomous reality affects how other actors view the EU. Expectations about its leadership and influence in international affairs are being shaped not only by its potential influence but also by its record in following through. Where the Commission has a clear degree of autonomy, or where it has taken the initiative to move forward within general mandates from the Council, EU accomplishments abroad are quite impressive in terms of leadership, agenda setting, and negotiating ability. Even the European Parliament, because of the co-decision procedure, has influenced the direction of EU foreign policy in some areas. However, where that semiautonomy does not exist for EU supranational institutions, member states have a tremendous ability to slow or sidetrack external policy efforts.

One of the more interesting observations that can be made in this context is that even when the Council has taken the lead in foreign affairs by issuing important new declarations of policy intent, it is the member states who often mire down plans to execute the substantive policy that results. In fairness, this is not that surprising, since even within individual nations governments are often faced with the same phenomenon. Broad policy declarations are generally not as controversial as the specific plans introduced to fulfill them. It is most common for interest groups to mobilize when their particular interests are threatened, and this usually occurs in the implementation phase of policymaking.

Even so, other actors are increasingly aware of the fact that in most policy areas the EU is not a cohesive actor, and their expectations regarding EU policy are being tempered by this reality. Its promise as an influential actor prompted Russian and CEEC national leaders to turn to the EU as a pivotal factor in their transition to democratic, market economies; the shape of the EU's response to those countries has in turn affected how others view its heterogeneous character and its resulting ability—or motivation—to respond to their own expectations.

An important qualification arises from this observation. Simply because the EU cannot take the kind of cohesive action that some advocates would like to see does not mean that it is an ineffective international actor. Often, individual nation-states frustrate their counterparts when they adopt certain foreign policies and are then prevented from pursuing them because of adverse domestic political consequences. Certainly many individual national governments have the centralized power to plunge ahead under such circumstances, but they often choose not to for domestic political reasons. This does not mean that they lack the institutional capability to act, but that political constraints have tempered their enthusiasm for action. Some would even go so far as to argue that domestic constraints on foreign policy adventurism are important checks against fundamentally flawed policies. Therefore, it is important that we distinguish a true *incapacity to act* in global affairs from a *capacity to act selectively.* There is no doubt that both the current institutional and decisionmaking structure of the EU and the heterogeneity of its member states exacerbate the tendency for state-level political issues to disrupt EU-level policy proposals; it remains true, nonetheless, that the EU's global role has continued to grow.

EU behavior in the international arena demonstrates that across a range of issue areas its potential for influence is considerable. Despite member state assertions of sovereignty, a wide range of activity in monetary, investment, commercial, and environmental affairs and in economic and political development assistance has clearly been shaped by EU-level policies. Although member state reluctance to develop a common defense policy has constrained the EU as an international actor, the EU has been influential in creating an impressive set of other types of bilateral relationships, as well as in shaping the direction of global affairs more generally. In fact, in light of this powerful evidence that the European Union is an increasingly active and influential actor in the world community, two important and related questions for further examination emerge from this set of comparative case studies: What prompts significant initiatives on the part of the Council in foreign affairs, and under what circumstances do the member states allow (or submit to) activities pursued under authority of the supranational institutions of the EU?

Acronyms

AASM	Association of African States and Madagascar
ACP	African, Caribbean, and Pacific countries
ALA	Asian and Latin American countries
APEC	Asia Pacific Economic Cooperation
ASEAN	Association of South East Asian Nations
CAP	Common Agricultural Policy
CCP	Common Commercial Policy
CEEC	Central and Eastern European Countries
CFSP	Common Foreign and Security Policy
CIS	Commonwealth of Independent States
CJTF	Combined Joint Task Force
CMEA	Council for Mutual Economic Assistance
CSCE	Conference on Security and Cooperation in Europe
DDR	German Democratic Republic
DG(s)	Directorate(s) General
EBRD	European Bank for Reconstruction and Development
EC	European Community
ECB	European Central Bank
ECHO	European Community Humanitarian Aid Office
ECOFIN	Economic and Finance Council of Ministers
ECSC	European Coal and Steel Community
ECU	European Currency Unit
EDF	European Development Fund
EEA	European Economic Area
EEC	European Economic Community
EFTA	European Free Trade Association
EIB	European Investment Bank
EMCF	European Monetary Cooperation Fund
EMS	European Monetary System
EMU	Economic and Monetary Union
EP	European Parliament

EPC	European Political Cooperation
ERM	Exchange Rate Mechanism
ESCB	European System of Central Banks
ESDI	European Security and Defense Identity
EU	European Union
FAO	Food and Agriculture Organization
FDI	foreign direct investment
GATT	General Agreement on Tariffs and Trade
G-7	Group of Seven
GCC	Gulf Cooperation Council
GSP	Generalized System of Preferences
IBRD	International Bank for Reconstruction and Development
IFOR	Implementation Force
IGC	Intergovernmental Conference
IMF	International Monetary Fund
LDCs	less-developed countries
MENA	Middle Eastern and North African countries
MEPP	Middle East Peace Process
NACC	North Atlantic Cooperation Council
NAFTA	North American Free Trade Agreement
NATO	North Atlantic Treaty Organization
NIS	Newly Independent States
ODA	official development assistance
OECD	Organization for Economic Cooperation and Development
OSCE	Organization for Security and Cooperation in Europe
PCA	Partnership and Cooperation Agreement
PHARE	Poland and Hungary Assistance for Economic Restructuring
SAIs	Structural Adjustment Initiatives
SEA	Single European Act
STABEX	Stabilization of Exports
SYSMIN	System for Mineral Products
TABD	Transatlantic Business Dialogue
TACIS	Technical Assistance Program for Commonwealth of Independent States
TEU	Treaty on European Union
TREM	trade-related environmental measures
UNCED	United Nations Conference on Environment and Development
UNCTAD	United Nations Conference on Trade and Development
USTR	United States Trade Representative
WEU	Western European Union
WTO	World Trade Organization

Bibliography

Allen, David. 1992. West European Responses to Change in the Soviet Union and Eastern Europe. In *Toward Political Union*, edited by R. Rummel. Boulder: Westview Press.

———. 1996a. Conclusions: The European Rescue of National Foreign Policy? In *The Actors in Europe's Foreign Policy*, edited by C. Hill. London: Routledge.

———. 1996b. The EU, the CFSP and the States of the Former Soviet Union: Does the EU Have a Coherent Policy? In *Foreign Policy of the European Union: From EPC to CFSP and Beyond,* edited by E. Regelsberger, P. de Schouteete, and W. Wessels. Boulder: Lynne Rienner.

Allen, David, and Michael Smith. 1990. Western Europe's Presence in the Contemporary International Arena. *Review of International Studies* 16: 19–37.

———. 1991–1992. The European Community in the New Europe: Bearing the Burden of Change. *International Journal* 47, Winter: 1–28.

Alter, Rolf. 1994. "Transplants: A Review of Economic Policy Issues." In *Trade and Investment*. Paris: OECD.

Anderson, Benedict. 1983. *Imagined Communities: Reflections on the Origin and Spread of Nationalism.* London: Verso.

Babarinde, Olufemi. 1994. *The Lomé Conventions and Development*. Aldershot, England: Avebury.

———. 1995. The Lomé Convention: An Aging Dinosaur in the European Union's Foreign Policy Enterprise. In *The State of the European Union, Volume 3: Building a European Polity?,* edited by C. Rhodes and S. Mazey. Boulder: Lynne Rienner.

Balassa, Bela. 1967. Trade Creation and Trade Diversion in the European Common Market. *The Economic Journal* 77: 1–21.

Baranovsky, V. 1994. The European Community as Seen from Moscow: Rival, Partner, Model? In *Russia and Europe: An End to Confrontation?,* edited by N. Malcolm. London: Pinter.

Becher, Klaus. 1994. Europe's Growing Responsibilities in International Security: Adapting the Tools. In *The International System after the Collapse of the East-West Order*, edited by A. Cleese, R. Cooper, and Y. Sakamoto. Dordrecht, Netherlands: Martinus Nijhoff.

Bertelsmann, Stiftung. 1995. *CFSP and the Future of the European Union*. Interim Report, Research Group on European Affairs (University of Munich) and Planning Staff of the European Commission (DG I-A), Munich/Brussels.

Bourgeois, Jacques H. J. 1995. The EC in the WTO and Advisory Opinion 1/94: An Echternach Procession. *Common Market Law Review* 32: 763–787.

Brewin, Christopher. 1987. The European Community: A Union of States Without Unity of Government. *Journal of Common Market Studies* 26: 1–24.

Brinkhorst, Laurens. 1994. The European Community at UNCED: Lessons to Be Drawn for the Future. In *Institutional Dynamics of European Integration: Essays in Honour of Henry G. Schermers*, edited by D. Curtin and T. Heukels. Dordrecht, Netherlands: Martinus Nijhoff.

Bull, Hedley. 1977. *The Anarchical Society: A Study of Order in World Politics*. New York: Columbia University Press.

―――. 1983. Civilian Power Europe: A Contradiction in Terms. *Journal of Common Market Studies* 21: 149–164.

Burghardt, Günter. 1994a. *The Potential and Limits of CFSP—Implementing Maastricht (What Comes Next?)*. Working Paper, EU Commission (DG I-A), Brussels.

―――. 1994b. The New Europe. Speech to the 16th World Congress of the International Political Science Association, Berlin, 23 August.

Burros, Williams, ed. 1996. *Global Security Beyond 2000: Global Population Growth, Environmental Degradation, Migration and Transnational Organized Crime*. Pittsburgh: Center for West European Studies, University of Pittsburgh.

Buzan, B., M. Kelstrup, P. Lemaitre, and O. Waever. 1990. *The European Security Order Recast: Scenarios for the Post–Cold War Era*. London: Pinter.

Cameron, Fraser. 1995a. Unpublished paper presented to the U.S. Defense Agency Conference on Regional Arms Control, Philadelphia, 12 June.

―――. 1995b. Europe Towards 1996: Developing the CFSP. EU-Commission (DG I-A). Paper presented at the Third Castelgandolfo Colloquium, CEPS, Brussels.

Caporaso, James. 1996. The European Union and Forms of State: Westphalian, Regulatory or Post-Modern? *Journal of Common Market Studies* 34: 29–52.

Carlsnaes, Walter, and Steve Smith. 1994. *European Foreign Policy: The European Community and Changing Perspectives in Europe*. London: Sage.

Carlton, David, Paul Ingram, and G. Tenaglia, eds. 1996. *Rising Tension in Eastern Europe and the Former Soviet Union*. Aldershot, England: Dartmouth.

Cecchini, Paolo. 1988. *The European Challenge: 1992*. Aldershot, England: Gower Press.

Chasek, Pamela. 1994. The Story of the UNCED Process. In *Negotiating International Regimes: Lessons Learned from the United Nations Conference on Environment and Development (UNCED)*, edited by B. I. Spector, G. Sjöstedt, and I. Zartman. London: Graham & Trotman.

Cini, Michelle. 1996. *The European Commission: Leadership, Organisation and Culture in the EU Administration*. New York: Manchester University Press.

Commission of the European Communities. 1989. *One Market, One Money*.

―――. 1992a. *Toward Sustainability: A European Community Programme of Policy and Action in Relation to the Environment and Sustainable Development*, Com (92) 27 March.

―――. 1992b. *Report of the Commission of the European Communities to the United Nations Conference on Environment and Development*. Luxembourg: Office for Official Publication of the European Communities.

―――. 1994. Interim Review of Implementation of the European Community Programme of Policy and Action in Relations to the Environment and Sustainable Development ("Toward Sustainability"), Com (94) November.

―――. 1995a. *Communication to the Council: The European Union and Russia, The Future Relationship*. Delegation of the European Commission in Moscow: EU Series no. 8, May.

————. 1995b. *White Paper on the Preparation of the Associated Countries of Central and Eastern Europe for Integration into the Internal Market of the Union.* Com (95) May.

————. 1997. Agenda 2000: For a Stronger and Wider Europe, 15 July. Com (97) 2000; Supplement 5/97, *Bulletin of the European Communities.*

Committee for the Study of Economic and Monetary Union. 1989. *Report on Economic and Monetary Union in the European Community.* (Delors Report) Committee for the Study of EMU, Brussels, 12 April.

Cooney, Stephen. 1994. *American Industry and the New European Union.* Washington, D.C.: National Association of Manufacturers.

Corcelle, Guy. 1993. 20 Ans après Stockholm: La conférence des nations unies de Rio de Janeiro sur l'environnement et le développement: point de départ ou aboutissement? *Revue du Marché Commun et de l'Union Européenne* 365: 107–131.

Cosgrove, Carol Ann, and Kenneth J. Twitchett, eds. 1970. *The New International Actors: The United Nations and the European Economic Community.* New York: St. Martin's.

Costigliola, Frank. 1984. *Awkward Dominion: American Political, Economic, and Cultural Relations with Europe, 1919–1933.* Ithaca: Cornell University Press.

Council of the European Communities Regulation 3906/89 of 18 December 1989 on Economic Aid to the Republic of Hungary and the Polish People's Republic. Official Journal L 375, 23.12.1989.

Court of Justice of the European Communities. 1971. Case 22/70, Commission of the European Communities v. Council of the European Communities [*ERTA*]. *European Court Reports*: 263–295.

————. 1976. Joined cases 3, 4, and 6/76, Cornelis Kramer and others. *European Court Reports*: 1279–1314.

————. 1977. Opinion 1/76, Re: Draft Agreement Establishing a European Laying-up Fund for Inland Waterway Vessels. *European Court Reports*: 741–762.

————. 1979. Opinion 1/78, Re: International Agreement on Natural Rubber. *European Court Reports*: 2871–2921.

————. 1994. Opinion 1/94. *Spicers Centre for Europe,* 21 November 1994.

Cowles, Maria Green. 1996a. The Collective Action of Transatlantic Business. Paper presented at the 1996 Annual Meeting of the American Political Science Association, San Francisco, California, 31 August.

————. 1996b. The EU committee of AmCham: The Powerful Voice of American Firms in Brussels. *Journal of European Public Policy* 33: 339–358.

————. 1996c. Organizing Industrial Coalitions. In *Participation and Policymaking in the European Union,* edited by H. Wallace and A. Young. London: Oxford University Press.

Cviic, Christopher. 1993. *Remaking the Balkans.* London: Pinter.

De la Serre, F. 1994. A la recherche d'une Ostpolitik. In *L'Union Européene: ouverture à l'Est?,* edited by F. De la Serre, C. Lequesne, and J. Rupnik. Paris: Presse Universitaires de France.

Demaret, Paul. 1993. Environmental Policy and Commercial Policy: The Emergence of Trade-Related Environmental Measures (TREMs) in the External Relations of the European Community. In *The European Community's Commercial Policy After 1992: The Legal Dimension,* edited by M. Maresceau. Dordrecht, Netherlands: Martinus Nijhoff.

Denza, Eileen. 1994. Groping Towards Europe's Foreign Policy. In *Institutional Dynamics of European Integration: Essays in Honour of Henry G. Schermers,* edited by D. Curtin and T. Heukels. Dordrecht, Netherlands: Martinus Nijhoff.

Deubner, Christian. 1994. *Deutschland, Frankreich und das Europa der Neunziger Jahre im Konflikt von Interessen und Wahrnehmungen*. Ebenhausen, Germany: Stiftung Wissenschaft und Politik AP 2847.

Deutsch, Karl W. 1957. *Political Community and the North Atlantic Area: International Organization in the Light of Historical Experience*. New York: Greenwood Press.

Devuyst, Youri. 1995. The European Community and the Conclusion of the Uruguay Round. In *The State of the European Union, Vol. 3: Building a European Polity?*, edited by C. Rhodes and S. Mazey. Boulder: Lynne Rienner.

Dinan, Desmond. 1994. *Ever Closer Union?* Boulder: Lynne Rienner.

Dunning, John H. 1991. European Integration and Transatlantic Foreign Direct Investment: The Record Assessed. In *Europe and America, 1992: US-EC Economic Relations and the Single European Market*, edited by G. Yannopoulos. Manchester: Manchester University Press.

Dyson, Kenneth, and Kevin Featherstone. 1996. France, EMU and Construction Européenne: Empowering the Executive, Transforming the State. Paper presented at the conference on L'Européanisation des politiques publiques, Paris, 21 June.

Emerson, M. 1994. Un peu d'histoire. Paper presented at L'Union Europeene et la Federation de Russie: des relations en mutation. Project of the Universite de Rennes and IMEMO.

European Parliament. *Debates of the European Parliament*. Various issues.

———. 1991. *Report of the Committee on the Environment, Public Health and Consumer Protection on EC Participation in the United Nations Conference on the Environment and Development (UNCED)*. Session Document A3–0363/91, 4 December.

———. 1995. *The European Parliament and the Environmental Policy of the European Union*. Directorate General for Research. Environment, Public Health and Consumer Protection Working Paper Series no. W-14.

Featherstone, Kevin, and Roy H. Ginsberg. 1993. *The United States and the European Community in the 1990s: Partners in Transition*. New York: St Martin's.

Frellesen, Thomas, and Roy H. Ginsberg. 1994. EU-US Foreign Policy Cooperation in the 1990s: Elements of Partnership. CEPS paper no. 58. Brussels: Centre for European Policy Studies.

Frenkel, Jacob A., and Morris Goldstein. 1993. Monetary Policy in an Emerging European Economic and Monetary Union: Key Issues. In *International Finance: Contemporary Issues*, edited by D. K. Das. London: Routledge.

Frey, Frederick W. 1985. The Problem of Actor Designation in Political Analysis. *Comparative Politics* 17: 127–152.

Funk, Albrecht. 1996. Policing Europe: Border Controls and European Integration. Paper for the Conference on Territoriality in Modern Society: Predicaments and Opportunities, University of North Carolina–Chapel Hill, 29–30 March.

Gardner, Anthony Laurence. 1997. *A New Era in US-EU Relations? The Clinton Administration and the New Transatlantic Agenda*. Brookfield, VT: Avebury.

Garret, Geoffrey. 1992. International Cooperation and Institutional Choice: The European Community's Internal Market. *International Organization* 46: 533–560.

———. 1994. The Politics of Maastricht. In *The Political Economy of European Monetary Unification*, edited by B. Eichengreen and J. Frieden. Boulder: Westview Press.

———. 1995. The Politics of Legal Integration in the European Union. *International Organization* 49: 171–181.

Gnesotto, Nicole. 1996. Common European Defence and Transatlantic Relations. *Survival* 38: 19–31.

Goetschel, Laurent. 1995. Die Europäische Union: Sicherheit durch zivile Integration. In *Tod durch Bomben: Wider den Mythos vom ethnischen Konflikt*, edited by Österreichisches Studienzentrum für Frieden und Konfliktlösung, 56–59. Chur/Zürich: Rüegger.

Gordon, Philip H. 1996. Recasting the Atlantic Alliance. *Survival* 38: 32–57.

Graham, Edward M. 1991. Strategic Responses of US Multinational Firms to the Europe-1992 Initiative. In *Europe and America, 1992: US-EC Economic Relations and the Single European Market*, edited by G. N. Yannopoulos. Manchester: Manchester University Press.

Graham, Edward M., and Paul R. Krugman. 1995. *Foreign Direct Investment in the United States*. Washington, D.C.: Institute for International Economics.

Groux, Jean, and Philippe Manin. 1985. *The European Communities in the International Order*. European Perspective Series. Brussels: Office for Official Publications of the European Communities.

Hallwood, Paul C., and Ronald MacDonald. 1994. *International Money and Finance*. Oxford: Blackwell.

Han, Sun-Taik. 1992. *European Integration: The Impact on Asian Newly Industrialising Economies*. Paris: OECD.

Harrison, Glennon J. 1994. *CRS Report for Congress: US-European Union Trade and Investment*. Congressional Research Service, The Library of Congress, 20 December.

———. 1995. *CRS Report for Congress: The Transatlantic Business Dialogue*. Congressional Research Service, The Library of Congress, 19 September.

Hayes-Renshaw, Fiona, and Helen Wallace. 1997. *The Council of Ministers*. New York: St. Martin's.

Hedetoft, Ulf. 1995. *Signs of Nations: Studies in the Political Semiotics of Self and Other in Contemporary Nationalism*. Aldershot, England: Dartmouth.

Hedetoft, Ulf, and Antje Herrberg. 1996. Russia and the European Other: Searching for a Post-Soviet Identity. *European Studies: Series of Occasional Papers* 17. Aalborg, Denmark: European Research Unit.

Henning, C. Randall. 1994. *Currencies and Politics in the United States, Germany, and Japan*. Washington, D.C.: Institute for International Economics.

———. 1996. Europe's Monetary Union and the United States. *Foreign Policy*, no. 102: 83–100.

Herrberg, A. 1996a. The European Union in Its International Environment: A Systematic Analysis. In *Rethinking the European Union: Interests, Institutions, Identities*, edited by A. Landau and R. Whitman. London: Macmillan.

———. 1996b. The Security Triangle: Germany, Russia and Europe. Paper presented at the colloquium Germany in Europe, Aalborg University.

Hession, Martin. 1995. External Competence and the European Community. *Global Environmental Change* 5: 155–156.

Hill, Christopher, ed. 1983. *National Foreign Policies and European Political Cooperation*. London: Allen and Unwin.

Hill, Christopher. 1994. The Capability-Expectations Gap, or Conceptualizing Europe's International Role. In *Economic and Political Integration in Europe: Internal Dynamics and Global Context*, edited by S. Bulmer and A. Scott. Oxford: Blackwell.

Hix, Simon. 1994. The Study of the European Community: The Challenge to Comparative Politics. *West European Politics* 17: 1–30.

Holland, Martin. 1995a. *European Union Common Foreign Policy: From EPC Joint Action and South Africa*. London: Macmillan.

————. 1995b. Bridging the Capability-Expectations Gap: A Case Study of the CFSP Joint Action on South Africa. *Journal of Common Market Studies* 33: 555–572.

Howard, Michael. 1995. 1945–1995: Reflections on Half a Century of British Security Policy. *International Affairs* 71: 705–716.

Hu, Y. S. 1973. *The Impact of U.S. Investment in Europe: A Case Study of the Automotive and Computer Industries*. New York: Praeger.

Hufbauer, Gary C. 1990. An Overview. In *Europe 1992: An American Perspective*, edited by G.C. Hufbauer. Washington, D.C.: Brookings Institution.

Imbrechts, Luc. 1986. Les effets internes des accords internationaux des Communautés Européennes. *Journal of European Integration* 10: 59–77.

Jackson, James K. 1992. American Direct Investment in the European Community. *Europe and the United States: Competition and Cooperation in the 1990s*. Study papers submitted to the subcommittee on International Economic Policy and Trade and the Subcommittee on Europe and the Middle East of the Committee on Foreign Affairs, U.S. House of Representatives, June.

Jackson, Robert H. 1986. Negative Sovereignty in Sub-Saharan Africa. *Review of International Studies* 12: 247–264.

————. 1987. Quasi-States, Dual Regimes, and Neoclassical Theory: International Jurisprudence and the Third World. *International Organization* 41: 519–549.

————. 1990. *Quasi-States: Sovereignty, International Relations and the Third World*. Cambridge: Cambridge University Press.

Jackson, Robert H., and Carl G. Rosberg. 1982. Why Africa's Weak States Persist: The Empirical and the Juridical in Statehood. *World Politics* 35: 1–24.

Jacquemin, Alex, and David Wright. 1994. Corporate Strategies and European Challenges Post–1992. In *Economic and Political Integration in Europe: Internal Dynamics and Global Context*, edited by S. Bulmer and A. Scott. Oxford: Blackwell.

Johnson, Stanley. 1992. Did We Really Save the Earth at Rio? *European Environmental Law Review* 1: 84–85.

Jopp, Mathias. 1992. Langer Weg—Kühnes Ziel. Gemeinsame Verteidigungspolitik. *Europa Archiv* 13/14: 397–404.

————. 1995a. After the Reflection Group. CFSP Forum, no. 4. Bonn: Institut fur Europaische Politik.

————. 1995b. Die Reform der Gemeinsamen Außen- und Sicherheitspolitik—institutionelle Vorschläge und ihre Realisierungschancen. *Integration* 18: 134–139.

Julius, DeAnne. 1991. *Foreign Direct Investment: The Neglected Twin of Trade*. Occasional Paper 33. Washington, D.C.: Group of Thirty.

Jupille, Joseph. 1996. Fewer States, Different Actors: The European Community and International Environmental Cooperation. Paper presented at International Studies Association West Conference, Eugene, Oregon, 10–12 October.

Kahler, Miles. 1995. *Regional Futures and Transatlantic Economic Relations*. New York: Council on Foreign Relations Press for the European Community Studies Association.

Kaiser, Karl. 1996. Reforming NATO. *Foreign Policy* 103: 128–143.

Kaufman Purcell, Susan, and Françoise Simon, eds. 1995. *Europe and Latin America in the World Economy*. Boulder: Lynne Rienner.

Keeler, John T. S. 1996. Agricultural Power in the European Community: Explaining the Fate of the CAP and GATT Negotiations. *Comparative Politics* 28: no. 2, 127–149.

Kelleher, Catherine McArdle. 1995. *The Future of European Security*. Washington, D.C.: Brookings Institution.

Kenen, Peter. 1992. *EMU after Maastricht*. Washington, D.C.: Group of Thirty.

Kenis, Patrick, and Volker Schneider. 1987. The EC as an International Corporate Actor: Two Case Studies in Economic Diplomacy. *European Journal of Political Research* 15: 437–457.

Keohane, Robert 1989. *International Institutions and State Power: Essays in International Relations Theory*. Boulder: Westview.

Keohane, Robert, and Stanley Hoffmann. 1990. Conclusions: Community Politics and Institutional Change. In *The Dynamics of European Integration*, edited by W. Wallace. London: Pinter.

Keohane, Robert, and Stanley Hoffmann, eds. 1991. *The New European Community*. Boulder: Westview.

Keohane, Robert, Joseph Nye, and Stanley Hoffmann, eds. 1993. *After the Cold War: International Institutions and State Strategies in Europe, 1989–1991*. Cambridge: Harvard University Press.

Kramer, Heinz. 1993. The European Community's Response to the "New Eastern Europe." *Journal of Common Market Studies* 31: 213–232.

Krause, J., and A. Jahr. 1995. Russia's New Foreign Policy. Study Undertaken for the European Commission. Final Report. Bonn: Research Institute of the German Society for Foreign Affairs, 15 May.

Krenzler, H., and A. Schomaker. 1996. A New Transatlantic Agenda. *European Foreign Affairs*, July: 5–22.

Krugmann, Paul. 1993. The Uncomfortable Truth About NAFTA. It's Foreign Policy, Stupid. *Foreign Affairs* 72: 13–19.

Lester, Jeremey. 1995. *Modern Tsars and Princes: The Struggle for Hegemony in Russia*. London: Verso.

Lieber, Robert. 1976. *Oil and the Middle East War: Europe in the Energy Crisis*. Cambridge: Harvard University Press.

Lodge, Juliet, ed. 1993. *The European Community and the Challenge of the Future*. London: Pinter.

Ludlow, Peter. 1991. The European Commission. In *The New European Community*, edited by R. Keohane and S. Hoffman. Boulder: Westview.

Lukin, Vladimir P. 1994. Russia and Its Interests. In *Rethinking Russia's National Interest*, edited by S. Sestanovich. Washington, D.C.: Significant Issue Series 16.

Malcolm, Neil, ed. 1994. *Russia and Europe: An End to Confrontation?* London: Pinter.

Marks, Gary. 1993. Structural Policy and Multilevel Governance in the EC. In *The State of the European Community Vol. 2: The Maastricht Debates and Beyond*, edited by A. Cafruny and G. Rosenthal. Boulder: Lynne Rienner.

Martin, Lawrence, and John Roper, eds. 1995. *Towards a Common Defense Policy*. Paris: WEU.

McCalla, Robert. 1996. NATO's Persistence After the Cold War. *International Organization* 50: 445–475.

McCulloch, Rachel. 1991. Why Foreign Corporations Are Buying into U.S. Business. In *Foreign Investment in the United States*, edited by M. Ulan. The Annals of the American Academy, July.

McGeehan, Robert. 1985. European Defence Cooperation: A Political Perspective. *The World Today* 41: 116–119.

McKinnon, Ronald I. 1993. The Rules of the Game: International Money in Historical Perspective. *Journal of Economic Literature* 31: 1–44.

McSweeney, B. 1996. Identity and Security: Buzan and the Copenhagen School. *Review of International Affairs* 22: 81–93.

Mearsheimer, John. 1990. Back to the Future: Instability in Europe After the Cold War. *International Security* 15: 5–56.

Menon, Anand. 1995. From Independence to Cooperation: France, NATO and European Security. *International Affairs* 71: 19–34.

Meunier, Sophie. Forthcoming 1998. *Divided but United: European Integration and EC-US Trade Negotiations 1962–1994*. Ph.D. diss., Department of Political Science, M.I.T.

Miall, Hugh, ed. 1994. *Redefining Europe: New Patterns of Conflict and Cooperation*. London: Pinter.

Miller, J.D.B. 1986. Sovereignty as a Source of Vitality for the State. *Review of International Studies* 12: 79–89.

Miller, Robert, and Mariusz Sumlinski. 1994. *Trends in Private Investment in Developing Countries*. Washington, D.C.: International Finance Corporation.

Moe, Terry M. 1984. The New Economics of Organization. *American Journal of Political Science* 28: 739–777.

Mommsen, M. 1996. *Wohin treibt Russland? Eine Grossmacht zwischen Anarchie und Demokratie*. Munich: Beck.

Moravscik, Andrew. 1991. Negotiating the Single European Act. In *The New European Community*, edited by R. Keohane and S. Hoffmann. Boulder: Westview.

———. 1993. Preferences and Power in the European Community: A Liberal Intergovernmentalist Approach. *Journal of Common Market Studies* 31: 473–524.

Morgan, Roger. 1994. The Prospects for Europe's Common Foreign and Security Policy. In *The International System After the Collapse of the East West-Order*, edited by A. Clesse, R. Cooper, and Y. Sakamoto. Dordrecht/Boston: Martinus Nijhoff.

Nanto, Dick K. 1992. The US-EC-Japan Trade Triangle. *Europe and the United States: Competition and Cooperation in the 1990s*. Study papers submitted to the Subcommittee on International Economic Policy and Trade and the Subcommittee on Europe and the Middle East of the Committee on Foreign Affairs, U.S. House of Representatives, June.

Neumann, Ivel B. 1996. *Russia and the Idea of Europe*. London: Routledge.

Neuwahl, Nanette A. 1991. Joint Participation in International Treaties and the Exercise of Power by the EEC and Its Member States: Mixed Agreements. *Common Market Law Review* 28: 717–740.

Nollkaemper, André. 1987. The European Community and International Environmental Co-operation: Legal Aspects of External Community Powers. *Legal Issues of European Integration* 2: 55–91.

Nugent, Neill. 1994. *The Government and Politics of the European Union*. London: Macmillan.

Nuttal, Simon. 1992. *European Political Cooperation*. Oxford: Oxford University Press.

Official Journal of the European Communities. 1973. Declaration of the Council of the European Communities and of the Representatives of the Governments of the Member States Meeting in Council of 22 November 1973 on the Programme of Action of the European Communities on the Environment. OJ C 112, 20 December: 1–53.

———. 1978. Written Question no. 174/77 by Mr. Maigaard. OJ C 56, 6 March: 1–2.

———. 1987. Resolution of the Council of the European Communities and of the Representatives of the Governments of the Member States, Meeting in the Council of 19 October 1987 on the Continuation and Implementation of a

European Community Policy and Action Programme on the Environment (1987–1992). OJ C 328, 7 December: 1–44.

———. 1992. [EP] Resolution on EC Participation in the United Nations Conference on the Environment and Development (UNCED). OJ C 67, 16 March, 156.

Okubo, Sumiye. 1995. Introduction and Overview. In *Foreign Direct Investment in the United States: An Update: Review and Analysis of Current Developments.* Report to the U.S. Congress in Response to Section 3(a) of the Foreign Direct Investment and the International Financial Data Improvements Act of 1990. U.S. Department of Commerce: Economics and Statistics Administration, Office of the Chief Economist, January.

Paarlberg, Robert. 1993. Why Agriculture Blocked the Uruguay Round: Evolving Strategies in a Two-Level Game. In *World Agriculture and the GATT*, edited by W. Avery. Boulder: Lynne Rienner.

Paemen, Hugo, and Alexandra Bensch. 1995. *From the GATT to the WTO: The European Community in the Uruguay Round.* Leuven, Belgium: Leuven University Press.

Partnership and Cooperation Agreement Between Russia and The European Union. June 1994. Outlined in Russia and European Union Reach Historic Agreement to Deepen Trade and Political Ties. *Rapid* 22 June 1994.

Piening, Christopher. 1997. *Global Europe: The European Union in World Affairs.* Boulder: Lynne Rienner.

Pelkmans, J., and A. Murphy. 1991. Catapulted into Leadership: The Community's Trade and Aid Policies Vis-à-Vis Eastern Europe. *Journal of European Integration* 14: 2–3.

Peters, Patrick F. H. J. 1996. The Development of the Euro as a Reserve Currency. Paper presented at the Annual Convention of the International Studies Association, San Diego, California, 18 April.

Peterson, John. 1993. *Europe and America in the 1990s: The Prospects for Partnership.* Aldershot, England: Edward Elgar.

Pierson, Paul. 1996. The Path to European Integration: A Historical Institutionalist Analysis. *Comparative Political Studies* 29: 123–163.

Pollack, Mark. 1997. Delegation, Agency, and Agenda Setting in the EC. *International Organization* 51: 99–134.

Putnam, Robert. 1988. Diplomacy and Domestic Politics: The Logic of the Two-Level Game. *International Organization* 42: 427–460.

Qvigstad, Jan Fredrik. 1992. *Economic and Monetary Union (EMU): A Survey of the EMU and Empirical Evidence on Convergence for the EC and the EFTA Countries.* Geneva: European Free Trade Association.

Ravenhill, John. 1985. *Collective Clientelism: The Lomé Conventions and North-South Relations.* New York: Columbia University Press.

Regelsberger, Elfriede. 1993. European Political Cooperation. In *The New Europe: Politics, Government and Economy Since 1945*, edited by J. Story. Oxford: Blackwell.

Rhodes, Carolyn. 1997. The Role of the European Union in the Global Arena as Model, Bandwagon and Agenda Setter: Identifying and Assessing Its Influence Abroad. Paper presented to the European Community Studies Association Biennial Conference, Seattle, Washington, 28 May–1 June.

Robins, Nick. 1992. The EC and the Earth Summit. *EIU European Trends* 2: 75–82.

Rosecrance, Richard N. 1993. Trading States in a New Concert of Europe. In *America and Europe in an Era of Change*, edited by H. Haftendorn and C. Tuschhoff. Boulder: Westview.

Ross, George. 1995. *Jacques Delors and European Integration*. Cambridge: Polity Press.

Ruhle, M., and N. Williams. 1995. NATO Enlargement and the European Union. *The World Today,* May: 84–88.

Rummel, Reinhardt. 1991–1992. Integration, Disintegration and Security in Europe: Preparing the Community for a Multi-institutional Response. *International Journal* 47, Winter: 64–92.

———. 1992. Regional Integration in the Global Test. In *Toward Political Union: Planning a Common Foreign and Security Policy in the European Community*, edited by R. Rummel. Baden-Baden: Nomos.

———. 1994. West European Cooperation in Foreign and Security Policy. *Annals of the American Academy for Political and Social Sciences* 531: 112–123.

Sack, Jörn. 1995. The European Community's Membership of International Organizations. *Common Market Law Review* 32: 1227–1256.

Sandholtz, Wayne. 1993. Choosing Union: Monetary Politics and Maastricht. *International Organization* 47: 1–39.

Sandholtz, Wayne, and John Zysman. 1992. Europe's Emergence as a Global Protagonist. In *The Highest Stakes: The Economic Foundations of the Next Security System,* edited by W. Sandholtz, et.al., Oxford: Oxford University Press.

Sawers, John. 1996. A New Approach to Europe's Common Foreign and Security Policy. Paper presented at the Center for International Affairs, Cambridge, MA.

Sbragia, Alberta M., ed. 1992a. *Euro-Politics: Institutions and Policymaking in the New European Community*. Washington, D.C.: Brookings Institution.

———. 1992b. Thinking About the European Future: The Uses of Comparison. In *Euro-Politics: Institutions and Policymaking in the New European Community*, edited by A. M. Sbragia. Washington, DC: Brookings Institution.

———. 1996. *Institution-Building from Below and from Above: The European Community in Global Environmental Politics*. Center for German and European Studies, University of California–Berkeley, Working Paper no. 2.40, November.

———. Forthcoming. The European Union and Compliance: A Story in the Making. In *Engaging Countries: Strengthening Compliance with International Environmental Accords,* edited by E. Brown-Weiss and H. K. Jacobson. Cambridge: MIT Press.

Schaetzel, J. Robert. 1975. *The Unhinged Alliance: America and the European Community*. New York: Harper & Row.

Schelling, Thomas. 1960. *The Strategy of Conflict*. Cambridge: Harvard University Press.

Schermers, Henry G. 1983. A Typology of Mixed Agreements. In *Mixed Agreements,* edited by D. O'Keeffe and H. Schermers. Boston: Kluwer Law and Taxation Publishers.

Schirm, Stefan A. 1994. *Macht und Wandel: Die Beziehungen der USA zu Mexico und Brasilien.* Außenpolitik, Wirtschaft und Sicherheit, Opladen: Leske & Budrich.

Schirm, Stefan A. 1996. Regionalisierung der Internationalen Politik? Gemeinsame Außen- und Sicherheitspolitik in Europa, Lateinamerika und Südostasien. *Zeitschrift für Politik* 43: 262–284.

Schott, Jeffrey. 1994. *The Uruguay Round: An Assessment*. Washington, D.C.: Institute for International Economics.

Senghaas, Dieter. 1993. Eine friedenstheoretische Leitperspektive für das Europa nach dem Ost-West Konflikt. In *Gesamt Europa: Analysen, Probleme und*

Entwicklungsperspektiven, edited by C. Jakobeit and A. Yenal. Opladen: Leske & Budrich.

Servan-Schreiber, Jean Jacques. 1968. *The American Challenge*. New York: Atheneum.

Shakhnazarov, G. 1995. East-West: The Problem of Deideologizing Relations. In *The Soviet System*, edited by A. Dallin and G. Lapidus. Oxford: Westview Press.

Sjöstedt, Gunnar. 1977. *The External Role of the European Community*. Swedish Studies in International Relations 7. Farnborough, England: Saxon House.

Skjœrseth, Jon Birger. 1994. The Climate Policy of the EC: Too Hot to Handle? *Journal of Common Market Studies* 32: 25–45.

Smith, Anthony. 1991. *National Identity*. Harmondsworth: Penguin.

Smith, Michael. 1984. *Western Europe and the United States: The Uncertain Alliance*. London: George Allen & Unwin.

———. 1994a. The European Community, Foreign Economic Policy and the Changing World Arena. *Journal of European Public Policy* 1, Autumn: 283–300.

———. 1994b. Beyond the Stable State? Foreign Policy Challenges and Opportunities in the New Europe. In *European Foreign Policy: The European Community and New Perspectives in Europe*, edited by W. Carlsnaes and S. Smith. London: Sage.

———. 1996. The European Union and a Changing Europe: Establishing the Boundaries of Order. *Journal of Common Market Studies* 34: 5–28.

Smith, Michael, and Stephen Woolcock 1993. *The United States and the European Community in a Transformed World*. London: Pinter.

Staniland, Martin. 1995. The Unites States and the External Aviation Policy of the EU. *Journal of the European Policy* 2: 19–40.

Stevens, Christopher. 1990. The Impact of Europe 1992 on the Maghreb and Sub-Saharan Africa. *Journal of Common Market Studies* 29: 217–241.

Tavlas, George S. 1993. The Deutsche Mark as an International Currency. In *International Finance: Contemporary Issues*, edited by D. K. Das. London: Routledge.

Taylor, Paul. 1983. *The Limits of European Integration*. New York: Columbia University Press.

Tourlemon, Robert. 1995. Kerneuropa—Deutsch-französische Aktionsgemeinschaft in Sicht? *Integration* 18: 61–67.

Trade Relations Between the European Union and Developing Countries. 1995. Luxembourg: Office for Official Publications of the European Communities.

Treaty of Amsterdam. 1997. June Draft.

Treaty Establishing the European Coal and Steel Community. 1950. Luxembourg: Office for Official Publications of the European Communities.

Treaty Establishing the European Economic Community. 1957. Luxembourg: Office for Official Publications of the European Communities.

Treaty on European Union. 1992. Luxembourg: Office for Official Publications of the European Communities.

United Nations Development Programme (UNDP). 1995. *Human Development Report 1995*. New York: Oxford UP.

United Nations. 1992a. *Status of the European Economic Community at the United Nations Conference on Environment and Development*. General Assembly Document A/Conf.151/PC/L.74, 2 April.

———. 1992b. *UNCED Provisional Rules of Procedure*. General Assembly Document A/Conf.151/2, 30 April.

————. 1992c. *Report of the Preparatory Committee for the United Nations Conference on Environment and Development on the Work of Its Fourth Session.* General Assembly Document A/Conf.151/PC/128, 12 May.

Van Heuven, Martin. 1994. *The U.S. Role in Post–Cold War Europe: Significance of European Views of the New U.S. Administration.* Prepared for the Office of the Secretary of Defense. Santa Monica: RAND.

Vernon, Raymond. 1992. *Are Foreign-Owned Subsidiaries Good for the United States?* Occasional Paper 37. Washington, D.C.: Group of the Thirty.

Viner, Jacob. 1950. *The Customs Union Issue.* New York: Carnegie Endowment for International Peace.

Vogel, David. 1995. *Trading Up: Consumer and Environmental Regulation in a Global Economy.* Cambridge: Harvard University Press.

Waever, Ole. 1996. European Security Identities. *Journal of Common Market Studies* 34: 103–32.

Waever, Ole, and the Center for freds-og Koufliktforskning, 1993. *Migration, Identity and the New European Security Order.* London: Pinter.

Wallace, Helen. 1992. What Europe for Which Europeans? In *The Shape of the New Europe*, edited by G. Treverton. New York: Council on Foreign Relations.

Wallace, Helen. 1994. European Governance in Turbulent Times. In *Economic and Political Integration in Europe: Internal Dynamics and Global Context*, edited by S. Bulmer and D. Scott. Oxford: Blackwell.

Wallace, William. 1983. Less Than a Federation, More Than a Regime: The Community as a Political System. In *Policy-Making in the European Community*, edited by H. Wallace, W. Wallace, and C. Webb. New York: John Wiley.

Wallander, Celeste A., ed. 1996. The Sources of Russian Foreign Policy After the Cold War. The John M. Olin Critical Issues Series. Boulder: Westview Press.

Weiler, Joseph. 1981. The Community System: The Dual Character of Supranationalism. *Yearbook of European Law* 1: 267–306.

————. 1983. The External Legal Relations of Non-Unitary Actors: Mixity and the Federal Principle. In *Mixed Agreements*, edited by D. O'Keeffe and H. G. Schermers. Boston: Kluwer Law and Taxation Publishers.

Wendt, Alexander. 1992. Anarchy Is What States Make of It: The Social Construction of Power Politics. *International Organization* 46: 391–425.

————. 1994. Collective Identity Formation and the International State. *American Political Science Review* 88: 384–396.

Wessels, Wolfgang. 1991. The EC Council: The Community's Decisionmaking Center. In *The New European Community: Decisionmaking and Institutional Change*, edited by R. O. Keohane and S. Hoffmann. Boulder: Westview Press.

Wessels, Wolfgang. 1993. Von der EPZ zur GASP—Theorienpluralismus mit begrenzter Aussagekraft. In *Die Gemeinsame Außen—und Sicherheitspolitik der Europäischen Union*, edited by E. Regelsberger. IEP, Bonn: Europa Union Verlag.

Wessels, Wolfgang, and Elfriede Regelsberger. 1996. The CFSP Institutions and Procedures. *European Foreign Affairs*, December: 65–73.

Winand, Pasculine. 1993. *Eisenhower, Kennedy, and the United States of Europe.* New York: St. Martin's.

Wolfers, Arnold. 1962. *Discord and Collaboration: Essays on International Politics.* Baltimore: Johns Hopkins University Press.

Woolcock, Steven. 1992. *Trading Partners or Trading Blows? Market Access Issues in EC-US Relations.* New York: Council on Foreign Relations Press.

Young, Oran R. 1972. The Actors in World Politics. In *The Analysis of International Politics*, edited by J. Rosenau, V. Davis, and M. A. East. New York: Free Press.

Zelikow, Philip. 1996. The Masque of Institutions. *Survival* 38: 6–18.

Zito, Anthony R. 1995. Integrating the Environment into the European Union: The History of the Controversial Carbon Tax. In *The State of the European Union, Vol. 3, Building a European Polity?*, edited by Carolyn Rhodes and Sonia Mazey. Boulder: Lynne Rienner.

List of Contributors

David Allen
Department of European Studies
Loughborough University
Loughborough, United Kingdom

Olufemi A. Babarinde
Assistant Professor
Department of International Studies
Thunderbird
The American Graduate School of International Management
Glendale, Arizona

Fraser Cameron
Foreign Policy Adviser
European Commission, DG I-A
Brussels, Belgium

James A. Caporaso
Virginia and Prentice Bloedel Professor
Department of Political Science
University of Washington
Seattle, Washingon

Antje Herrberg
Research Associate
European Research Unit
Aalborg University
Aalborg, Denmark

Madeleine O. Hosli
Visiting Scholar

Netherlands Institute of International Relations "Clingendael"
The Hague, Netherlands

Joseph Henri Jupille
Department of Political Science
University of Washington
Seattle, Washington

Alan Mayhew
Leuven Institute for Central and East European Studies
Catholic University of Leuven
Leuven, Belgium

Sophie Meunier
Lecturer in Management Studies
Graduate School of Business
University of Chicago
Chicago, Illinois

Carolyn Rhodes
Associate Professor
Department of Political Science
Utah State University
Logan, Utah

Alberta Sbragia
Director, Center for West European Studies
University of Pittsburgh
Pittsburgh, Pennsylvania

Stefan A. Schirm
Research Associate
Stiftung Wissenschaft und Politik
(Research Institute for International Affairs)
Ebenhausen, Germany

Michael Smith
Professor of European Politics
Department of European Studies
Loughborough University
Loughborough, United Kingdom

Index

About the Book

Although the European Union as a supranational entity is the subject of much academic and policy analysis, there is little disagreement that the Union significantly shapes the policy orientations of member states toward one another. In the realm of foreign policy, however, the assessment of the EU's role in affecting or replacing member state behavior is much more mixed. This volume analyzes the character of the EU as an actor in international affairs.

The authors consider the following questions: Does the EU have an identity of its own in global affairs, distinct from that of its member states? What is its relationship with other major international actors? What constraints and opportunities exist for this unique entity? And what gives the EU authority and legitimacy in international affairs? Collectively, the authors explore how the EU is shaping international relations beyond its borders in security, diplomatic, economic, and environmental affairs.

Carolyn Rhodes is associate professor of political science at Utah State University. She is author of *Reciprocity: U.S. Trade Policy and the GATT Regime* and coeditor of *The State of the European Union: Building a European Polity?*